I0800953

Making The Children's Year

Seasonal Waldorf Crafts with Children

Marije Rowling

Hawthorn Press

Hawthorn Press

Published by Hawthorn Press, Hawthorn House,
1 Lansdown Lane, Stroud, Gloucestershire, GL5 1BJ, UK
Tel: (01453) 757040
E-mail: info@hawthornpress.com
Website: www.hawthornpress.com

Cover photography by Faisal Khouja
Design by Lucy Guenot
Reprinted 2018 by Everbest Printing Co Ltd, China

Printed on environmentally friendly chlorine-free paper sourced from renewable forest stock.

British Library Cataloguing in Publication Data applied for

ISBN 978-1-907359-69-9

Making The Children's Year

Seasonal Waldorf Crafts with Children

Marije Rowling

Fully updated revised edition of *The Children's Year* (1986)
by Christine Fynes-Clinton, Stephanie Cooper and Marije Rowling

Hawthorn Press

Contents

Author's Note

The original *The Children's Year* was written in the early 1980s by Christine Fynes-Clinton, Stephanie Cooper and me. We were brand new young mothers keen to create a meaningful home life and to share our ideas. Now after all these years, our individual lives as home-makers and crafters, artists and teachers have been woven from the Waldorf thread into a very rich tapestry. Out of all our experiences we realise that our first book now has the potential to be updated.

As the only one of the original group who has the possibility to free up time, I have had the honour and pleasure to thoroughly revise the book and add many new projects.

Marije Rowling

Foreword

The original *The Children's Year* has continued to delight for over three decades since its first publication. This second edition, *Making the Children's Year: Seasonal Waldorf Crafts with Children*, has been lovingly updated and completely refreshed by Marije Rowling, who has added many new projects. She brings to it the eye of an artist, a parent, a grandparent and a professional; deepening our understanding of colours throughout the seasons and highlighting the importance of craft and beauty. *Making the Children's Year* is enlivened with captivating colour illustrations and clear instructions.

For young children there is a sense of magic as they encounter these images, drawings and activities. Older ones will find creative projects suited to their skills and enjoyment. For adults also the book offers a wide choice of craft, from tissue paper lanterns, a bee house and the old gnome, to a May flower crown and lavender bags, just to name a few. The book aims to encourage everyone's creative expression. It reminds us that making things by hand brings inner and outer rewards. Moreover, its use for sharing through creativity can bring us together; whether friends, household, family or community.

These days the limitations of mass production and our consumer society are perhaps more widely recognised than in the mid-1980s, when the first edition appeared. Since then the need to re-connect with nature and its rhythms and processes has become even more urgent. The importance of making and self-expression with a seasonal background resonates throughout the year, offering simple yet deeply satisfying pleasures. This is a resource to use personally and with children; a book to bring elements of nature indoors and help us look again at changes outdoors. Here, in a refreshingly new form, is a book to be thoroughly enjoyed.

Judith Large

Introduction

A Colour Year with Seasonal Crafts

When astronauts look down to the Earth they see the most marvellously beautiful planet – the blue planet Earth.

Since the 1970s the concept of Gaia has gained acceptance again – Mother Earth, who has had so many different names in different early cultures.

We saw one aspect of her in Botticelli's beautiful *Primavera* and in a different guise as Venus draped in gorgeous flower gowns. In spring she shows a tender, gentle, fresh and tentative mood of pale, clean pink or yellow.

As the plants start to grow faster, an outward and upward movement appears to be accelerating. Faster and faster, more and more plants show this joy of growth till midsummer. Colour-wise we are within the active orange and joyous golden, orangey-red mood.

In autumn when the days are getting shorter the Earth breathes in again – everywhere it contracts. Finally all the dried-up brown leaves have floated down to earth and the seeds have been scattered wide into the soil; a sombre violet indigo mood hangs over the land. A dying down like Persephone going into the Underworld.

Around midwinter the mood can be magical as a grand crisp night sky, speckled with stars, looks down onto a very quiet and expectant crystallised Earth. This is a beautiful, deep ultramarine mood, offset with festive red for celebration.

This in turn is followed by a quiet pale royal magenta in anticipation of the appearance of the first shoots, and then the yearly dance can start all over again. Slowly we begin to sense Nature's moods when we live in the seasons.

This book is about our participation in the majestic seasonal cycle of the year through the nature table with all its craft possibilities.

You will find four large sections, each setting the mood for the season with a description, and a large seasonal festival table and a small nature table.

These are followed by a wide variety of gorgeous, simple projects for children and experienced crafters to make. There is no more heartfelt and joyful way of connecting with children than through doing crafts together. A flickering screen can entertain children so well, but we are seeing its very negative effects so clearly too.

Children are born doers and learn through physical play, imitating people around them (enjoying dusting, washing up, making the bed) and making things. Remember: nimble fingers make nimble minds.

In order for children to feel secure and at home on this precious Earth they need to feel connected to the rhythms of nature. Celebrating the festivals with the nature table is a beautifully creative way of doing this.

I hope that this book will inspire you to make a highly enjoyable journey through the seasons.

Regions, Seasons, Festivals and Crafts

When the plant saps rise in the morning in the east, they start to fall in the evening in the west. A midsummer in the northern hemisphere is a midwinter in the south.

In some regions the seasons are very distinct; in others they only show relatively small differences.

In the original *The Children's Year* and now in this *Making the Children's Year*, the starting point was our experiences and traditions from north-west Europe.

Here, as everywhere else, seasons, religious festivals and craft traditions have been firmly intertwined until fairly recently. But wherever you are on this Earth you should be true to your time. Your own experiences with the festivals should guide you and become the tool to research into new ways of celebrating them. It is wonderful to see the energy with which more and more people are creating vibrantly new festivals out of the traditional ones.

The Colour Year

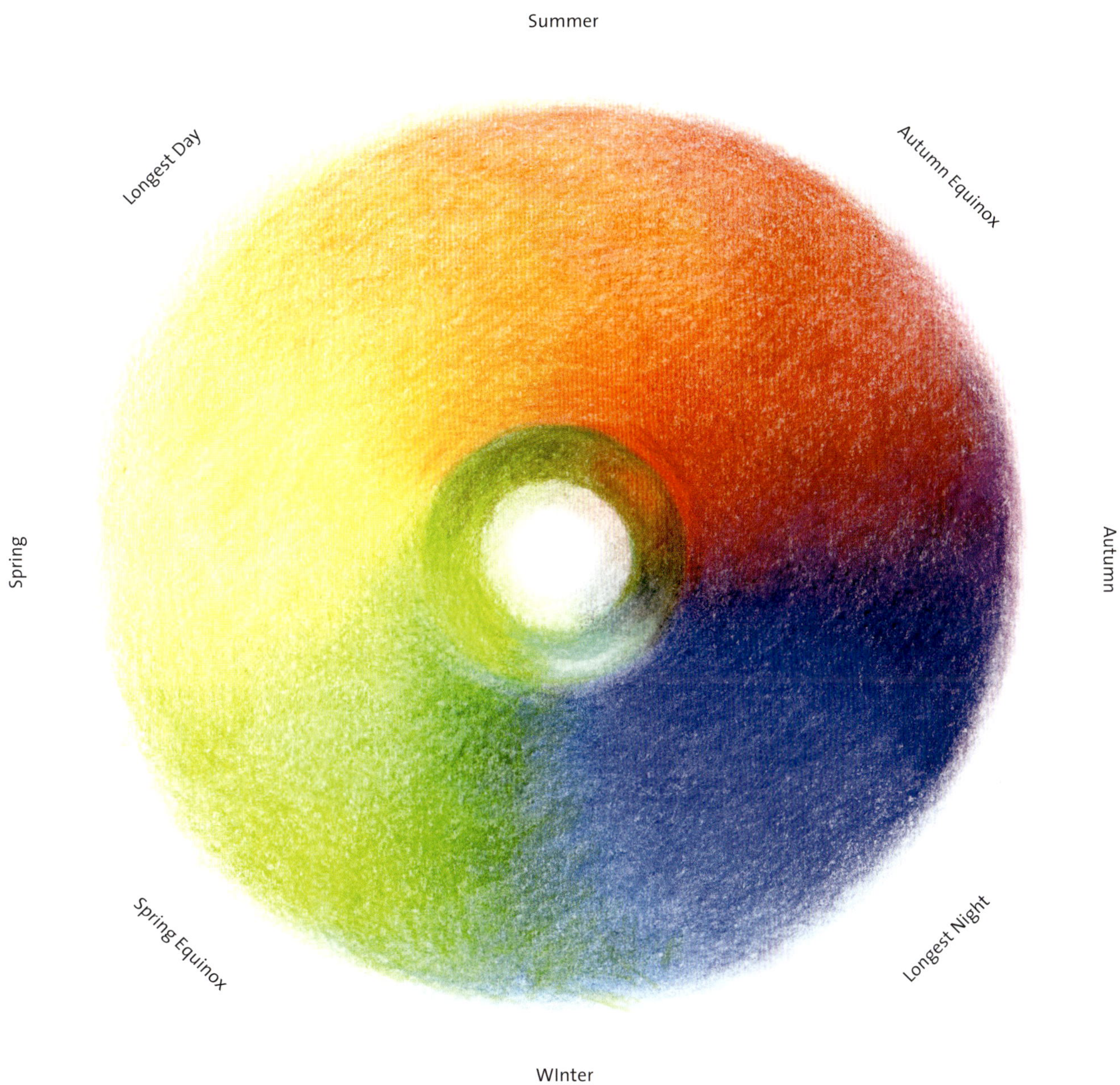

However, some festivals have such magnitude that their influence can be felt all over the world at the same time.

You can take the appropriate projects described in this book and use them for your own, adjusted seasonal festival table.

Making the Children's Year can be a guide for you and your children to develop a love for this amazingly mysterious Earth.

Happy Crafting!

Craft Materials

Quality and colour

Little children are very curious about the world they find themselves in. They love to investigate everything they meet in many and various ways.

An important way is through the sense of touch. Their little fingers remember the feel of the cat's hair, the keys on Grandma's piano, rust on a garden spade.

The materials we give them speak of soft or smooth or grainy qualities intrinsically bound up with that one particular substance. Therefore natural fabrics like pure wool, cotton and silk speak of the real world, which is rich and varied and full of life.

Children are also acutely sensitive to colour. Again we can help by giving colours that are suitable for them.

And what joy it is to work with these rainbow colours. They contain a whole gamut of emotions: jolly yellow, fiery red, inward violet, expansive blue, quiet green and all the just-in-between hues. Colours can be pastel for winter and spring or full-bodied for summer, autumn and Christmas. Remember, beige is boring for a child, and black and grey only really suit the serious artist – neither brings joy to the child.

Most patterned fabrics are too sophisticated and fashionable for little ones. They speak a confused language – plain is best.

Supply box

When you get a sudden inspiration to create, the last thing you want to do is to go shopping for the 'YOU WILL NEED' section. Always be on the lookout for good deals and the 'right' fabric and colour.

It is good to have several boxes or drawers containing essentials. Be on the lookout for seasonal colours of table mats and larger pieces of fabric to place under your simple and larger seasonal nature tables. For the small nature tables the easiest material to use are felt squares in the colours below. You can use a 30 x 30cm/12 x 12" square, and round off the corners or make a circle out of it.

I recommend the following colours for each season:

Spring	pastel yellowish green (ground) and pastel pink (sky)
Summer	plain rich green and orange
Autumn	rich golden brown and red
Winter	white and pastel blue/violet
Christmas	rich red and deep ultramarine blue

See also the Colour Year on page 9

The following materials are always handy:

- Pins and needles
- Sewing cotton in various rainbow colours
- Sharp scissors and children's scissors
- Knitting needles – size 3.5 is very useful
- H and 2B pencils
- Coloured pencils
- Sharpener and a good rubber
- Thin printer paper and drawing paper – A4
- Plain coloured tissue paper
- Non-toxic watercolours and a brush
- Off-cuts of 100% natural fabric – plain rainbow colours, pastel and full-bodied
- Knitting wool, double-knit thickness (see above for 'natural' and 'rainbow' colours)
- Short-cut dyes for wool only food dyes (and even some strongly coloured fizzy drinks if you are really desperate)
- Wooden beads
- Craft knife and cutting mat or board
- Thin, stiff card
- Glue – glue stick, PVA and UHU
- String
- Ribbons (various)
- Ruler, set-square, compass
- Paper fasteners, drawing pins, Blu-Tack
- Tape measure
- Wool tops (long strands of carded wool, about 5cm wide). These are a wonderfully woolly shortcut
- Roving (similar to wool tops but narrower)
- 4 large clear plastic boxes with lids to keep your precious seasonal crafts safe for next year.

Where to find these materials

The secret is to turn into a hunter! Wherever you go, always have the question in the back of your mind, 'Is that what could inspire us?' I found a mixture of local craft shops, larger craft supermarkets and online shops supplied me with all I needed for this whole book. See the Resources section (page 236) for help in finding materials.

Nature Table Scenery

Each of the season sections in this book starts with a large festival table and a small nature table. Seasonally coloured veils add magic to these. Each season has its own colours, and dyed veils (page 15) are the most satisfying material to bring out nature's moods.

Nature tables can be made in any size from just a few seasonal flowers and objects on a small placemat on the dining room table, to a large display in classroom. Little quiet corners at home are ideal: a shelf, part of a bookcase unit, a deep window recess, a low corner table, an unused fireplace, for example. For these you just need smaller veils to make a backdrop and ground. Very often a bit of Blu-Tack is enough to fix the veils to the wall.

However, on large festival tables at home, playgroups and schools, you can use a pre-made stand over which veils can be draped (see page 15). The ground can be made 'hilly' or 'mountainous' by placing bricks or small boxes underneath the veils.

Once you start building your set, your imagination has a starting point and can guide you to create beautiful scenery. When one seasonal celebration has passed, the veils can be replaced with the next ones, or you can give the table a little 'rest'.

Nature Table Backdrop Stand

Two backdrop sizes are given – the smaller for your home and the larger for a playgroup or school. Place it where it is not in the way, but where it can still be enjoyed. Perhaps the corner of a sideboard, a small table against the wall, or in a deep, large window recess.

You will need some carpentry skills, so it is not suitable for children to make.

YOU WILL NEED

- Panel of hardboard or mdf – 6mm/¼" thick – about 50 x 50cm/20 x 20" for home use or 70cm x 70cm/28 x 28" for school use
- Piece of wood for the foot – any type – size about 5 x 12cm/2 x 5" wide* and 50cm/20" long for home use or 70cm/28" long for school use
- 3 screws (3mm/size 6), about 2.5cm/1" long
- Wire – about 2mm diameter/US gauge 12, at least 40cm/16" long or a wire coat-hanger (not plastic or wood)
- Wood off-cut – about 2.5 x 5cm/1 x 2", 8cm/3" long
- 2 screws (3mm/size 6), 2cm/¾" long
- Handsaw
- Sandpaper
- Drill and bits
- Screwdriver
- Pliers or wire-cutters
- White paint (water-based) and a paint brush

*If you cannot find a piece of wood this thickness for the foot, then use a thinner piece and put a weight on it to stabilise the arrangement. The weight (which could be a brick) will be covered by the veils.

Cut the top corners off the panel to soften the shape (about 5cm/2" down and 15cm/6" across). Drill three holes in the panel and screw the base on to the front. It should stand firmly on a flat surface. If necessary, put a brick on it to keep it steady. Sand all the edges to remove any roughness. Position the small wooden block on the back of the panel at least 6cm/2½" below the top edge. Mark the position.

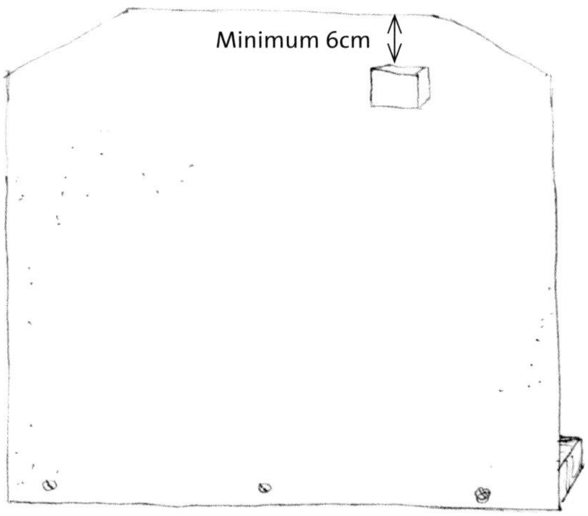

Drill a hole in the middle of the thin edge of the wood block which is just big enough to take the wire (at least 3cm/1¼" deep), but not right through the block. (NB: There should be room for the fabric to drape behind the panel and in front of the wire.) Drill two holes in the panel and fix the wood block onto the back of it with the hole facing upwards. Insert the wire into the hole and bend it neatly so that the end comes in front of the panel by about 15cm/6". If the wire is a bit too loose, stabilise it with some Blu-Tack on the block. Remove the wire and form a little hook in the front end.

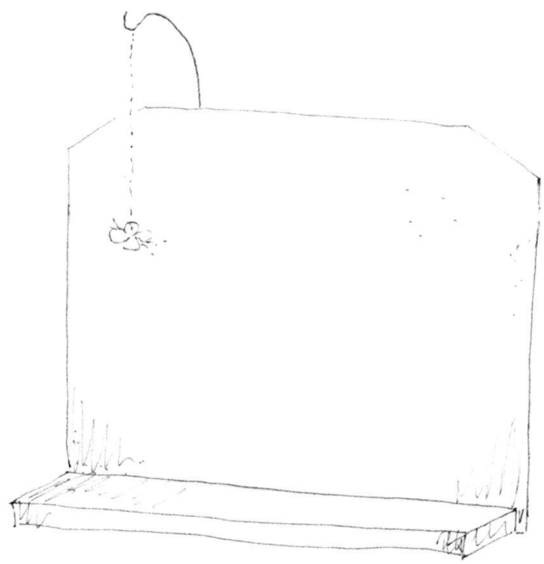

Replace it and test it by hanging a fairy or a butterfly on it. Adjust the shape of the wire till it works nicely. Paint it all white

The backdrop is ready for you to decorate.

Nature Table Veils and Play Veils

Pure, clear rainbow or spectrum colours bring warmth to any soul. Children love them. Colour can shine with happiness, excitement, peace, inwardness and many more subtle moods.

Each season has its own quality and colour mood. Delicate pinks and yellowy greens conjure up spring, whereas full-bodied fiery reds evoke autumn. Warm yellows speak of summer, whereas pale grey purples express winter (see the Colour Year on page 9 for more information).

White silk or pure cotton can be dyed easily in a myriad of colours. You can use dyed muslin (very cheap and beautifully transparent) for all purposes or you can select different fabrics for different uses – cotton sheets (not too old) for rough-and-tumble camps and castles, muslin for cloaks and wings, and the thinnest silk for nature tables.

When you use these veils as a background and a base for a nature table you set the mood straight away.

They are also evocative in simple fairy tale puppet shows on a table top. Skies, mountains, forests, fields and rivers can be created simply with them.

They can also be used as roofs for camps (page 115), castles and shops. They can be used over and over again endlessly in many different situations.

When not used as scene-setters these veils are a key part of imaginative play and are therefore one of the most important projects in the book. They are wonderful for dressing up as fairies (with scrunchy hairbands, page 106), princesses and princes (crowns, page 233) and pirates.

Each nature table is built up out of various colours of veils; for example in autumn you can have a large opaque strong red background with a transparent lighter warm orange draped partly over it. To avoid buying too many expensive dyes you can mix your own colours – green, orange, purple, brown, grey etc – with just three colours (see colour mixing, page 16).

You could prepare for the full year of seasonal tables in one dyeing session. Teenagers and adults can have fun making them.

Below are instructions for different dyeing projects – the first for large quantities (a camp, perhaps) and for smaller quantities, for example silk or muslin for a seasonal table.

NOTES ON DYE

The fresher the dye, the stronger the colour; the dye loses its strength with use. For a deeper colour use fresh dye and leave the material in for a long time. The quicker you dye, the lighter the colour. For a very delicate colour, dilute the dye with water. The autumn and Christmas colours are the strongest; spring and summer and the snow scenes are paler.

For larger quantities of fabric

YOU WILL NEED

- Very fine 100% cotton or silk (synthetic fabric will not take dyes), about 150cm/60" long and as wide as possible. As many pieces as the number of colours you want (you might need to order silk online)
- Hand dyes in 3 primary colours – mid red, mid blue and lemon yellow (for 'in between' colours see colour mixing, page 16)
- Rubber gloves
- Apron
- Wooden spoons (which will be stained forever!)
- Saucepans or buckets to contain the dyes – one per colour

Cut out and hem the fabric pieces by hand or machine. Wearing the gloves and apron, hand wash the fabric to remove any starch (these fabrics are too delicate for machine washing). Follow the manufacturer's instruction to make three different containers of the three primary colours. Modern dyes tend to be very harsh so be careful. Test the suitability of the colours by dipping small samples of your fabric in each dye. First dye all the yellow pieces, then the red pieces and finally the blues. These later ones are very strong and can easily stain everything else. For making orange, green, purple and brown dyes, follow the colour mixing directions on page 16. Hang out to dry, preferably outside but not in full sun

Before you start dyeing, think of other items you might want to colour at the same time, like bits of wool fleece.

For smaller quantities of fabric

YOU WILL NEED

- Very fine 100% cotton or silk (synthetic fabric will not take dyes). As many pieces as the number of colours you want
- Watercolours in three primary colours – mid red, mid blue and lemon yellow (or if you want more, see colour mixing, page 16)
- Apron
- A bowl big enough to comfortably contain the fabric and dye

Follow the instructions above for larger quantities of fabric, up to where you will start to dye your fabric. Dilute each watercolour in just enough water to cover the fabric. Test the suitability of the colours by dipping small samples of your fabric in each dye. When you're happy with the result, submerge the fabric and agitate it a bit so that all of it is dyed. Hang it out to dry, preferably outside but not in the sun.

Please note: Using watercolours will make these dyes impermanent and they will fade over time.

Colour mixing

If your dyes are true mid-range colours (for example, red should be not too orange or too purple) then mixing is easy. But this is seldom the case.

For GREEN, mix Prussian blue (slightly greenish blue) and lemon yellow (slightly greenish yellow)
For PURPLE – mix ultramarine blue (slightly purple blue) and carmine red (slightly bluish red)
For ORANGE – mix vermillion red (orangey red) and yellow
For BROWN – mix red, yellow and a tiny amount of blue – the warmer the yellow the warmer the brown
For DULL GREEN – mix ultramarine blue and lemon yellow
For PALE GREY – mix light ultramarine blue, a tiny bit of carmine red and an even smaller amount of lemon yellow (this is good for winter)

Always mix your new colours in small amounts in small containers first, to avoid losing all your dye if it is wrongly proportioned. Consult the Colour Year for the whole year (page 9) to see which colours are most suitable for each season.

Sewing and Knitting

Throughout the book there will be projects that require a varying degree of sewing and knitting skills. Here are some basic tips and skills that may help if you're a beginner.

Sewing tips

Be careful when using 'one-way' fabric, such as velvet or corduroy, as all pieces of the garment need to run in one direction. Lay and pin the pattern pieces on your fabric. For finishing and neatening edges there are three easy ways so choose which suits you best:

1. Use a sewing machine to zigzag closely to the edge of the fabric.
2. Cut out with pinking shears, although this method is not very satisfactory when working with very thick fabrics that fray easily.
3. Oversew all the raw edges by hand (this method is of course more time consuming but works well on all fabrics).

Knitting abbreviations

st(s)	stitch(es)
k	knit
p	purl
m	make one stitch
st st	stocking stitch
g st	garter stitch
rep	repeat
cont	continue
sl	slip
tog	together
rds	rounds
inc	increase
dec	decrease
psso	pass slipped stitch over
DK	double knitting wool

Tips for Using this Book

PATTERNS

Patterns in this book either include dimensions or an instruction as to the precentage of enlargement required. Some patterns appear in their actual size. In these instances you may trace patterns or scan them and then print them out. These patterns and toy designs are for personal use only. The projects in this book are not intended to be made for commercial production or sold for personal gain.

HOW TO TRACE

There are three alternative methods:

1. By far the simplest way to trace is to make a photocopy – this allows you to easily change the size.
2. Lay very thin paper like greaseproof baking paper, lightweight copy paper or tracing paper over the original and follow the line with a pencil. Hold your paper steady on the original with paper clips or masking tape.
3. Hold the original against a window with your paper over it and follow the line with a pencil. You can use a light box instead of a window for this method too.

HOW TO TRANSFER

There are three alternative methods:

1. If your shape is simple, cut around the trace and make it into a template. Fix that onto your fabric with pins or, if on paper, small bits of Blu-Tack and cut out the shape. A template allows you to repeat a shape very easily.
2. If your original is complicated (for example the Advent calendar on page 213) first trace it to make a copy. Place your trace onto the cardboard that you plan to cut out and fix it with paper clips. Draw over your trace with a slightly blunt pencil, pressing firmly. This will make a shallow groove in the cardboard which will form your guide for cutting. You may need a resilient backing to work on, like a writing pad or magazine – this should make your groove a bit clearer.
3. If the 'groove' method does not work (perhaps because the base material is too hard) take your trace and turn it over and cover the back of the trace lines with a broad shaded line using a very soft pencil (at least 2B). Turn over and fix it onto your cardboard, right side up. Draw firmly over your trace lines again with a hard pencil (at least 2H). Remove your trace to see the outline transferred to the card.

Spring

Very soon after Christmas deep darkness makes way for light. The lengthening days seem refreshed and brighter, an early prelude to spring. What a contrast to the dark days of late autumn! But the cold winter wind still blows and keeps its chill. The buds on the trees all seem quiet and still. But look deeper and a lot of them are red – they cannot wait to start growing.

Amongst the tired old grass and rotten leaves from last year the first flowers are showing. They are small, keeping their heads out of the freezing breezes. Snowdrops hang theirs down; no snow can get inside. Pert daffodils send their shoots straight up and stand prettily and defiantly as forerunners for the grand flower show to come. A little later the crocuses and primroses dare to peek at the sun. The trees have already sent out tiny little blossoms and soon the patient buds unfurl their delicate leaves with vigour.

Not only is the plant world renewing itself; everywhere the animals are preparing for their offspring with their searching for mates and nest-building. Little lambs have already been jumping in the meadows with spring joy. Soon it will be the equinox: the days will be as long as the nights. Acceleration seems to be the key word: quickly the sun climbs higher and higher in the sky. Change is speeding up. The world starts to grow warmer. This is the nature mood of Easter.

Eggs, with their sun-like centre, have been used for centuries as symbols of new life and what an abundance of new life surrounds us now!

Easter Festival Table

Easter is a movable feast. It takes place on the first Sunday after the first full moon after the spring equinox. So in essence it is about the returning of light. It is celebrated in different ways in most cultures. How to capture this mighty event in a project?

The Easter festival table is a good starting point. As with all season tables you can either keep it very simple or you can go to town and incorporate lots of details. It all depends who it is for – for teenagers and adults a simple scene is often sufficient. However, little children love the fun of a real abundance.

For building up the background, refer to nature table veils (page 14), the backdrop stand (page 12), the veils (page 15) and the Colour Year (page 9). Start with veils in pastel pink or yellow and fresh green for the ground, with or without backdrop elevations (little boxes to put under the veils). Freely lay the veils with a few natural folds where they want to be. A stream can be indicated by a narrow blue veil. For the centre piece you can use a large (about 30cm/12") flower-pot saucer – clay is best but plastic will do. Protect your table if you use a clay saucer, as water will seep through.

Fill the saucer up with houseplant compost and cover with moss, which you can find outside in shadowy damp places. Or, if you start two weeks before you need it, you can sow it with grass seed. If you do, make sure you keep it moist all the time. If you only have about four days, you can use cress seed.

Now for your actors on the scene: see the following chapter for spring flower fairies (page 24), Easter chicks (page 28), chickens and cockerels (pages 29 and 30), Easter hares (page 32), lambs (page 30), Easter candles (page 34). Crystals and a small vase with flowers, and Easter eggs on Easter morning, can complement the scene. Behind all this you can have a larger vase with freshly sprouting branches from which hang beautifully painted Easter eggs (page 36).

Let your imagination guide you. The most important figure, out of which all this magic appears, is the figure of Mother Nature (page 22), who can be hung centrally over the table. As with all nature tables, the figures can be played with by children, but in order to keep the magic it is good to respect them. Therefore items should not be removed but placed perhaps in an even better place. And when flowers fade it is easy to replace them, as they are increasingly more and more available.

When the festival time is over, it is good to give the table a rest so that when the time comes for the next one it will be interesting again.

Simple Spring Table

Start with a place-mat, small cloth or, easier still, use a 30 x 30cm/12 x 12" felt square in pastel pink or pastel yellow and either round off the corners or make a circle out of it. Put it where it will not be constantly moved. Display a few flowering branches and perhaps some flowers in a vase. Pick them from your garden, if you're lucky enough to have one, or from the wild – but remember only to pick the flowers from common species and never uproot them.

A spring art postcard in a simple card stand, a candle, a few Easter eggs and a pale-coloured crystal are often sufficient to set the mood.

Please note: Never leave a lit candle unattended.

Mother Nature

Mother Nature, like Persephone, presides over the return of light and warmth in spring. She can take centre stage on the nature table. Here she is the queen of nature and therefore made out of the queen of materials – pure silk. She weaves a new spring out of the four basic elements, so her garment is made out of two layers – one representing earth (violet) and water (pale blue) and one representing air (pale yellow) and fire (pale peach-red).

YOU WILL NEED

- The thinnest silk available (you may have to go online for this) – 90 x 45cm/36 x 18"
- Good quality water colour paint: violet, ultramarine blue, golden yellow, vermillion
- 4 small containers for the liquid watercolour (eg eggcups, small jam jars, mini snack boxes)
- Soft painting brush – large flat-topped
- A clean white plastic or glass work surface
- Jar of water
- Small ball of wool, for head and hands
- White cotton thread
- Needle and scissors
- Wool tops (pale yellow, 20cm/8" long, for hair)
- Ribbon with tiny embroidered flowers for hairband and flower 'string' about 6mm/¼" wide and 20cm/8" long

1. Make a paper pattern circle (20cm/8" radius). Pin it onto the silk and cut two circles.

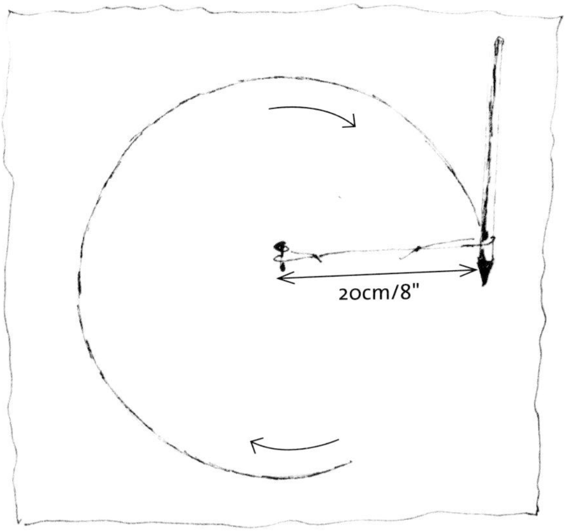

2. Wash the silk gently by hand to remove any starch. While the silk is still wet, spread it out on the clean flat surface and remove all air bubbles by gently spreading them out to the edges with your fingertips. Mix up small quantities of liquid pale watercolour paint in the small containers – one for each colour. Test for strength on a scrap of silk (it should not be too strong). On the first circle paint the outside (10cm/4") with yellow and fade the colour towards the centre. Paint the centre of the circle with pale vermillion and fade outwards into the yellow (with a soft dry brush) so that all transitions are smooth. On the second silk circle paint the outside 10cm/4" with light violet and fade the colour towards the centre. Paint the centre of the second circle with pale ultramarine blue and fade outwards into the violet (with a soft dry brush) so that all transitions are smooth. Leave to dry completely to create a beautiful smooth texture.

3. Lay the two circles on top of each other. Make a tightly wound ball of wool for the head (2½cm/1" diameter) and place it under the dry circles in the very centre. Then gather the silk around the ball to form a neck and tie the thread firmly around the neck (take care not to give her wrinkles).

4. Lay the yellow wool tops symmetrically over the head to create the hair. Fix it with a few stitches in the 'centre parting' right over to the back.

5. Make two tightly wound balls of wool (1cm/½" diameter) and place them under the top silk in the middle of the sides and tie them into place, just as you did for the neck. This makes two arms and two hands.

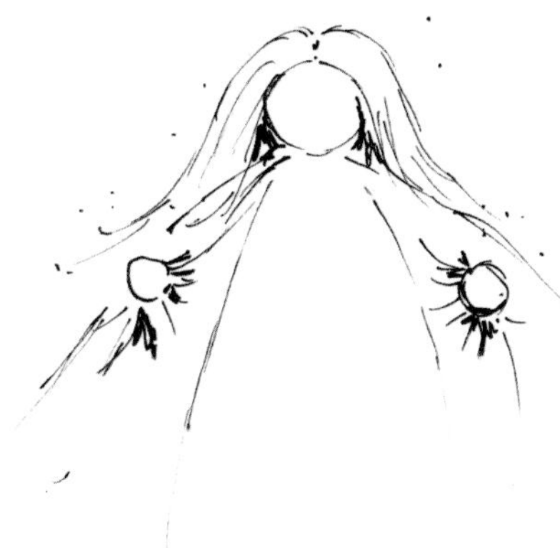

6. Sew the hairband in place with a few stitches and attach the flower 'string' between the two hands.

7. Suspend Mother Nature from the crown of her head with a length of sewing thread and hang her as the focal point over your table. She is now ready to spread her spring bounty over the table.

Spring Flower Fairies

When it is very cold outside with perhaps snow on the ground, it is magical to see the first small shoots of snowdrops tentatively but determinedly pushing up out of the cold earth. We can anticipate the arrival of the pretty flowers by making snowdrop flower fairies. When the flowers unfold outside we have more work to do because soon the crocus, primrose and violet will want our attention.

These fairies are quite quick and not difficult to make but do require nimble fingers for fine cutting, sewing and tying.

Snowdrop fairy

YOU WILL NEED

- 1 piece white felt (12 x 12cm/5 x 5")
- 2 pieces green felt (12 x 7cm/5 x 3") and a circle (3cm/1¼" diameter)
- Pipe cleaner
- 1 bead (2cm/¾" diameter)
- Glue
- Thread – white and green

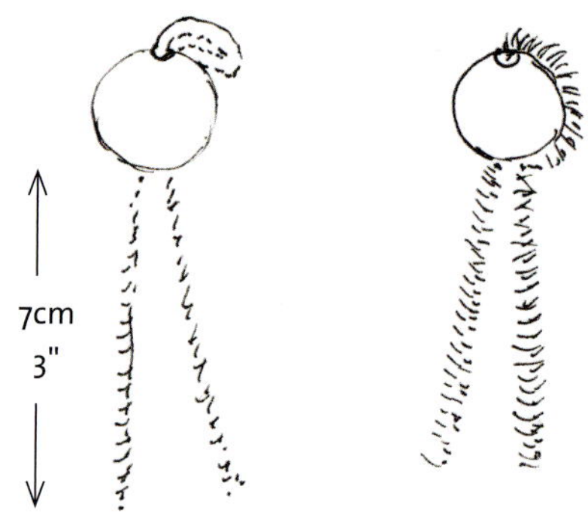

1. Fold the pipe cleaner in half, push the folded end through the bead and fold over 1cm/½" to stop the bead falling off, and secure with glue. If the pipe cleaner is too thick, push it through singly and fold it back over the bead and twist in place.

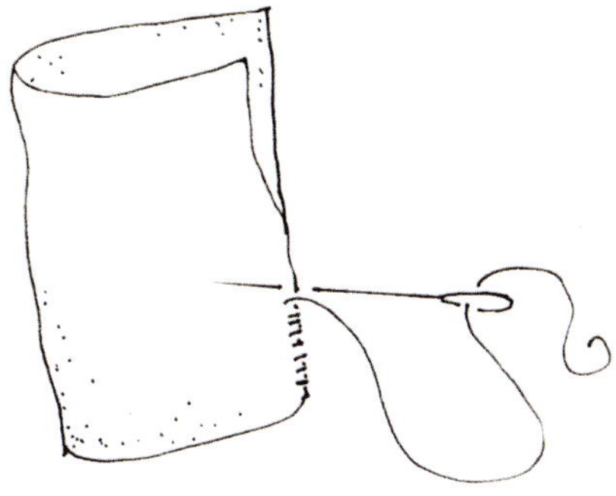

2. Cut a strip of white felt for the dress (7 x 12cm/3 x 5") and sew the short sides together using a tiny overstitch.

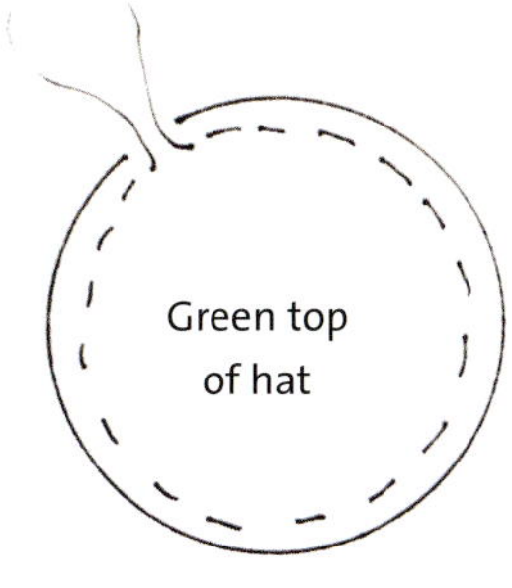

5. Cut a circle of green felt (3cm/1¼") for the top of the hat and fold the green circle as shown and fix with a few stitches.

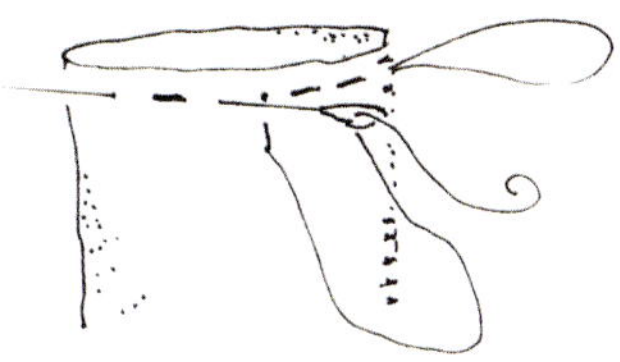

3. Gather the neck edge and pull tight around the pipe cleaner and tie around the neck.

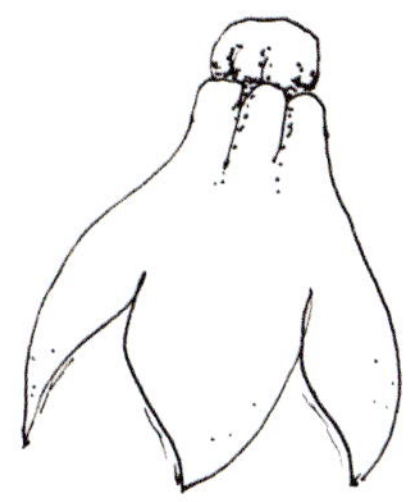

6. Sew the white felt as for the dress and gather tightly around the green felt stalk.

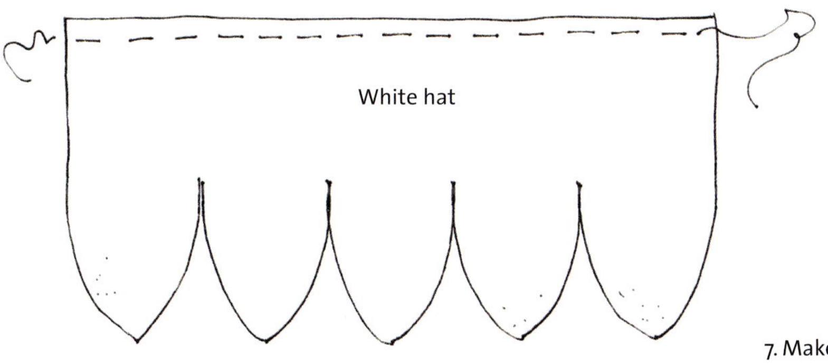

4. To make the hat, cut a piece of white felt 8 x 4cm/3¼ x 1½" and shape the petals.

7. Make the leaves from the piece of green felt 5 x 12cm/2 x 5". (NB: Pull up the gathering threads tightly and secure them before fixing around the stalk and/or neck.)

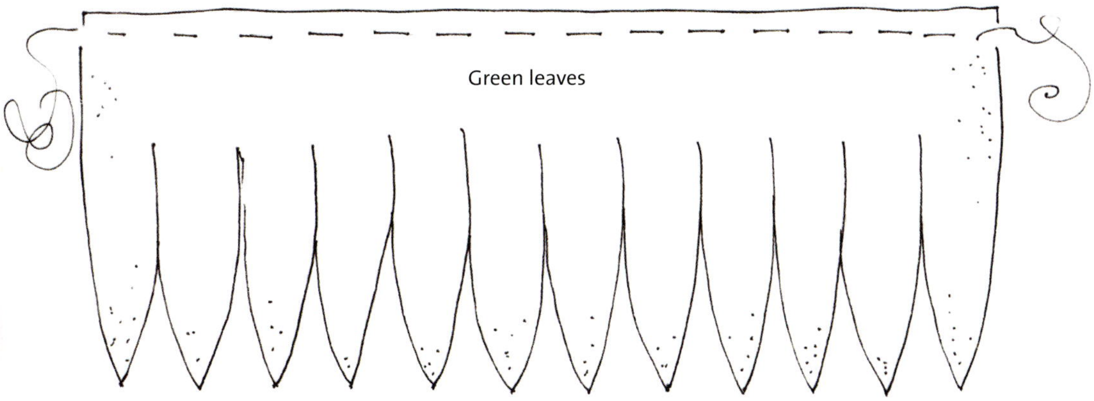

NB: All pattern pieces for the flower fairies are actual size.

8. Gather the top edge with green thread and join together round the neck over the dress then glue the hat onto the head.

Crocus fairy

YOU WILL NEED

- Purple felt (12cm/5" square)
- Green felt (12 x 5cm/5 x 2")
- Scraps of golden yellow felt
- Pipe cleaner
- Bead for head – 2cm/¾" diameter
- Purple thread
- Glue

1. Follow the instructions given for the snowdrop but make the dress and hat from purple felt.

2. Cut a scrap of golden yellow felt, as below, to show the characteristic saffron stamen of the crocus and gather the hat tightly round the stamen, as below. The leaves are the same as for the snowdrop.

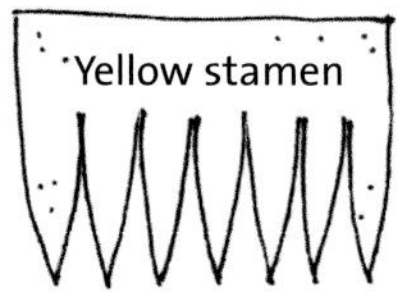

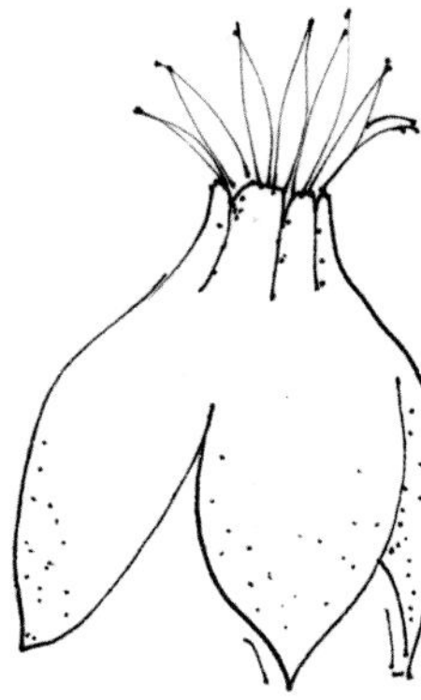

Primrose fairy

YOU WILL NEED

- Light yellow felt (12 x 12cm/5 x 5")
- Green felt (12 x 5cm/5 x 2")
- Pipe cleaner
- Bead for head (2cm/¾" diameter)
- Yellow thread
- Glue

1. Make this fairy as for the previous two but make the dress and hat from the light yellow felt. To make the hat, cut another piece of light yellow felt (8 x 4cm/3¼" x 1½"), as shown below.

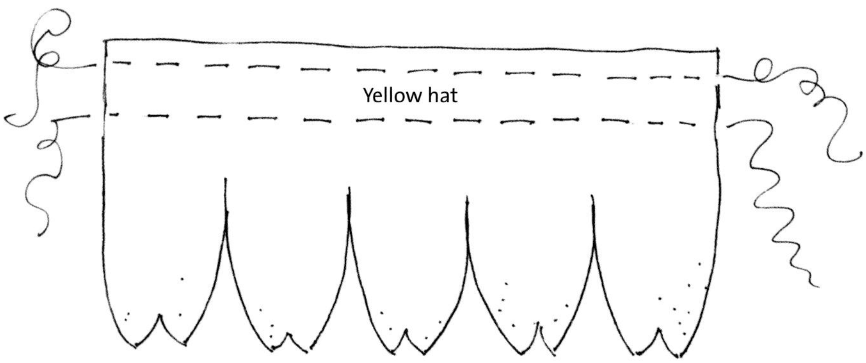

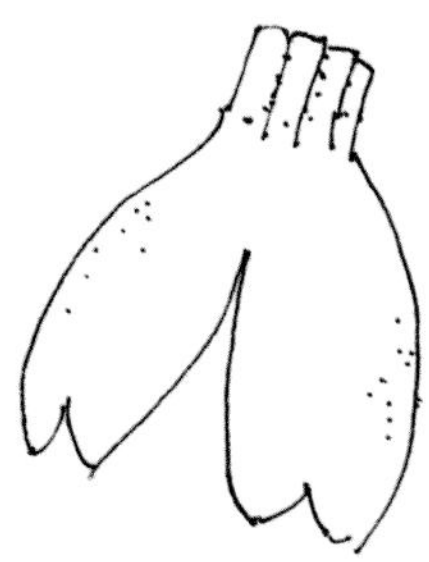

2. Gather tightly at the top and 1cm/½" below the top of the hat, as shown above.

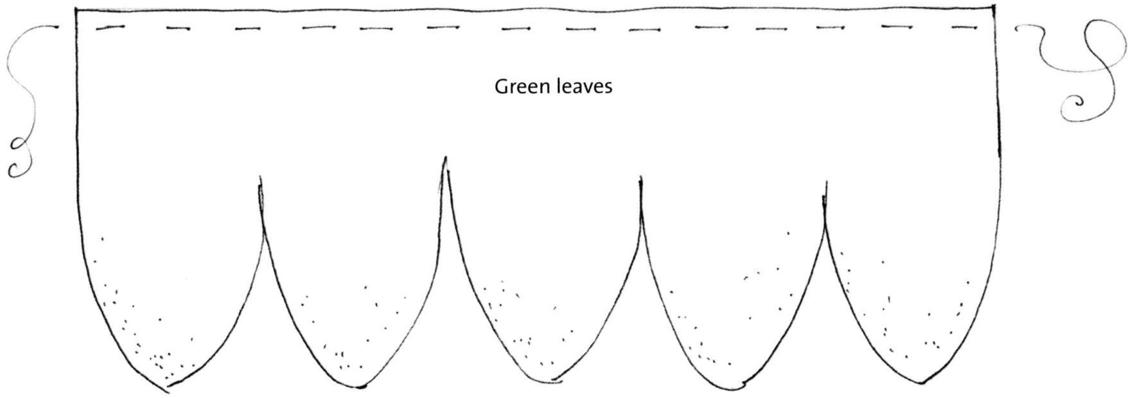

3. Follow the diagram (above) for cutting the leaves from the green felt and secure them over the dress, as described for the snowdrop.

Violet fairy

YOU WILL NEED

- Dark violet felt (12 x 12cm/5 x 5")
- Green felt (12 x 5cm/5 x 2")
- Pipe cleaner
- Bead for head (2cm/¾" diameter)
- Violet thread
- Glue

1. Follow the instructions as for the snowdrop but to make the dress and hat, use the dark violet felt. Cut and sew the hat as shown.

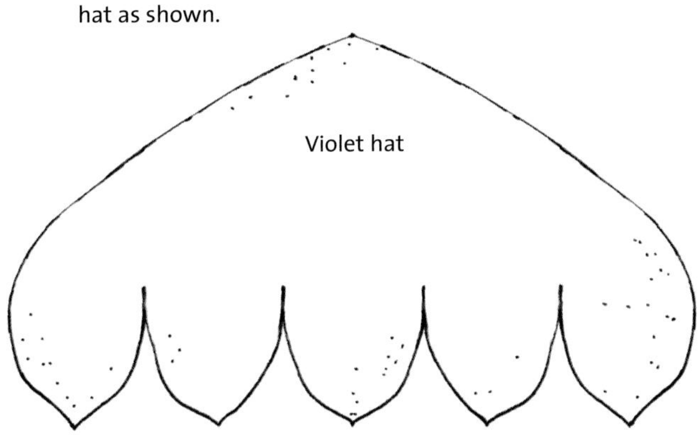

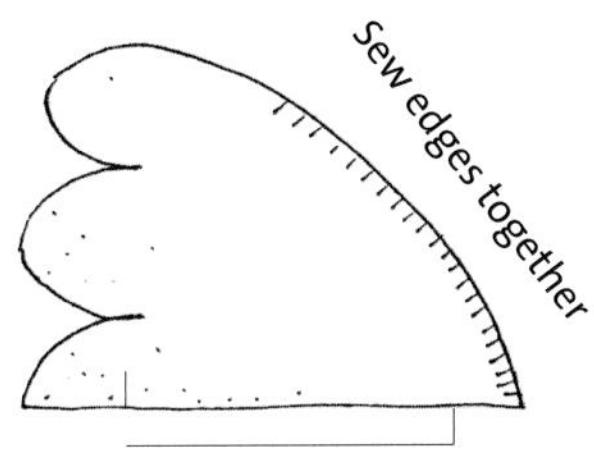

2. Cut the leaves from green felt as shown and secure over the dress as described for the snowdrop.

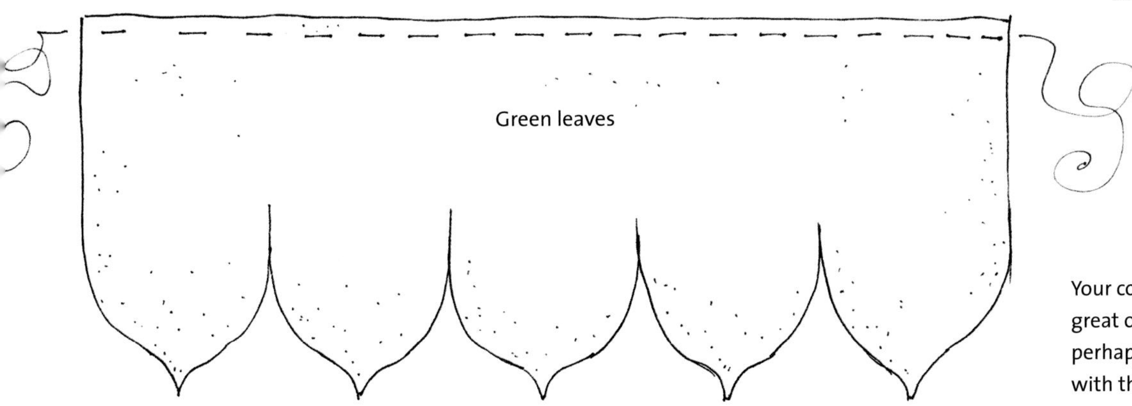

Your colourful fairies will look great on your spring table, perhaps with a very small vase with the actual flowers in it.

Easter Chicks

Suitable for knitting beginners, these charming little chicks are ideal for an Easter table. They are quick, easy and bring a smile to anyone's face. A slightly more experienced crafter may need to help with the finishing details.

YOU WILL NEED

- Double knit yellow wool
- Knitting needles (3mm/US size 3)
- Scrap of orange felt
- Fleece or cotton wool for stuffing
- Embroidery thread – dark blue
- Wooden or matching button for the feet

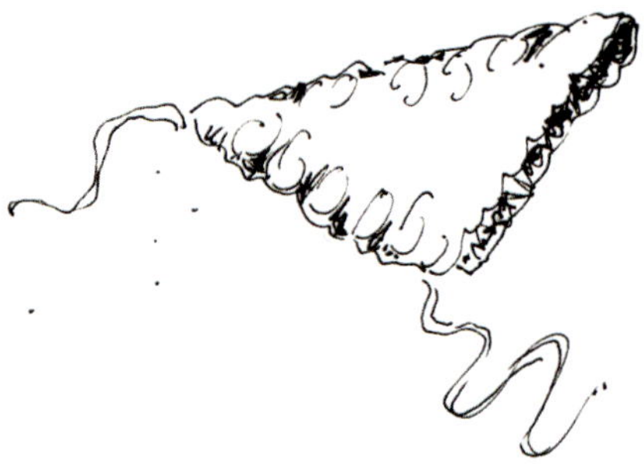

1. Cast on 14 sts and k 24 rows or till you have a square. Cast off and fold into a triangle.

2. Sew up on one side and stuff the chick lightly with fleece or cotton wool. Sew up the other side of the triangle, pull the top corner slightly inwards to make a rounded head and then shape the head with a few stitches round the neck.

3. Cut the orange felt into a beak shape and sew into place

4. Embroider the eyes with the dark blue thread (these are set close to the beak on either side) and sew the button upside down onto the chick so that it will stand up.

See how easy – now how about its little sisters?

Cheeky Chicken

Here is an opportunity to knit a whole farmyard set, which can be used in the spring table. They are quick and simple to make for beginners in knitting and crocheting. A little help may be needed for the finishing touches.

YOU WILL NEED

- Small amount of white or yellow double knit wool
- Small amount of red and yellow double knit wool for comb, wattle and beak
- Pair 3mm/US size 3 knitting needles
- 3½mm/US C crochet hook
- Fleece or cotton wool for stuffing
- Button – wood or matching your bird colour

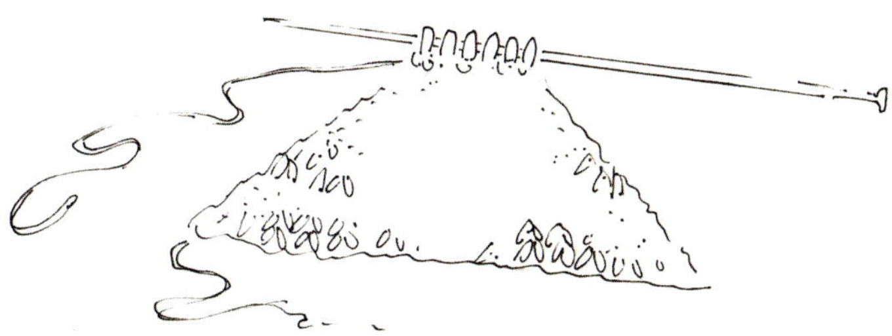

1. Cast on 18 sts and work in garter stitch. K 3 rows. On the fourth, and every following row, k the first 2 sts together. Continue until there are 6 sts left.

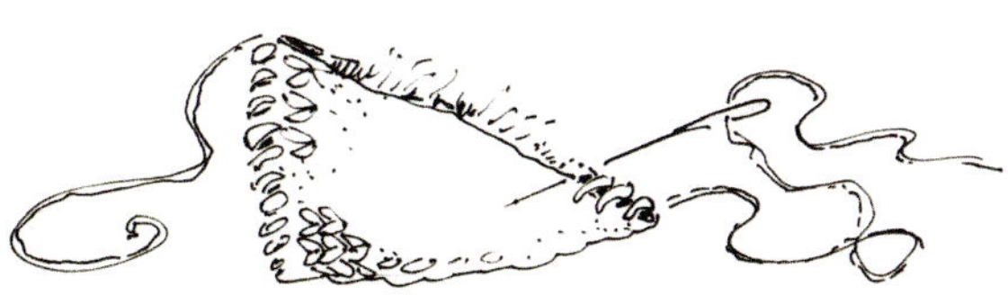

2. Cast off and fold this triangular piece in half and sew up one side. Stuff the triangle and sew up the other side.

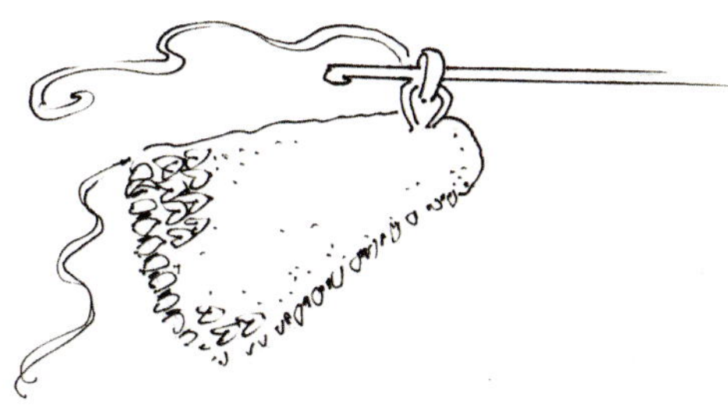

3. With the red wool, crochet the chicken's comb by making 3 sts into the same place.

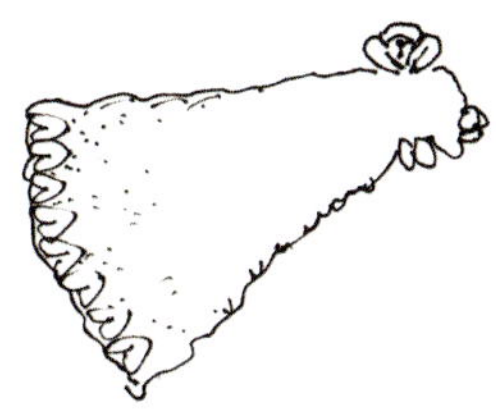

4. Neaten up and embroider the beak with yellow wool and the wattle with red wool.

5. For the tail, use the same wool as for the body then crochet four rings with 5 chain sts each.

6. Sew on the button with the hollow side facing downwards to make the chicken stand.

Cockerel

YOU WILL NEED

- Small amount of reddish brown double knit wool
- Small amount of red, green and yellow double knit wool
- Pair 3mm/US size 3 knitting needles
- 3½mm/US C crochet hook
- Fleece or cotton wool for stuffing
- Button about 2cm/¾" diameter

Knit and make up the cockerel in exactly the same way as the chicken but cast on 20 sts. The main difference is in the tail. Use red, green and yellow wool and use chain st to make several feathers, 8 sts each. Sew in the end of the threads.

Knitted Lamb

YOU WILL NEED

- White alpaca bouclé (yarn with little loops) is best because it makes the lamb extra woolly, but any mohair or soft wool will be fine too. (Note: bouclé wool is not suitable for beginners, as the loops are too confusing.)
- 3.5mm knitting needles, but check the instructions on the wool packet before you start
- Clean wool fleece for stuffing
- Pipe cleaner
- Large-eye darning needle (several would be useful but you can manage with one)

A little knitted lamb is perfect for your festival table. Here is a little soft cuddly one.

This is suitable for beginners who have just mastered the craft of knitting, perhaps with a little help.

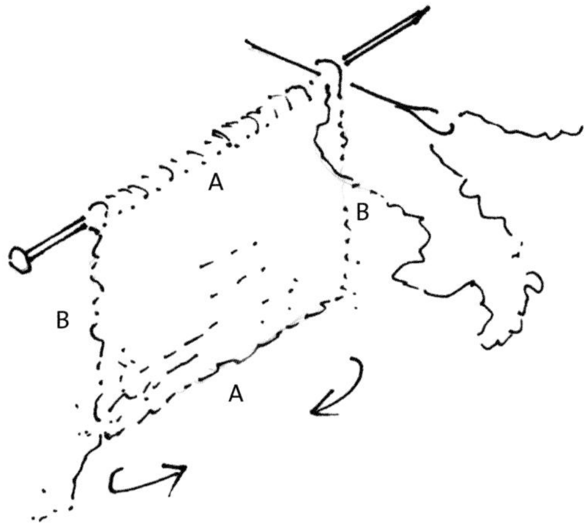

1. For the body, cast on 20 stitches and knit 24 rows then cut the yarn with 30cm/12" to spare. Do not cast off, but pick up the stitches with the darning needle. This is the tail end of the body.

2. Sew up the bottom seam (B).

3. Stuff the body, making sure you do not overdo it, so the lamb stays soft and cuddly, then gather up the stitches around the front, pull them together and sew the front closed.

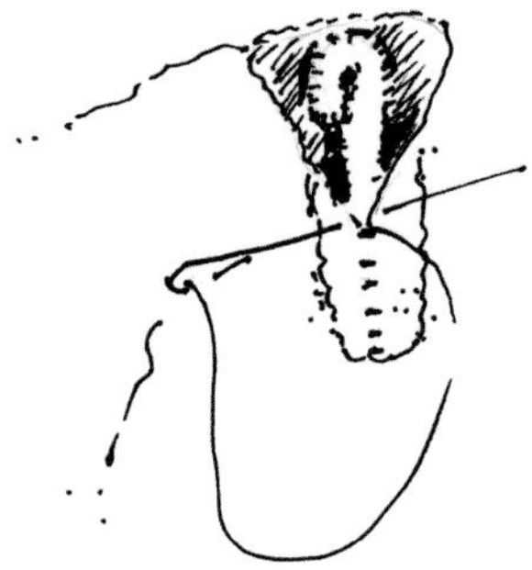

4. For the head, cast on 10 stitches and knit 12 rows. Cut the yarn with 15cm/6" to spare and with the darning needle pick up the stitches as above. Sew up the two sides and stuff the head and sew it up.

For the legs, cast on 4 stitches and knit 10 rows. Cut the yarn with 15cm/6" to spare. Do not cast off, but pick up the stitches with the darning needle. Cut a slightly longer piece of pipe cleaner and fold over a tiny piece at each end. Wrap the knitted leg around it and sew it up then repeat three more times.

5. To make the ear, cast on 2 stitches and knit 2 rows. Cut the yarn with 10cm/4" to spare but don't cast off; pick up the stitches with the darning needle. Repeat one more time. Then to make the tail, cast on 2 stitches and knit 3 rows. Cut the yarn with 10cm/4" to spare. Do not cast off, but pick up the stitches with the darning needle.

To finish, firmly sew the legs in place on the body with the same wool so they are able to stand up and attach all the other pieces.

Now you have mastered the first woolly wonder, the rest of the flock will follow very quickly – as all good lambs do.

Quickest-Ever Easter Hare

YOU WILL NEED

- Thin card – cereal packet is ideal
- Scissors
- Carded wool tops, mainly light brown and a small bit of white for the tail – roughly 30gm/1 oz
- Light brown felt for the ears (10 x 7cm/4 x 3")
- Iron-on interfacing
- Strong crochet cotton, any colour

Here is a golden opportunity to create a very lifelike and cuddly hare in no time. Best of all, it is very easy to make. The design is based on the traditional pompom (page 231) but uses wool tops instead of knitting wool.

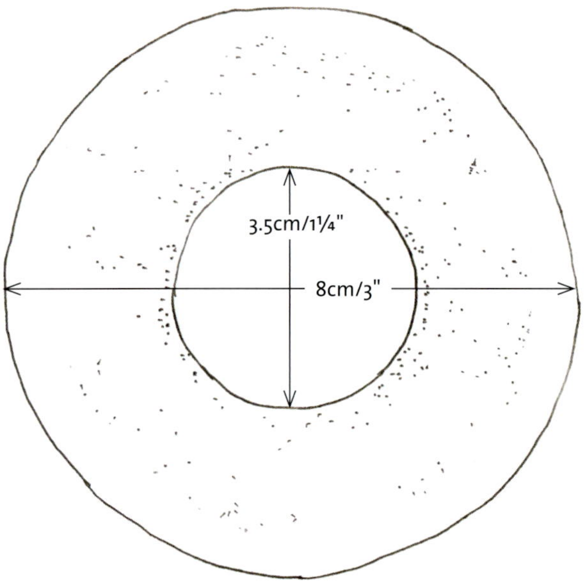

1. Cut out two circles of card for the body.

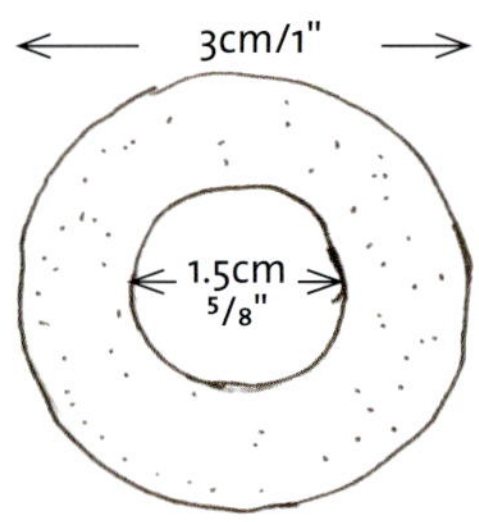

3. Cut out two circles of card for the tail.

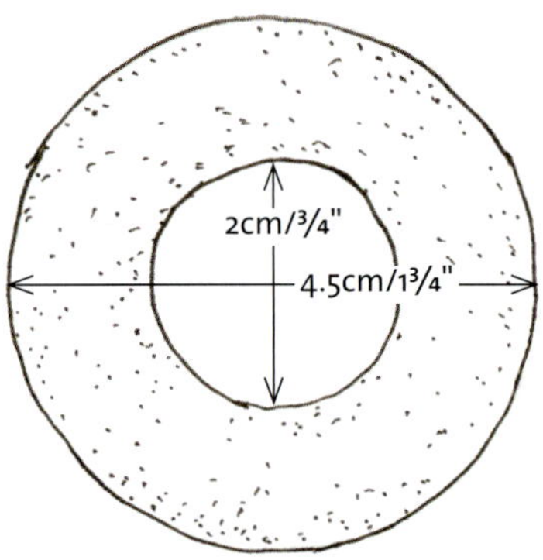

2. Now cut out two circles of card for the head.

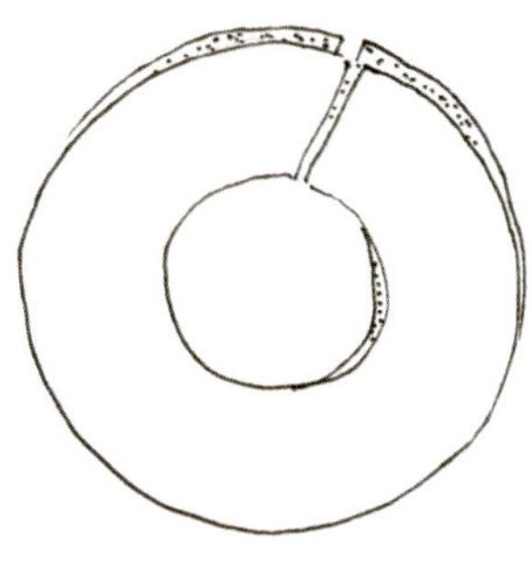

4. Cut through all circles at right angles and line them up in pairs.

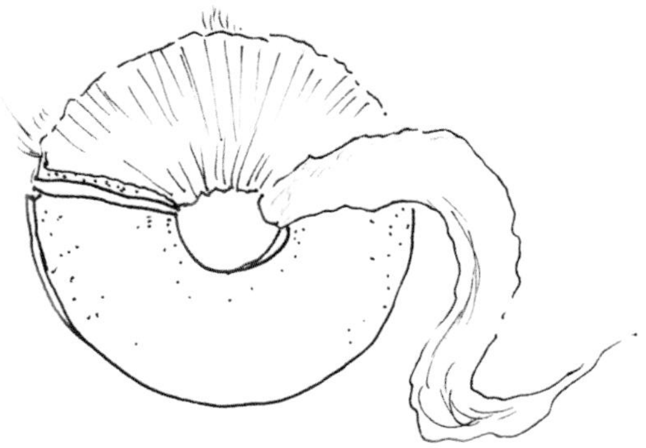

5. To make the body, begin by splitting one carded tops strand into four thinner ones. Wrap one strand tightly around the two circles, always going in the same direction. Do not twist it, and tie the end firmly. Use the cut in the card to open up the circles when it gets tight.

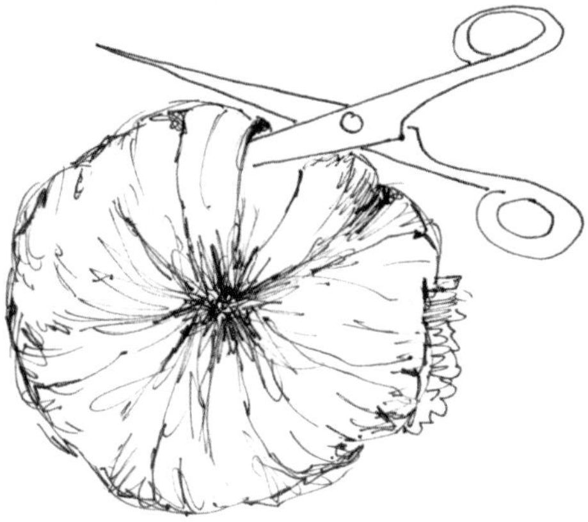

6. When there is no more space for tying, cut the wool tops following the gap between the two pieces of card.

7. Tie the cotton very tightly in between the two pieces of card. Secure with a double knot, as above.

8. Repeat this method for the head and tail.

9. To make up the hare, sew the body firmly to the head using the cotton. Go backwards and forwards several times between the two pompoms. Trim the overall shape. It's good to remember that the head of a hare has flat sides when seen from the front. Also the body is quite long so trim from the sides as well.

10. For the final details, firmly sew the tail in place.

11. To make the ears, cut the felt in half to make two pieces, then iron these together with the iron-on interfacing between them. Cut out two ears from this 'sandwich' using this template (below) as a guide

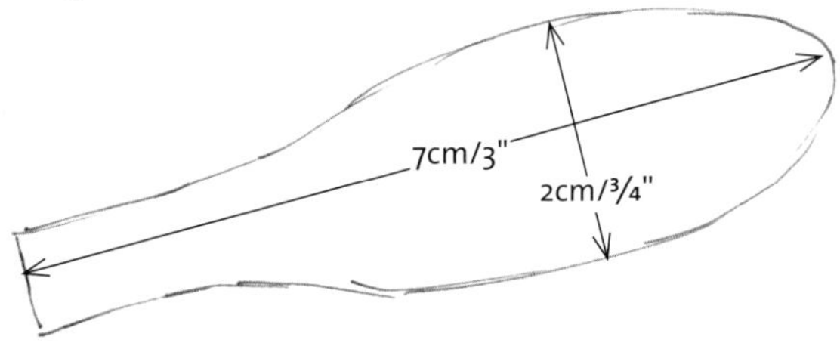

12. Sew the ears in place, facing outwards on top of the head.

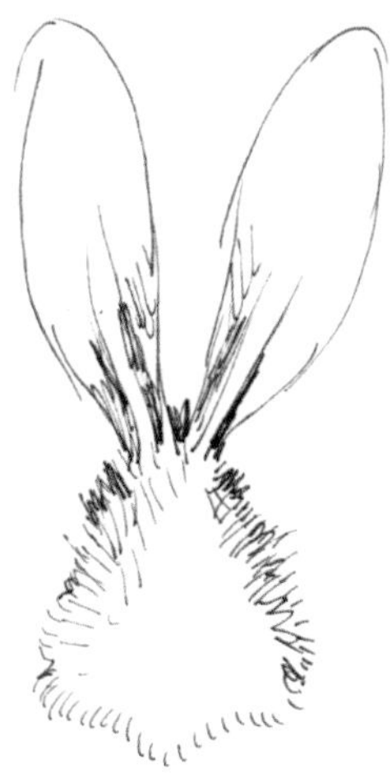

He is ready to run!

Easter Candles

Candles in the shape of an egg are fun to make. It is a great moment when you can crack the eggshell and find a new candle egg inside the cracked one!

You can make them from candle wax that is available in most craft shops or from old candles that you have melted down. To colour the candle, you can use wax dye or bits of broken wax crayon. You can make charming candle eggs using plain or light-colour wax eggs decorated with little transfers of spring flowers.

This is suitable for teenagers and adults to make.

YOU WILL NEED

This is to make one candle.

- A blown egg (see page 36)
- Egg cup
- A little cooking oil
- A small paint brush
- A candlewick (narrow size, about 8cm/3" long)
- Plasticine
- Melted wax (enough to fill an egg)
- Wax dye (optional)
- 2 matches
- Craft knife
- Nail scissors
- Aluminium cooking foil

1. Enlarge the hole at the top of the egg to about 2½cm/1" diameter. You can use nail scissors for this. Wash the egg and dry it thoroughly upside down. Paint the inside of the egg very thoroughly with oil using the small brush. Melt the wax in a container that is standing in boiling water. Add colouring if you like.

2. Dip the whole wick in hot wax, remove it and pull it straight while it is still soft. Then thread the wick through both holes in the egg and seal the small hole by putting some plasticine around the wick. Line an egg cup with aluminium foil and stand the egg in it (large hole on top). Slowly pour some wax into the egg, holding the wick in the middle. Fill it to the top. Keep the wick in place with two matches and let the wax set for about 15 minutes.

3. When you see that a well has appeared around the wick, break the surface skin of the wax with a skewer and top up with more hot wax around the wick. This topping up process may need to be repeated, as wax shrinks when it cools. When the candle has finally cooled and set (after a few hours or overnight), crack the eggshell and gently remove it. Trim the wick and level the base of the candle with a knife. You can decorate the candle with transfers or by gluing small, pressed flowers all around the sides.

Short-cut Easter candle

This one lacks some beauty but is still charming. It is ever so quick to make, even for quite young children.

YOU WILL NEED

- A pale eggshell left over from boiled eggs for breakfast
- Tea light
- Egg dye or food dye
- Scissors

1. Gently cut off the most uneven edges of the shell and wash it in warm water and let it dry.

2. Dye the egg shell and dry it again. Pop in the tea light. Ready!

Please note: Never leave a lit candle unattended.

Egg Decorations

Most Easter eggs are made of delicious chocolate wrapped in delightfully shiny paper and meant for immediate consumption! They are great fun to spot amongst the dull green grass.

However, the traditional eggs are hen-laid ones, beautifully decorated in many different ways. They are a symbol of new life and meant for keeping for one whole year.

Some eggs are hard-boiled and these can only be displayed lying in a bowl. Blown eggs can be hung up. For all methods of decoration, use the palest eggs available. Local suppliers may sell pale chicken eggs, or duck eggs, which are great to use too.

How to blow an egg

This is a task for careful fingers!

YOU WILL NEED

- White or very pale eggs
- A dash of vinegar
- Darning needle
- Small bowl or mug

1. Wash the egg in water with the vinegar in it then dry it. Carefully bore a hole at each end with the darning needle and make the hole at the pointed end slightly larger than the other one.

2. Break the yolk with the needle and hold the egg over a bowl and blow through the smaller hole until the liquid egg runs into the bowl and the shell is empty.

3. Wash the eggshell again very carefully. Dry the egg with the big hole at the bottom.

Tissue-paper dyed eggs

YOU WILL NEED

- Pale blown eggs (see above)
- Aprons for all
- Several old newspapers
- Small pieces of tissue paper, several different colours
- Small bowls of water, the same number as you have colours
- Vinegar
- Egg box
- Furniture wax and a cloth

This is a very easy method but potentially very messy. Little fingers (and many other things in the area) can get stained by the strong colours from wet tissue paper. But it is great fun with quick results and very young children (kindergarten upwards) can do it.

1. Cover your work surface with old newspaper and put on the aprons. Put a small quantity of water and a couple of drops of vinegar into each bowl and dip a piece of tissue paper into the water (don't leave it to soak). Lay the paper onto the egg so that it sticks and keep dipping and sticking. However, only dip one colour into each bowl, otherwise the colours will mix together in the bowls.

2. Keep to related colours for each egg – for instance, yellow and orange and red, or yellow and green and blue, or blue and red, etc – and continue dipping and sticking until the whole egg is covered. Don't worry about multi-coloured hands – it all washes off eventually. Leave the egg to dry in the egg box with the big hole at the bottom. When the egg is dry, peel off the paper and polish the egg delicately with some wax.

A SIMPLE VARIATION

Just dab damp tissue paper onto a clean egg and repeat with a few matched colours. Dry and wax as above.

A less messy variation

These are less messy but consequently much less fun for some people! It is a good method to use with children who are able to use a small paint brush with reasonable precision.

YOU WILL NEED

- Pale, blown eggs (see page 36)
- Aprons for all
- Several old newspapers
- Food colouring
- Small coffee cup
- Plain white vinegar
- Craft paint or gouache
- Very small paint brush or felt pens
- Thin knitting needle
- Blu-Tack

1. Protect your work surfaces and put on your aprons. Dye the eggs in a very light overall colour and leave them to dry with the big hole at the bottom.

2. When an egg is thoroughly dry, insert a thin knitting needle through the bottom and top holes, with some Blu-Tack above and below it to hold it in place. Begin painting or use felt pens to draw your design.

You can use the traditional patterns, but your little artists will want to design their own! Suggest a hare, rising sun, small birds, little flowers – anything to do with the mood of new spring.

HOW TO DYE AN EGG WITH FOOD COLOURING

1. Mix about 20 drops of food dye with a tablespoon of vinegar and half a cup of hot (not boiling) water in the small coffee cup.
2. Place your clean egg in the warm mixture.
3. Lift the egg out with a spoon after a minute or two to see if you have the required colour strength.
4. To make it stronger put the egg back in the mixture.

You may want to test your colour strength before dying a large number of eggs.

Batik eggs

This is a very simple way of using the batik technique on eggs. You can do this with children from seven years old onwards so long as you supervise them with the hot wax and the candle flame.

For the authentic batik technique you need the proper *tjanting* tools, which you can get from a craft shop.

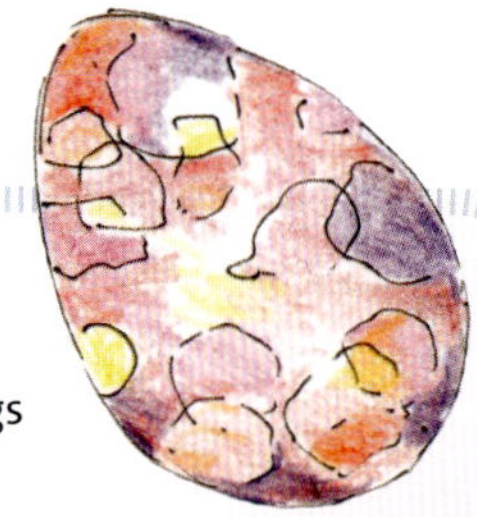

YOU WILL NEED

- Pale blown or hardboiled eggs
- Aprons for all
- Several old newspapers
- Matches
- Candle in a holder
- Dye or food colouring in 3 colours (a good combination is yellow, red and violet)
- Vinegar
- Paper tissues or toilet paper

1. Wash the eggs in water, that has a dash of vinegar in it. Dry them very thoroughly with the big hole at the bottom to make sure no water is left inside the blown eggs. Light the candle and then tilt it slightly to allow liquid wax to drip sparingly over the egg, making an even spread of spots over it – mind your fingers; hot wax is HOT.

2. Let it dry and then dye it in the lightest colour (yellow). After this had dried, drip some more wax spots onto the egg, this time onto the coloured base. Dye the egg again in a slightly darker colour (red). Repeat the wax drip process once more and dye the egg in the darkest colour (violet). Leave the egg to dry thoroughly.

3. When it is dry, hold it next to the candle flame, but not in it (mind your fingers). As the wax melts, quickly wipe it off with the paper tissue. Repeat this till all the wax is removed.

You will be surprised at the colour effects and the sheen on the egg!

Scratched eggs

This method is not so easy but some older children can do it.

YOU WILL NEED

- Pale hard-boiled eggs are best (they are firm and do not crack so easily – this method requires some force)
- Food colouring, batik dye or egg dye – dark colours only. Deep red was often used traditionally
- Sharp knife or nail (ideally a dentist drill bit –ask your dentist for old ones – held in a clutch pen)
- Black pencil and rubber
- Rubber band

1. Dye the eggs a deep colour and dry them. The traditional design divides the egg in halves horizontally. Mark this line with the pencil – if you do not have a steady hand you can use the rubber band as a guide. Gently scratch away the pencil line with your tool to reveal the white underneath. After making the horizontal lines, divide the egg vertically. Repeat this at right angles to your first vertical division.

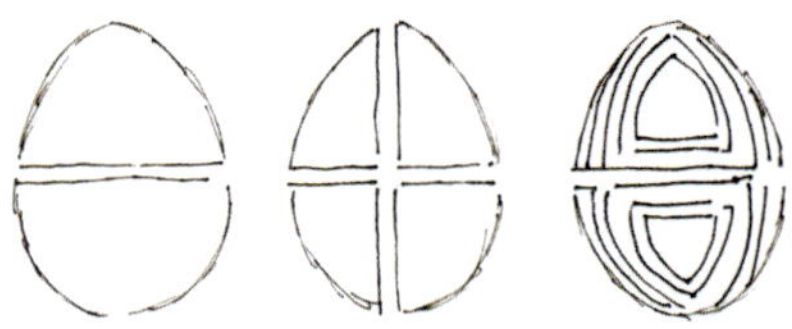

2. You now have eight parts. To finish the basic structure of the design, make a triangle in each part, as shown. You can now use your imagination and design an Easter figure or pattern in each triangle. First draw it and then gently scratch it out. When it is done you can wax it with furniture wax polish to give it a beautiful, deep sheen.

Tie-dyed eggs

This is not suitable for small children to attempt, but teenagers can have a go.

YOU WILL NEED

- The palest eggs available
- Food dyes or egg dyes (or you can use lots of onion skins, for a rich golden brown colour)
- Tiny flowers and leaves
- An old nylon stocking
- Strong cotton thread
- Glue
- Furniture wax and a cloth

1. Follow the instructions on the egg dyes. Or boil your eggs till hard if you are using food dyes. But, if you use onion skins, do not boil your eggs yet. Cut a rectangular piece of stocking big enough to easily wrap the egg and firmly tie up one end. Carefully arrange the flowers and leaves around the egg with tiny dabs of glue. Put the egg inside the stocking, pull the nylon tightly over it and secure firmly. Your parcel is ready for dyeing.

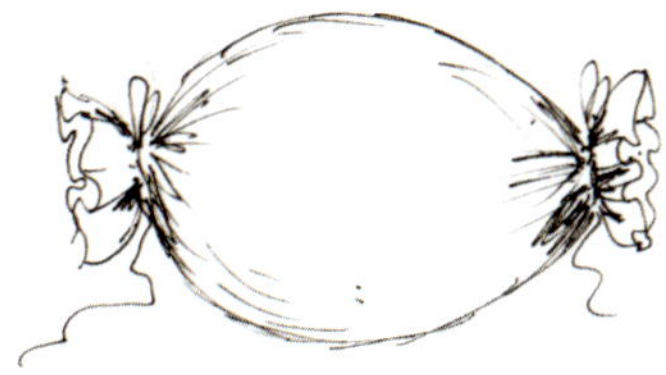

2. Use either the egg dye or the food dye but take care not to dye it too strongly otherwise the delicate patterns will be lost. If you use onion skins, first boil them in water in a saucepan for 10 minutes then put your wrapped eggs, raw or blown, in with the skins and boil them all together for at least another ten minutes. Onions take longer to dye. When done, unwrap the eggs and let them dry in an egg box with the big hole at the bottom. When fully dry, rub the egg with furniture wax to give it a deep sheen.
The delicate patterns show up beautifully on the coloured eggs. These eggs look beautiful on the Easter table.

Here are some Easter egg motifs to get you started.

Easter Tree

On Easter morning a festive Easter tree can set the mood for the day and the time to come.

We decorate a fir tree for Christmas. For Easter you can hang beautifully decorated eggs on fresh branches that are just about to sprout, or already have blossom on them. Birch and forsythia are good examples.

You can put these into a deep vase or in a deep flowerpot filled with houseplant compost. This compost can be covered with moss. Or, if you start early enough, you can use grass seed – it will take at least 10 days to sprout; cress is a bit quicker.

YOU WILL NEED

- Blown eggs (see page 36; quantity is up to you and the size of your tree)
- Coloured wool, embroidery cotton or split raffia or coloured string
- Coloured beads
- Long, large-eyed darning needle
- Scissors

How to hang a blown egg

1. Thread the wool or string through the darning needle. Hold the egg in your hand and push the needle first through the small hole at the bottom and then the larger hole at the top. You may have to make the small hole slightly bigger.

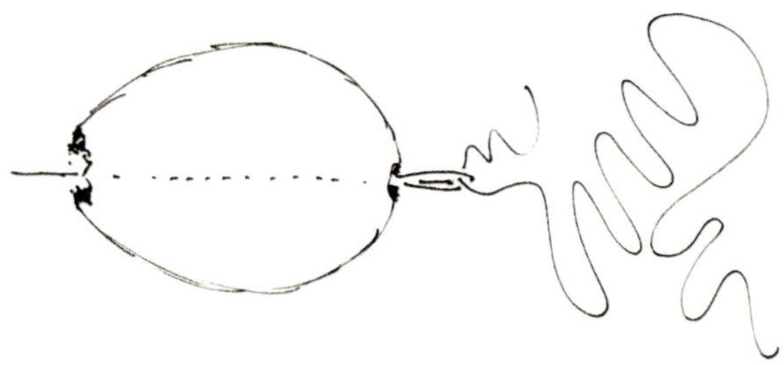

2. Push the needle back down through the holes again, leaving a loop at the top and tie a bead at the bottom to stop the egg sliding off. Or you could just tie a large knot.

3. The waiting tree can now be decorated.

Paper Boxes

These boxes are ideal for collecting Easter eggs but they have many other uses too. They make very nice presents if you put a little treasure in them – some sea shells, a polished stone, beads, some pretty ribbons, little biscuits or sweets. You could even use the oblong box as a bed in a doll's house if you add a tiny pillow and blanket.

They can be made any size – remember a big one will need thicker paper than a small one. Neat paper-folding skills are the only requirement.

YOU WILL NEED

- Strong paper (about 120gsm) or thin card. A4 copy paper, 80gsm, is only suitable for very small boxes but is very good for practising any size.)

Oblong box

1. Fold the paper in half lengthwise to find the centre and open flat again. Fold in both long edges to the centre crease and open flat again. You now have three parallel creases.

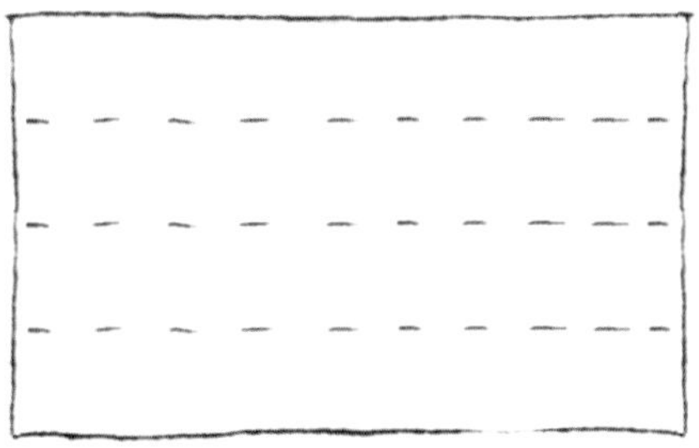

2. Turn the paper sideways and fold again to make two creases running at right angles to those you have just made. Leave the two ends folded into the middle

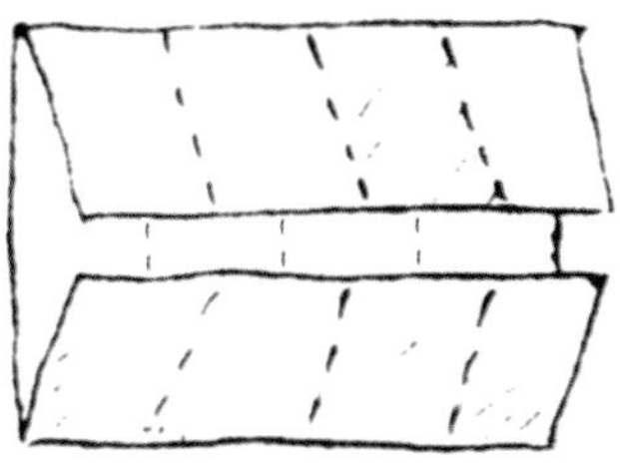

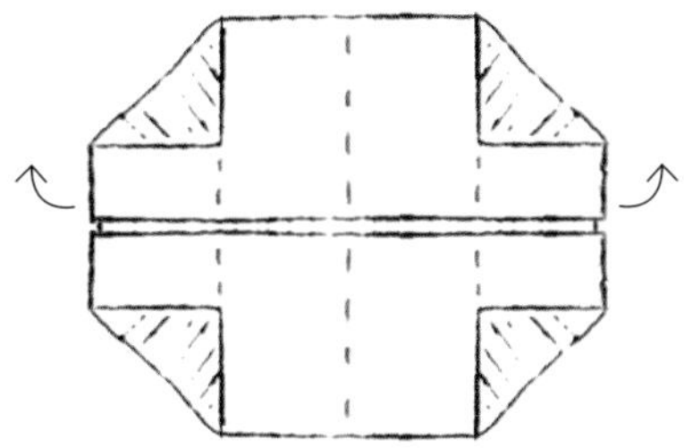

3. Fold over all four corners to line up with the creases.

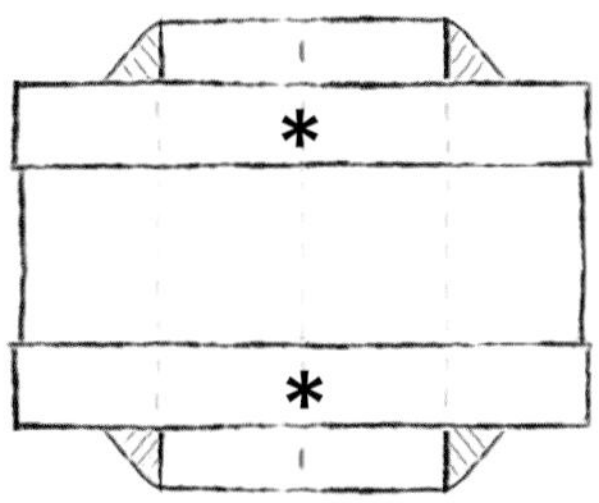

4. Fold the two centre flaps to cover the four corner folds.

5. Lift up at the two points marked * and the box will start to appear. Gently refold the corners to give it its final shape. You can make the box into a basket by fixing a strip of folded paper to either side to make a handle – use glue, staples or paper fasteners. This will also help to strengthen the sides.

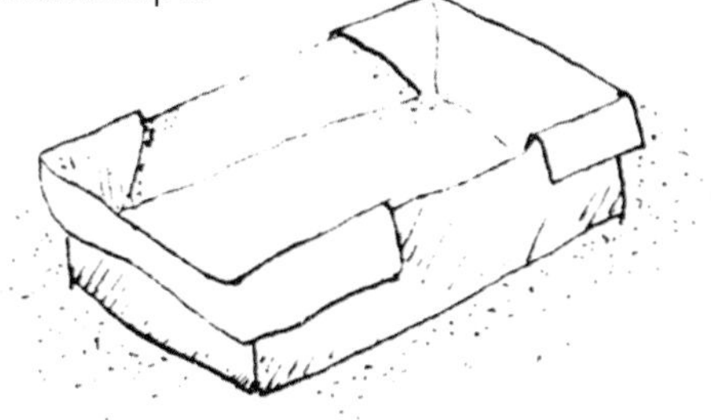

Square box

1. Fold a square of paper in half diagonally (if you use a piece of paper 20 x 20cm/8x 8" you will make a 7 x 7cm/3 x 3"box).

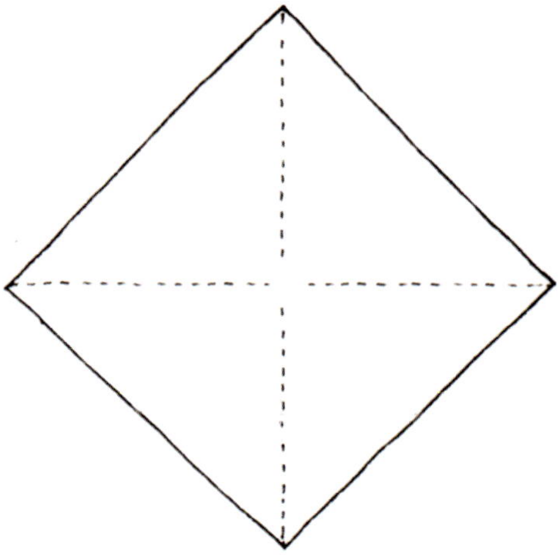

2. Fold all four corners in to the centre and open them out again.

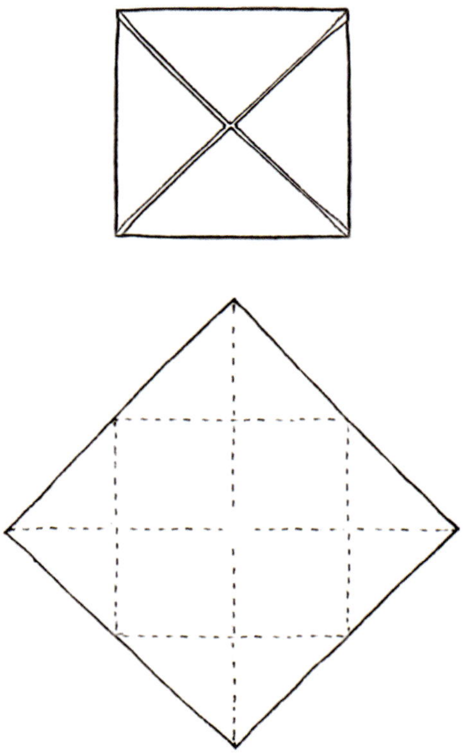

3. Fold corner C to Y and, after opening the square up again, fold C to Z, thus making more creases.

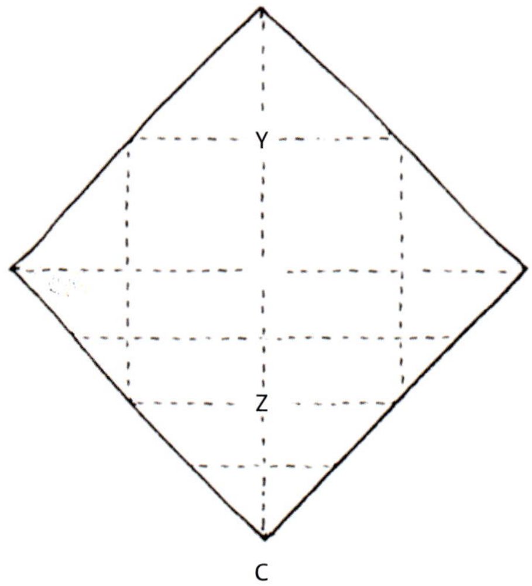

4. Repeat the same procedure with corners A, B and D. Cut along the two solid lines shown below.

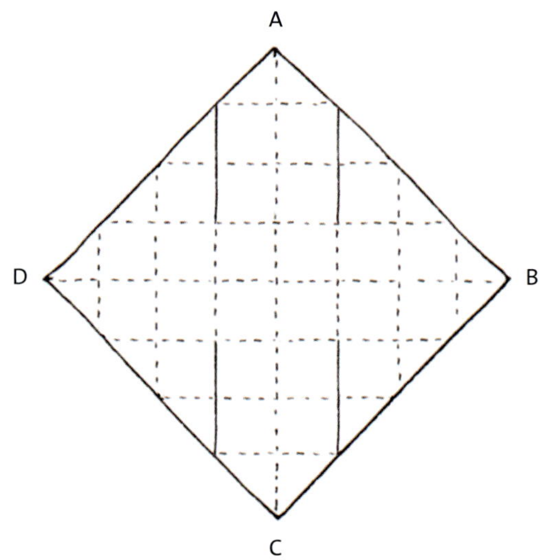

5. Fold corners D and B into the centre and turn the paper through 90°. Lift and fold the upper flaps to form three loose sides of the box.

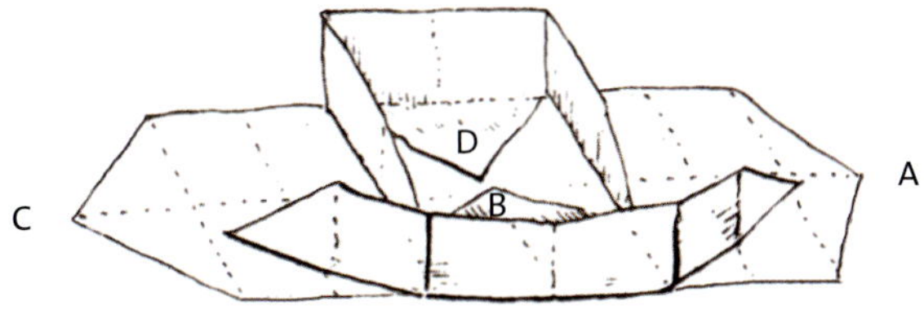

6. Repeat with the lower flaps. Lift corners A and C over the four loose sides and fold them down into the box, bringing them together in the centre of the 'floor' of the box.

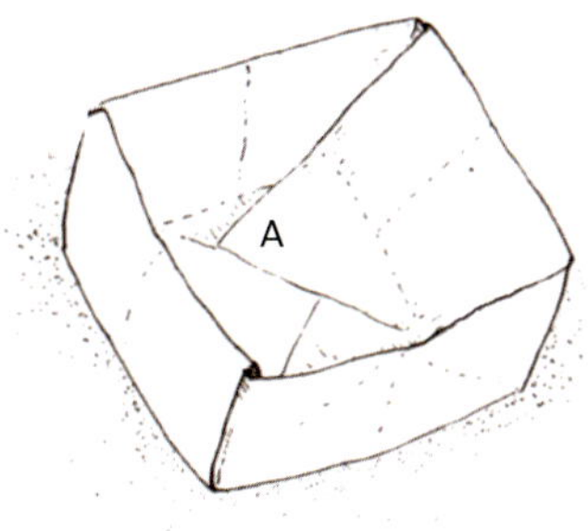

7. You may need to fix all four corners where they sit on the floor of the box – use a small dab of glue under each. If you choose to make a lid for your box, make it in the same way but start with paper that is 1cm/½" bigger than the one you used for the base box.

The completed paper box can be decorated with cut-out paper shapes – a heart for Valentine's Day, a star for Christmas, a hare for Easter or some flowers for a birthday or Mother's Day.

Pop-up Easter Card

This is a special card that can make the Easter hare appear! For adults and teenagers to make, for little ones to decorate.

YOU WILL NEED

- Two A4 pieces of light-coloured card
- Hard pencil, eg 2H
- Paper and pencil for tracing
- Cutting knife and underlay
- Coloured pencils
- Glue

1. Trace or copy twice the egg template as for the Easter egg wheel card (page 45), and trace twice the tab (as shown right).

2. The top egg card has a window, the bottom one does not, so cut out the two eggs and two tabs but only cut out one window. Place the two eggs together and lightly trace the window opening onto the bottom egg.

3. Draw and colour a sunrise onto the bottom egg's window space. Make it slightly larger than the window on the top card. Place the tab underneath the window and lightly trace its outline. Remove the tab and draw on it your own hare or use the printed one, and then colour it in.

4. Rub out the tracing lines and colour the whole top part of the tab. Glue the two tabs together for strength. When the glue is dry place the 'double' tab onto the bottom egg and put 1cm/1/2" of glue around the outer edge of the egg. You must not put glue where the tab is.

5. Stick the two eggs together and leave to dry – you may want to hold it firmly with paper clips until it is dry.

6. You can decorate the front egg with a simple colour haze by sharpening a light-coloured pencil over the card and gently rubbing the filings into it. And/or you can draw spring motifs like little flowers, a hare, eggs or lambs.

7. When all the glue is dry, the Easter hare can appear by just pushing the tab up and before you know it he can disappear again!

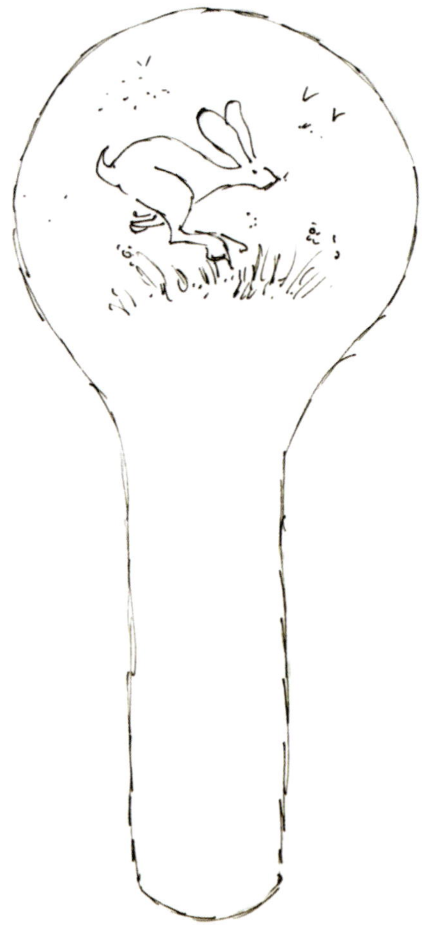

Easter Egg Wheel Card

A lovely moving image card for nimble little fingers to turn at Easter time. The decorating can be done by little ones.

YOU WILL NEED

- 2 similar pieces of light-coloured, firm card
- Hard pencil and a soft pencil
- Printer paper (for tracing)
- Coloured pencils
- Paper fastener
- Cutting knife and underlay
- Thick pin

1. Trace the egg shape and the window A onto the card. Mark the point B for the paper fastener.

2. Cut out the egg and the window A.

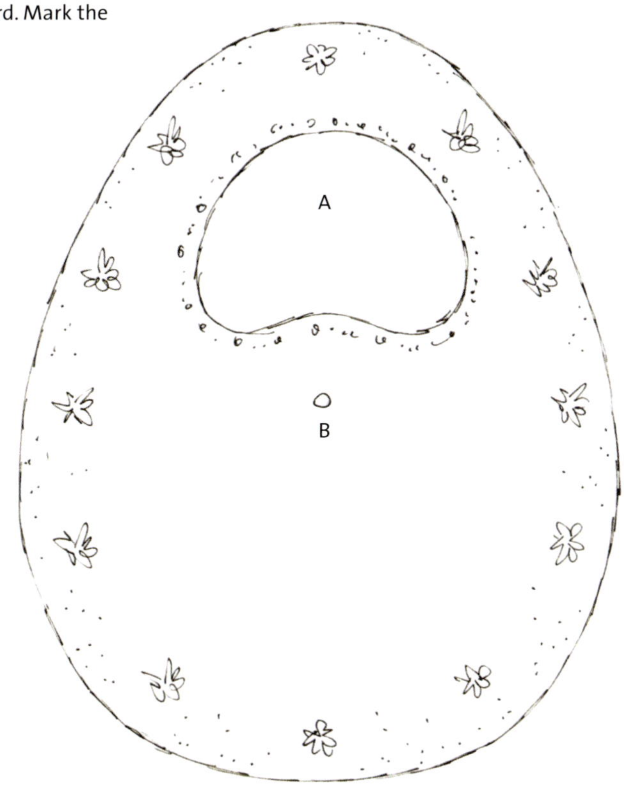

3. Trace the wheel onto the card. Cut it out and mark the centre C. Slightly enlarge the holes B and C with the thick pin and temporarily fix the wheel behind the egg by pushing the paper fastener through B and C.

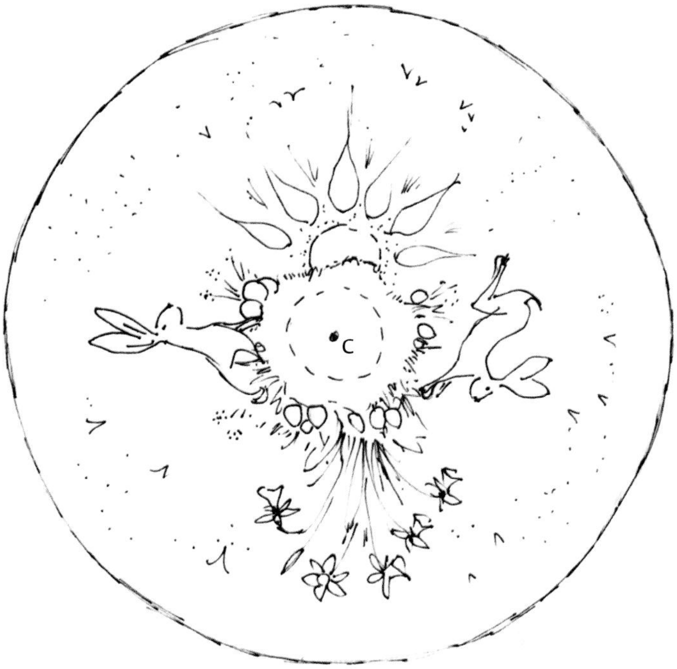

4. Lightly mark through the window the top and bottom where your images will be visible. Turn the wheel and continue lightly marking right around.

5. Take it apart again and lightly draw the pictures on the wheel as shown, or draw your own pictures of hares, sunrise, daffodils, etc. Rub out the demarcation lines and extend the picture all round slightly, so that the edges are not visible through the front window.

6. Colour in the images when you are happy with the layout. Decorate the front simply, for example with little flowers around the outside or, even simpler, sharpen a pale-coloured pencil and gently rub in the filings to make a colour haze.

7. Fix the wheel behind the egg with the paper fastener.

Turn the wheel and watch the hare jumping on Easter morning!

The Sprouting Spring Card

Whoever receives this card can grow their own cress with it. Now that is what I call a 'green' card! The little ones can help the adult with this one.

1. Cut out and fold a piece of the card to make a greeting card (A) that will fit into a standard-size envelope; cut another piece that is the same size as the front of your greeting card (B).

2. Make a circle on B by drawing around a circular shape. With the craft knife cut out this circle, discard it and use the hole in the card as a stencil. At this point you can decorate card A with paint or coloured pencils if you like. Place B onto A and secure it all the way round with the paper clips.

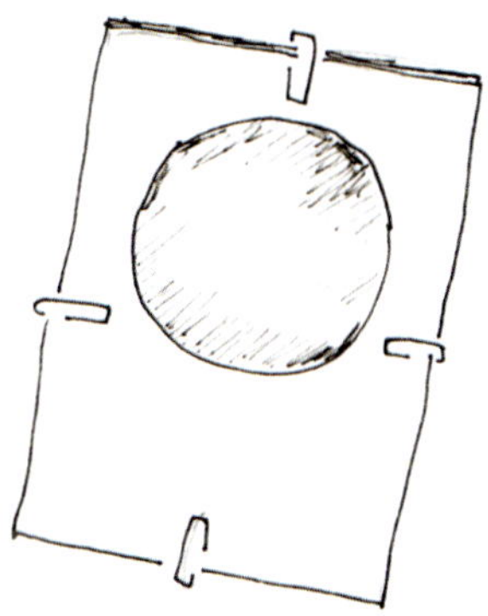

YOU WILL NEED

- Cress seed
- Pale-coloured card
- Craft knife and cutting underlay
- 4 paper clips
- Small paintbrush
- Small round shape like a small jar
- 3 tablespoons of white flour
- 1 tablespoon of white sugar
- Small saucepan and flat bottomed stirrer
- Water

3. To make the glue, mix the flour and sugar in the saucepan. Gradually add a little water and stir vigorously until smooth. Cook over a very low heat, stirring constantly, adding a little water, when needed, to prevent lumps. Simmer till clear and gloopy and leave to cool.

4. Then, using the paintbrush, spread the glue all over the inside of the circle on A. Sprinkle the cress seed on top of the glue, making sure it is well covered. Remove the stencil card (B) and leave the card (A) to dry. When it is completely dry you can write these instructions for the recipient on the back of the card:

Cut 1cm or ½" around the seed circle and lay it flat in a small bowl on a bed of damp fine compost. Sprinkle some more damp compost over the top. Lightly flatten it. Put it in a bright window but not in direct sunlight, making sure that it is always slightly damp. Soon your card will start to sprout delicious cress. Enjoy!

Easter Egg Cosy

This cosy will keep your Easter egg nice and warm. Moreover, its jolliness will bring cheer to any breakfast table. It is very easy to make with a little sewing skill.

YOU WILL NEED

- 2 pieces of golden yellow felt – 9 x 9cm/3½ x 3½"
- Scraps of yellow, orange and red felt
- Embroidery cotton – dark brown, yellow, or bright red if you are confident with the blanket stitch
- Needle
- Scissors
- Thin paper and a pencil

1. Trace the chicken shape (see below) onto the paper. Cut it out and pin onto a double layer of felt.

2. Cut the felt and embroider the eyes on the front and the back with the brown thread.

NB: All pattern pieces for the chicken are actual size.

3. Using the templates (below), trace the orange beak, red comb and three tail feathers (one of each colour) onto paper and cut out the felt. Pin the beak, comb and feathers into place onto the bottom yellow chicken, using the drawing (right) as a guide.

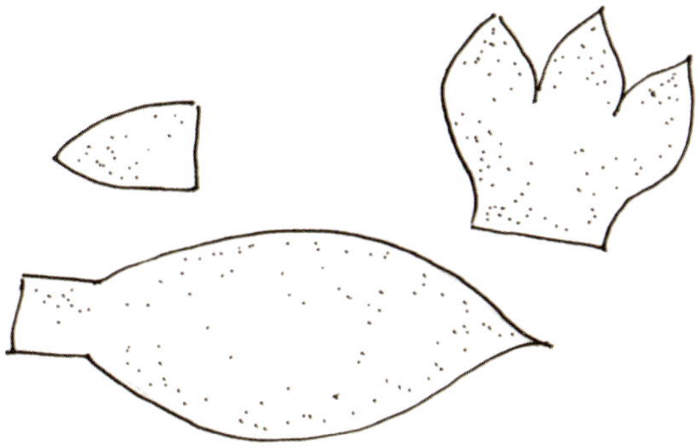

4. Sew so that you will not see the stitches from outside (underneath). Place the second chicken onto the first, wrong sides together, and sew around the outside (not the bottom!) with blanket stitch. Pick up the inner layer of felt when you meet the tail, comb and beak.

Blanket stitch

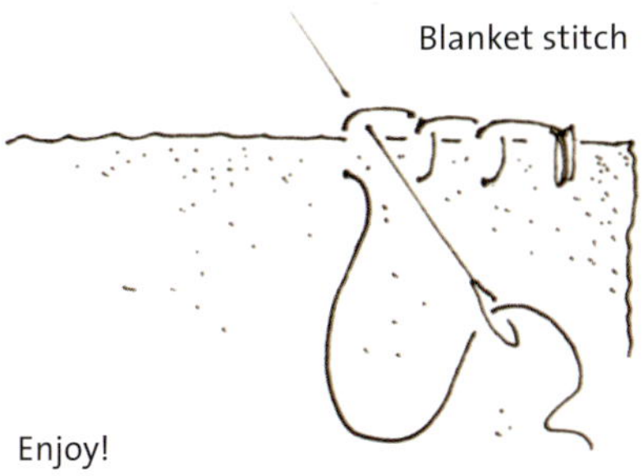

Enjoy!

Pecking Hen Card

Grannies and grandchildren alike will be very happy to receive a contented clucking hen card! It is easy to make for children with a little drawing and cutting skill.

YOU WILL NEED

- White card, heavy quality – size A5 (21 x 15cm/8 x 6")
- Pencil
- Scissors
- Cutting knife and mat
- Pin and paper fastener
- Coloured pencils
- Thin printing paper and a soft black pencil if you want to transfer the drawing from the book (see page 17)

NB: These drawings are to scale for making an A6 sized card (A5 piece of card folded in half).

1. Cut the card in half. Lightly draw (or transfer) the hen and chicks onto one piece of card. Leave just enough space in front of her for clucking. Draw the head again the same size, on the second piece of card, but extend the neck to 10cm/4".

2. Cut slot A in the top card; the tightness of the curve allows easy movement.

3. Insert the tab into slot A to fit the head into place. Push the pin through B (two layers!) and try it for movement. When it's right, replace the pin with a paper fastener and fold the ends flat against the back of the card.

4. Colour the card to create a warm spring day full of clucking contentment.

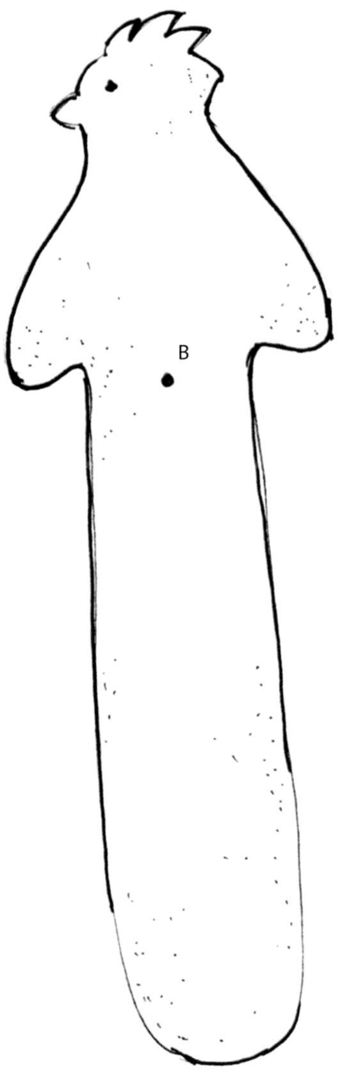

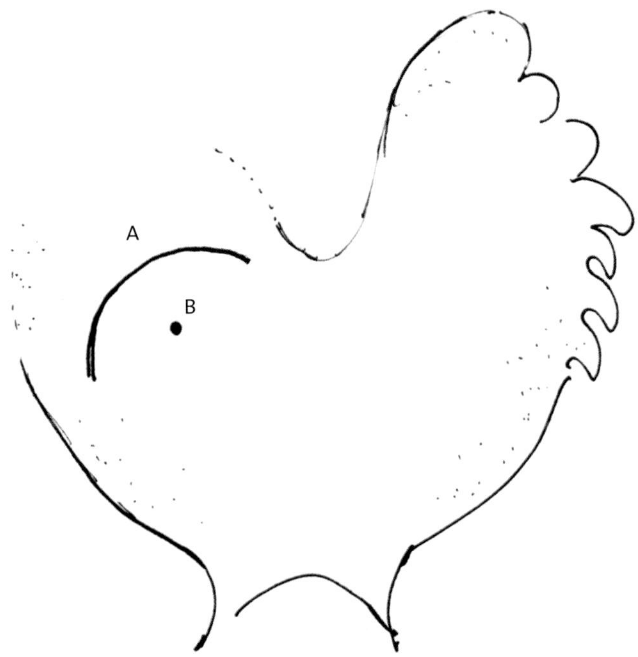

God's Eye

These colourful crosses originate in Mexico and are an Easter symbol. Dry branches become interesting from simply winding wool around them. They are easy to make and young children can have ago once they have seen the instructions.

As always, everything depends on the colour combinations. Go for joyous ones and be daring – forget all about grey, brown and black! You could make a rainbow sequence.

You can make a single cross and then, when you have mastered that, you could venture into an elaborate one with five crosses.

YOU WILL NEED

- 2 pieces of stick – thin, straight and dry – roughly 18cm/7" long
- Secateurs
- Wool – various matching colours
- Darning needle
- Scissors

1. Cut off all the side shoots and rub all the dust off the sticks. Select your wool colours and firmly tie the two sticks into a symmetrical cross shape.

2. Start work on the front and tie the wool anti-clockwise – winding it once round a stick over the left front to the right back and again to the left front of the next stick. Repeat till you want to change colour.

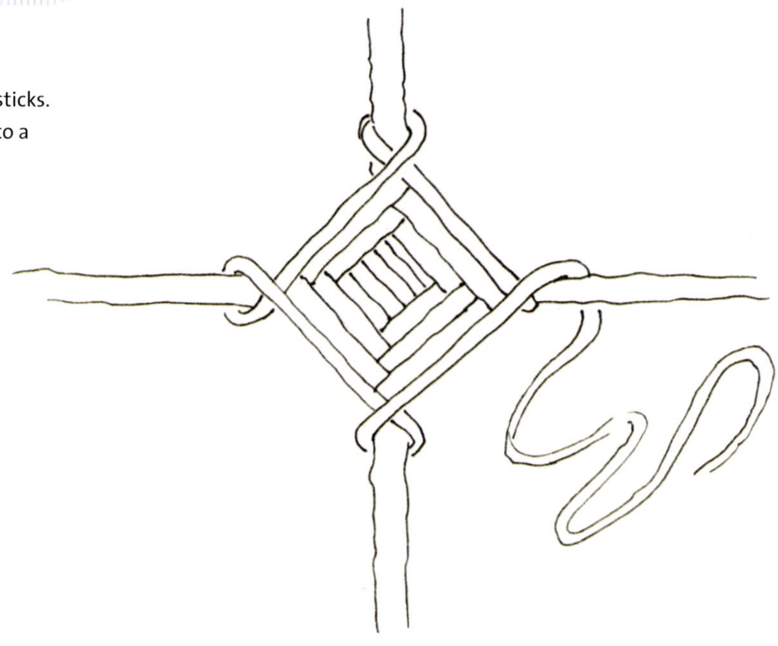

3. On the back sew the thread ends into the windings. fix the new colour there too, and continue.

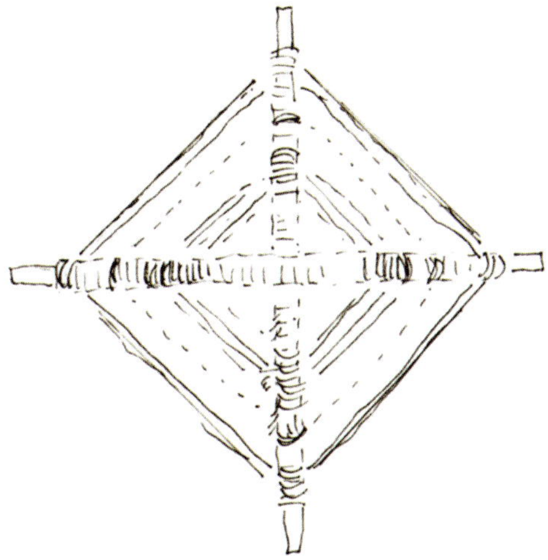

If you are bitten by the winding bug you can try something more ambitious.

Larger cross

YOU WILL NEED

- The same materials as for God's eye (page 52) but with 6 sticks – 2 longer and thicker, and 4 shorter.

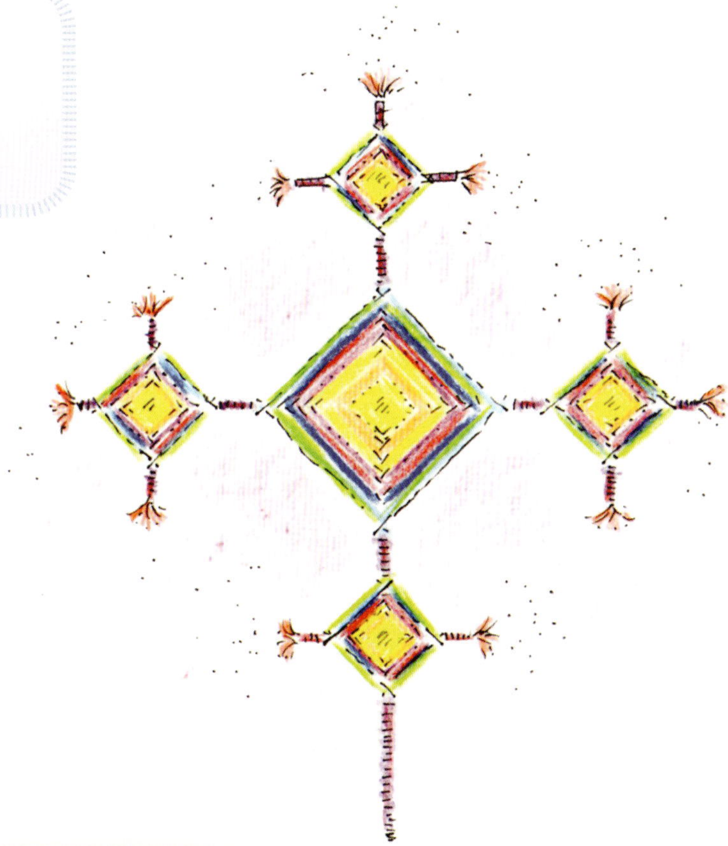

1. Make the central cross by tying the two larger sticks firmly together. Start winding wool, as before. Make the central cross larger than the outside ones.

2. When it is finished, firmly fix a short stick directly onto the large one to make another small cross. Start winding as for the large cross. Repeat for the three other crosses.

3. When all five crosses are finished, bind the exposed sticks with matching wool. If you like, you can make tassels on each end.

Whichever one you have made it can be enjoyed as part of your Easter table, or it can be hung on the wall or placed in a tall narrow vase.

HOW TO MAKE A TASSEL

- Wind about 130cm/50" wool loosely around 4 fingers of one hand.
- Ask a friend to tightly tie a 30cm/12" piece of wool around the windings, by going through the middle gap between fingers 2 and 3.
- Snip the loops where they go round the outside of fingers 1 and 4.
- Ease the cut ends together so they form your tassel.

May Flower Crown

This is a flower crown fit for a May Queen! For an adult to make and for a child to wear with pride – some adults too, especially Maypole dancers.

YOU WILL NEED

- Medium-hard gardening wire or florists wire, green-coated if possible – about 1m/3'
- Green garden twine – about 3m/10'
- Secateurs, pliers and scissors
- Greenery, such as lavender, rosemary or other sprigs. Not Christmas tree or any other spiky material (it's going on someone's head)
- Flowers or florets of whichever are available – primroses, cherry blossom, cow parsley, marguerites, bluebells etc.

1. Make a small loop at one end of the wire, with the pliers. Push the other end through the loop to make a wire circlet. Gently place it on your princess's head so that it fits generously. You need to allow a little extra space for the greenery, which will be added later.

2. Fix the size by twisting the free end back on its self. Cut off the excess wire with the pliers.

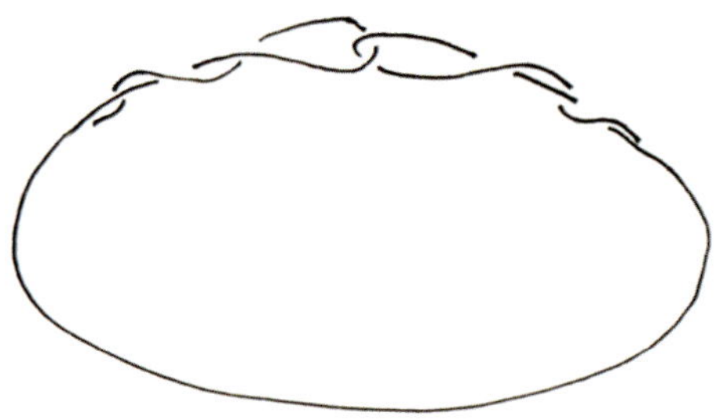

3. Cut the greenery into roughly 10cm/4" lengths with the secateurs. Firmly tie one piece of greenery onto the circlet with the garden twine. Lay the next piece of greenery so that it covers half of the first piece (especially the stems) and tie it on. Continue firmly tying the greenery around the circlet, making sure it is all facing the same way.

4. The stalk of the last bit should slide under the leaves of the first bit. Bind and knot firmly. Your base is ready – now for the fun bit! Cut the flowers into roughly 10cm/4" sprigs. Tie them onto the leafy base in the same way as you have done before with the greenery. This time you can let your imagination guide you. You could place all the large flowers at the front, or alternate different shapes all around, or play around with different colour combinations.

Are you ready for the dance?

Whitsun Dove Ring

It is a very special surprise for children to find this ring of doves spiralling down to earth on Whit Sunday! When they're hanging over the breakfast table, the slightest draught or the heat of a candle flame makes them move softly.

It is easy to make with a little paper-cutting and folding skills.

If you find making 12 doves a bit daunting, just start with one and hang that. There is always next year!

YOU WILL NEED

- Wooden ring – 20cm/8" diameter (available in craft shops) if you want to make a flock
- Smooth white card about 10 x 6cm/4 x 2½" for one, or 30 x 24cm/12 x 10" for 12
- Sheet of white tissue paper
- White thread – better still use gold or silver thread
- Nail scissors and a craft knife

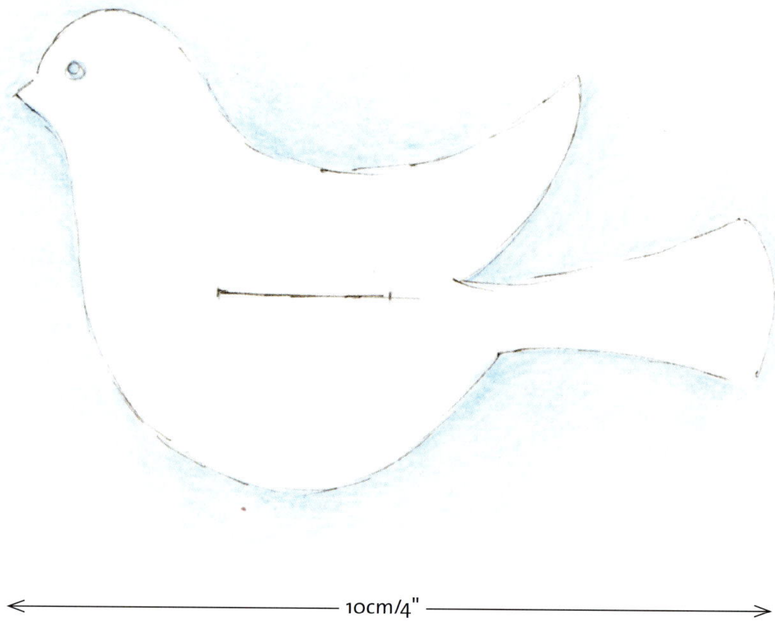

1. Cut out the dove from the card as shown above.
With some fine nail scissors or a sharp craft knife cut a slot for the wings where indicated.

2. Cut a piece of tissue paper – 13 x 10cm/5 x 4". Fold down the length like a concertina and trim the corners as shown.

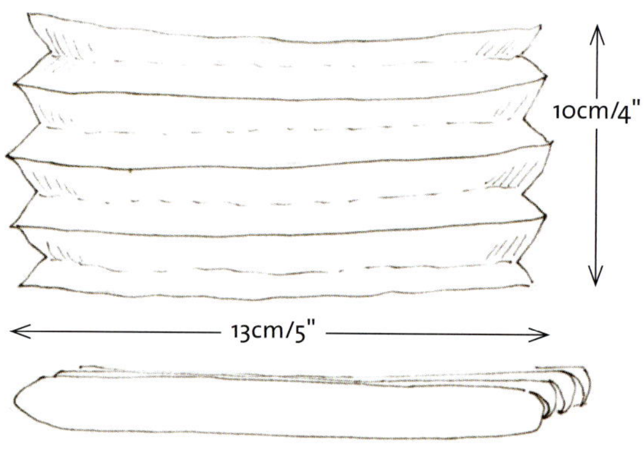

3. Insert the folded tissue paper through the slot in the body piece and open it up like a fan on either side. Pull up the wings so that they meet in the middle and join them together by carefully threading a length of cotton through each side.

4. The dove can now be hung up on that thread.

That was so easy you won't feel daunted about making the other eleven now!

5. Tie the first dove to the ring so that it hangs 5cm (2") below the ring. To achieve the spiral, the thread of each following dove needs to be about 4cm/1½" longer than the one before. Space out the doves evenly around the ring. Hang the ring with three threads.

Rhododendron Flower Stick

Around the end of spring and the start of summer rhododendrons show off their exuberant clusters of flowers – purple, magenta, pink and white. A walk with little children can become a flower feast when fresh blossoms are collected from the ground and simply put on a stick. They will last until bedtime.

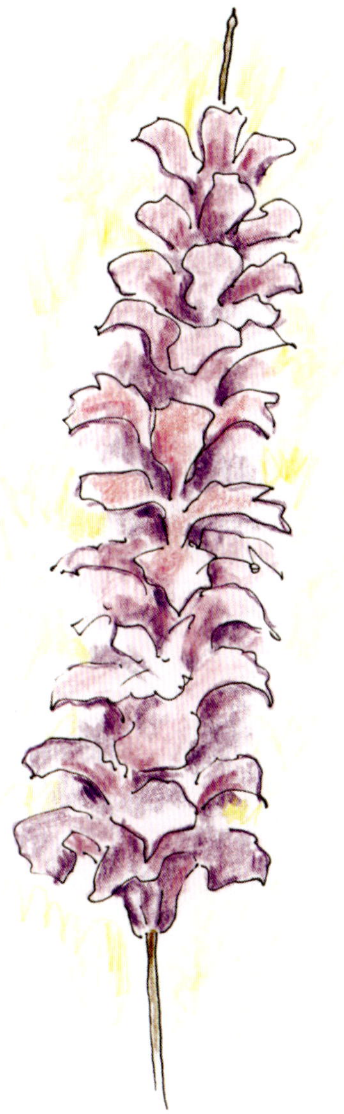

YOU WILL NEED

- A straight thin stick, with no side shoots, roughly 40cm/16" long
- Freshly fallen flowers under a rhododendron bush

1. Gently pull out the pistil and stamen from a flower, thus making a small hole at the base of it. Carefully slide the flower (facing upwards) onto the stick and repeat this as many times as you have patience for.

2. Later in the summer you can make flower sticks with flowers from bindweed (convolvulus).

3. In the autumn you can make leaf sticks, especially with leaves from maple trees. And there are always other possibilities that you can try.

Soft Dolls

These beautiful soft dolls are one of the most important toys for girls and boys alike. Children can play out their daily discoveries and experiences with these dolls as their alter egos and friends. They are relatively simple to allow room for the child's imagination, and they are rich in texture, colour and association. They simply ask to be loved!

As far as making soft dolls go, these are ideal to get started with, as the body and limbs can be made in one go, out of one piece of material. The heads and hair have also been simplified.

It is very rewarding to make one specifically for your child, your grandchild or a little friend. You can personalise the doll by using the child's skin and hair colour as well as their favourite colour tops.

Little Brother, Sister and Baby Doll

This little family love to live in the doll's house (page 82) and they want to be together. The dolls are easy to make and older children could sew them for smaller children.

They are about 10cm/4" tall.

YOU WILL NEED

- Piece of stockinette (flesh-coloured cotton jersey, 25cm x 25cm/10 x 10")
- Piece of velour or soft towelling (30 x 25cm/12 x 10")
- Wool fleece for stuffing
- Wool for the hair
- Scraps or material and braid for finishing
- Sewing cotton

Brother

1. Starting with the head, cut out a piece of stockinette, 9 x 9cm/3½ x 3½". Stuff it firmly with wool so that it makes a little ball (2.5cm/1" diameter) and tightly tie a thread around the neck.

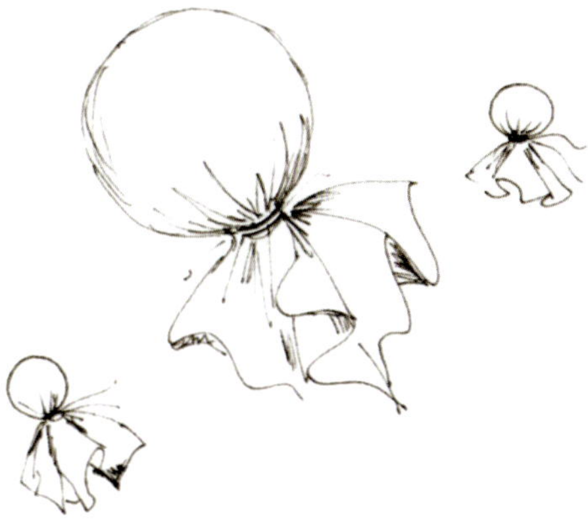

2. For the body, cut 2 pieces using the template below.

3. Put the right sides together and sew around the edge with a 5mm/¼" seam allowance. Leave an opening at the neck and cuffs.

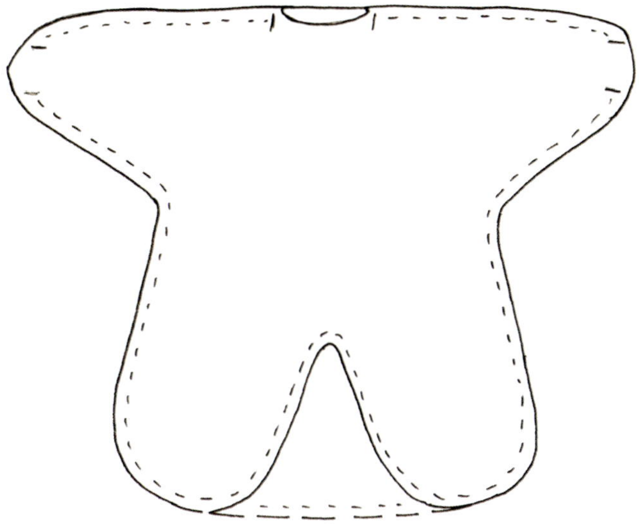

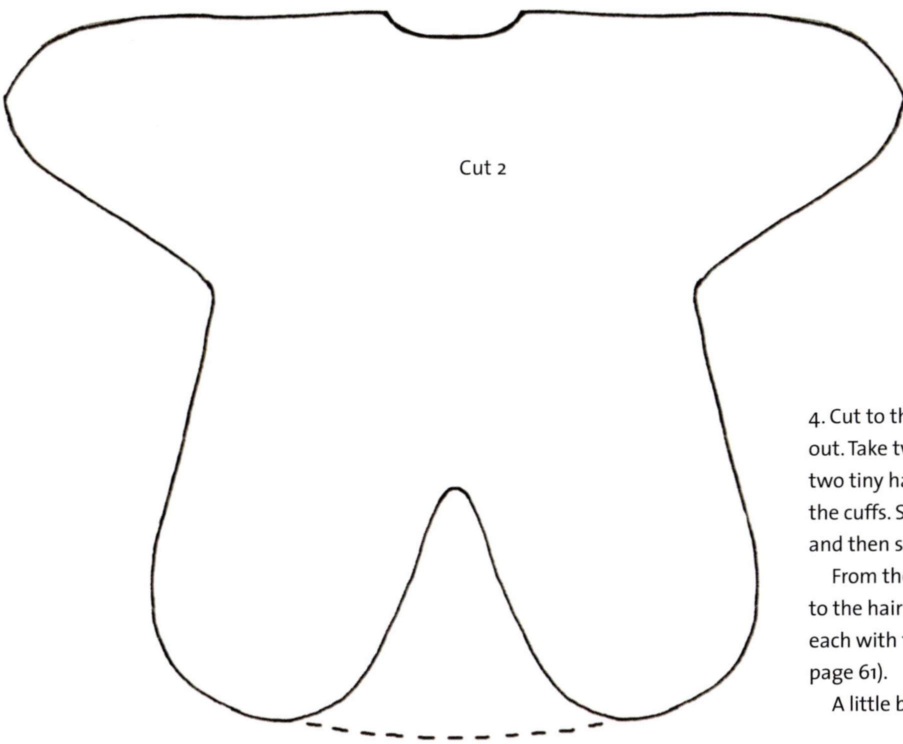

NB: This body template is actual size.

4. Cut to the seam in between the legs. Turn it inside out. Take two little pieces of stockinette and make two tiny hands stuffed with wool. Sew them into the cuffs. Stuff the body with wool, keeping it soft, and then sew on the head.

From the crown of the head sew with wool down to the hairline all around. Make the eyes and mouth, each with three stitches of cotton (see star doll, page 61).

A little bit of braid looks great as a finishing touch.

Sister

Follow the same method for the brother but make her a little shorter with a slightly smaller head. Give her a little skirt by following the same pattern, but omit the trouser legs (see right). Just sew straight along the bottom line.

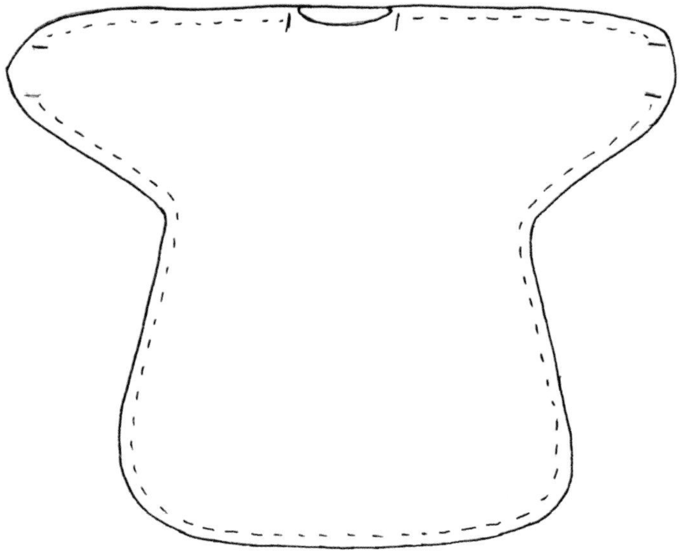

Baby

1. Make the head in the same way again, slightly smaller. From the velour cut the shape as shown below, about 7 x 6cm/3 x 2½".

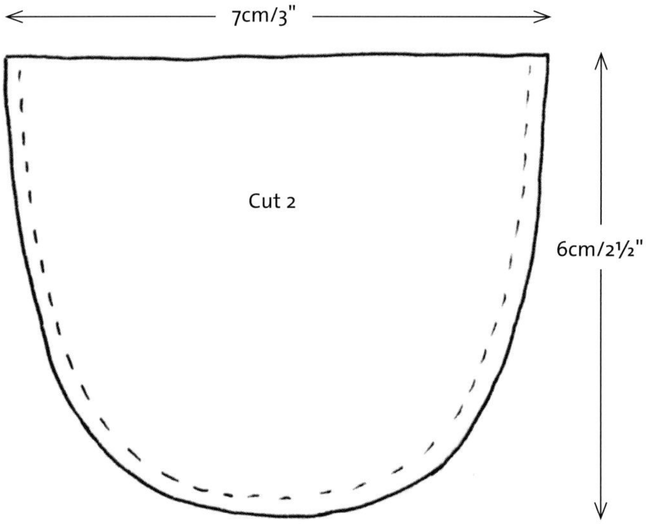

2. Put the right sides together and sew around the edge leaving the top open. Make two tiny hands with stockinette and sew them on each end.

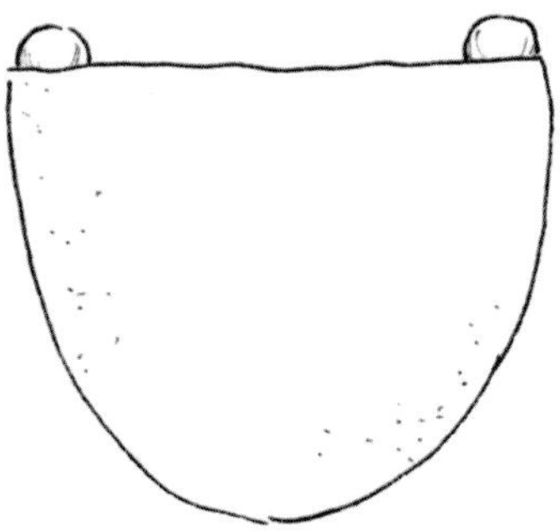

3. Insert the head in the middle and sew up the rest of the top seam. Gather the material a little so that the hands are pulled towards the head.

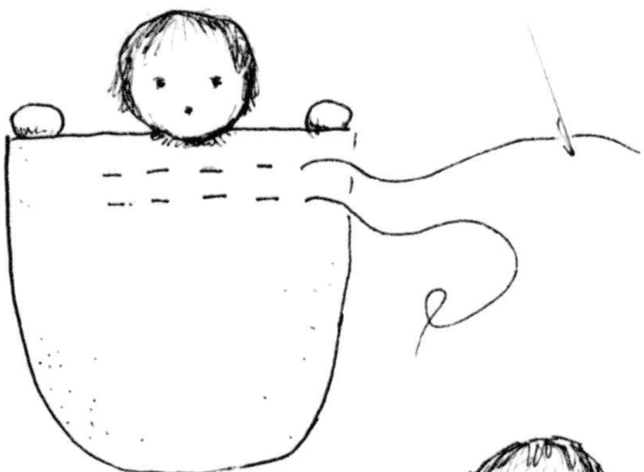

The family is now ready to play with.

Star Doll

This is the lovely baby of the larger doll family. You can make her with or without a sleeping bag. This doll has a carefully shaped head and needs experienced crafting skills.

YOU WILL NEED

- Gauze bandage, 3 or 4cm/1¼ or 1½" wide and 13cm/5" long (available from craft shops, specialist chemists or online)
- Strong sewing thread or thin crochet cotton – white
- Needle
- Stockinette fabric in skin colour, 13 x 13cm/5 x 5" for head
- Slightly stretchy fabric (cotton velour, recycled woollen jumper, good quality T-shirt) – 46 x 13cm /18 x 5" for hat and body
- Felt in contrasting colour to body, 10 x 10cm/4 x 4"
- Embroidery cotton in the same colour as body
- Fleece for stuffing
- Small ball of wool, firmly wound, any colour
- Embroidery cotton for eyes and mouth
- Thin paper and pencil for tracing

1. To make the head, tie off the tubular gauze at one end and turn it inside out. Wrap up the ball of wool in a thick layer of fleece to make a larger ball and stuff it into the tube. You should end up with a firm ball about 4cm/1¼" diameter.

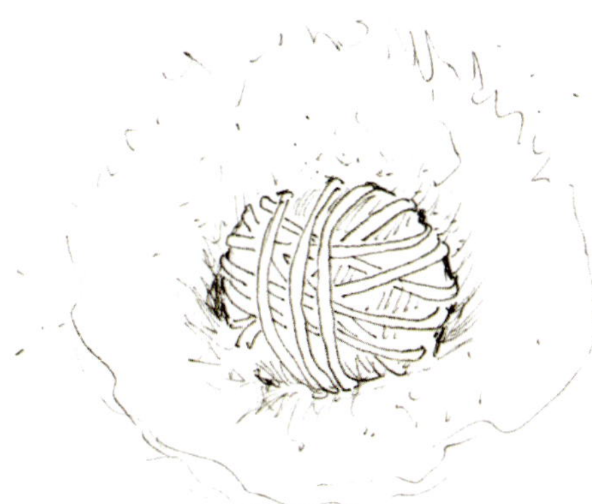

2. Tie off the tube securely just below the ball, making sure some of the fleece hangs down below the neck

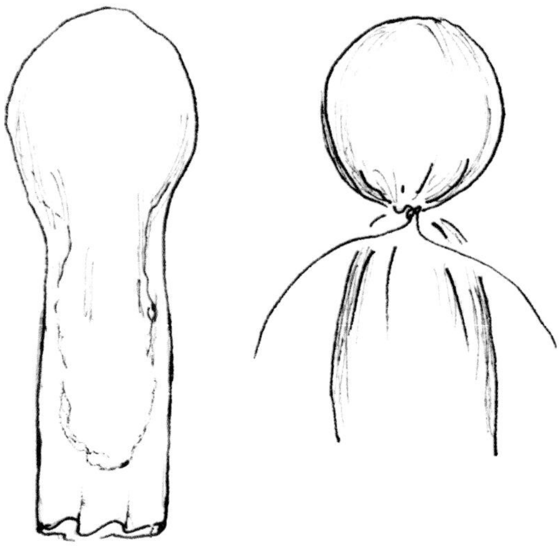

3. Use a length of strong white thread to make a stitch at the point where the ear would be – halfway down the head. Run the thread horizontally around the ball to the ear point on the other side and make a small stitch and pull tight to form a groove. Continue to run the thread around the back of the head to the first point and pull tight again. Knot the thread and cut it off. There should be a groove right around the head.

4. Pull down the back thread towards the neck whilst gently easing the fleece stuffing under it to form the back of the head.

5. Stuff more fleece into the tube below the head – it needs to be softer than the head. It should be about 6.5cm/2½" long. Sew up along the bottom to make a sort of torso.

6. Cover the head with stockinette fabric – it should be stretched horizontally around the head to follow the shape of the face closely. Make sure that the grain of the fabric runs from top to bottom. Overlap the fabric at the centre of the back of the head and pin in place.

Sew around the top edge of the fabric with a running stitch – pull together and sew to the top of the head. Sew up the pinned seam on the back starting at the top.

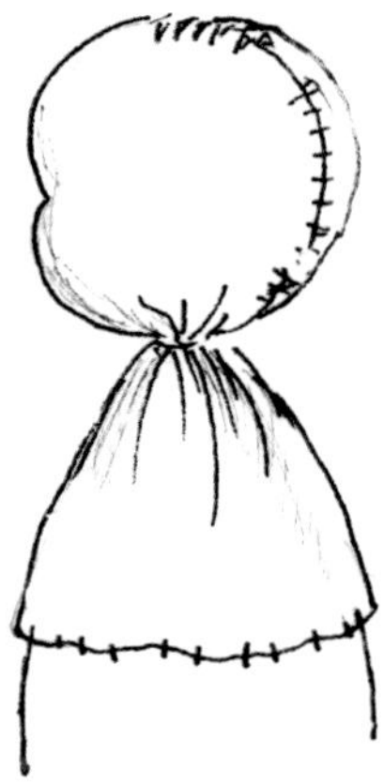

7. Tie off the head under the chin, making sure the wrinkles are at the back to avoid a premature wrinkly neck!

Sew the face fabric (stockinette) to the torso below the neck. The eyes are positioned on the 'groove' created earlier – they should be equidistant from the centre and not too close together. Mark the final position with two pins pushed into the head.

Thread a long fine needle with eye colour embroidery cotton, make a knot at one end and enter on the right side of the head, coming out where the nearest pin is. Remove the pin and embroider the eye with two or three horizontal stitches. Go across the head as deeply as possible to come out where the other eye is – remove the pin and embroider the second eye to match the first. Push the needle through the head to come out on the left side then secure the thread firmly so the eyes cannot come undone. Mark the mouth position halfway down the lower half of the head with pins – if is too low it will look grumpy! Embroider the mouth in the same way as the eyes.

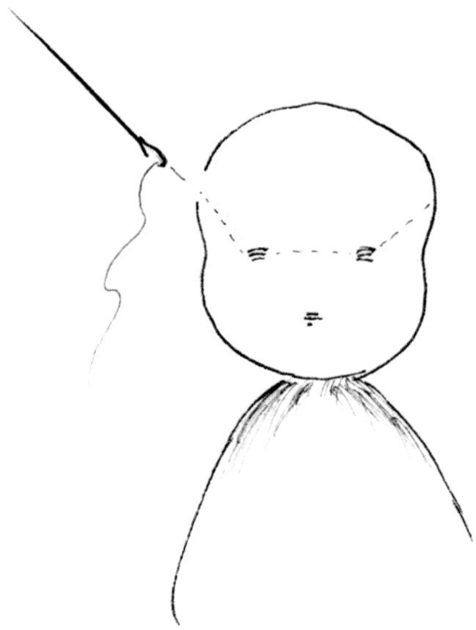

8. For the body, hat and collar, trace all three patterns onto paper and cut them out.

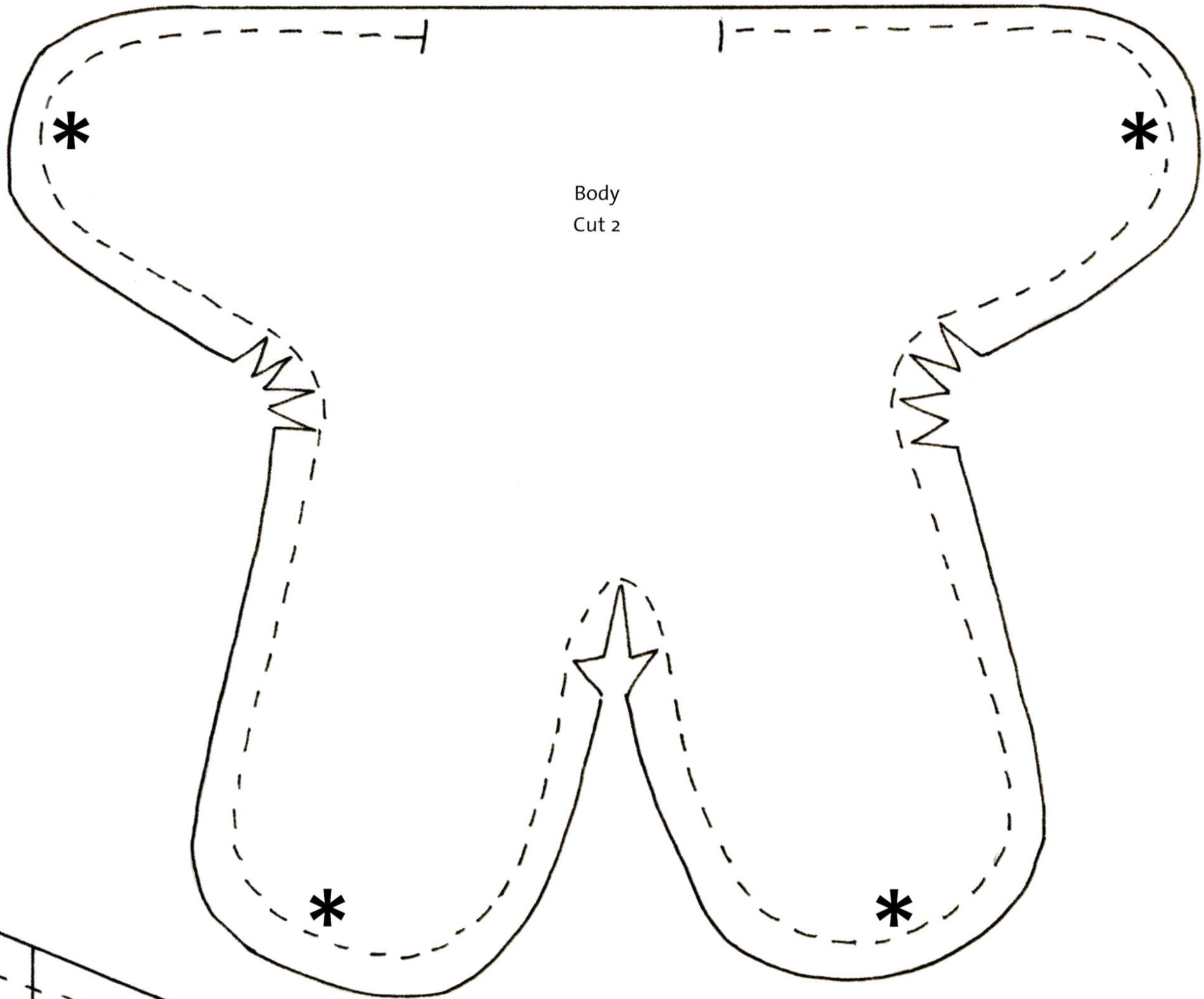

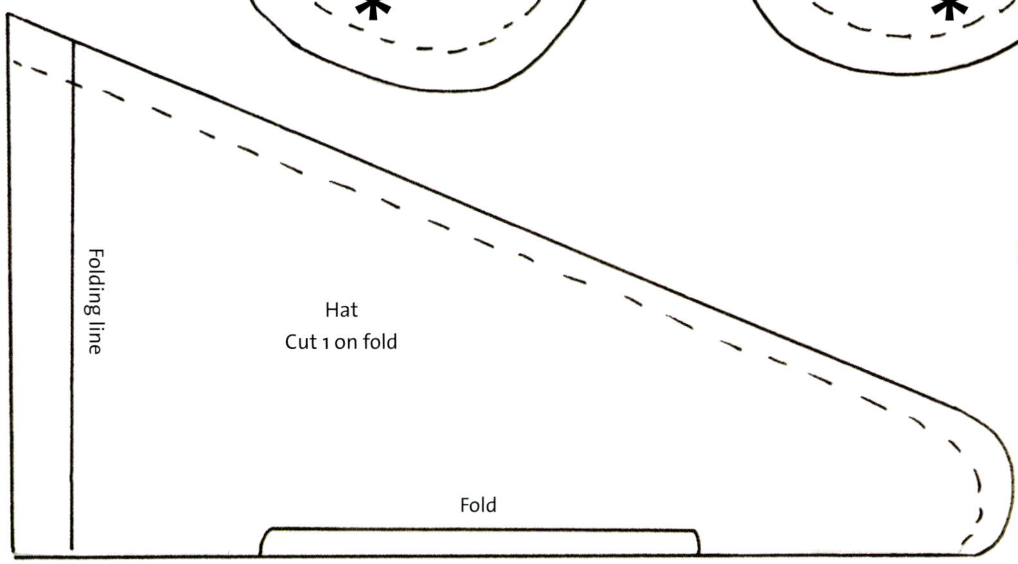

NB: All pattern pieces for the doll are actual size.

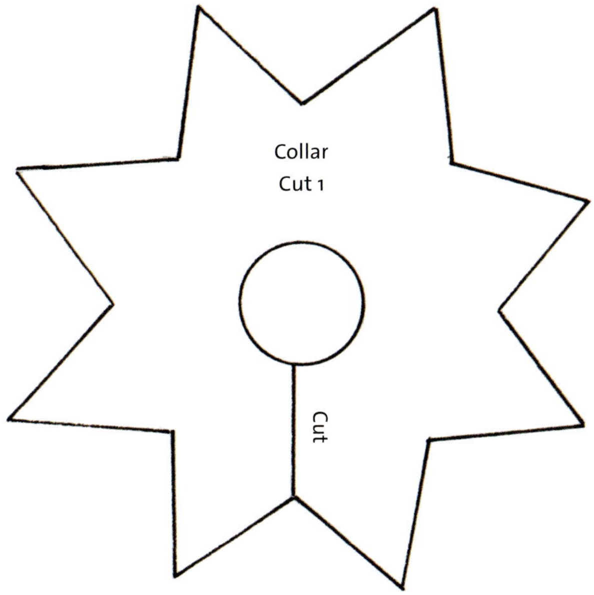

9. Pin the collar pattern to felt and cut it out then lay it aside. You may choose to embroider the collar. If so, it's best to do it before doll assembly. Fold the body fabric in half, right sides together, and pin the patterns to the fabric and cut out the hat and body. Use a zigzag stitch to keep the stretch (when machine sewing) and sew the body pieces together along the sewing lines. Don't sew across the neck openings.

10. Clip the fabric under the arms and in the crotch, as shown on pattern. Sew up the hat along the sewing lines.

11. Turn the body and hat inside. Roll the fleece into two small, firm balls about 1cm/3/8" for the hands and 1.5cm/5/8" for the feet. Place each ball at the points marked * on the pattern and tie off with the strong thread.

10. Make another very small fleece ball, stuff it into the end of the hat and tie it off with strong thread, to make a bobble. Lightly stuff the arms and legs with fleece but keep them feeling soft. Insert the torso through the neck opening and stuff more fleece around the body if needed, and still keep it feeling soft. Turn under the body fabric around the neck opening and gather it in with a running stitch.

11. Sew the body to the head with small stitches, using strong thread and ensure the face looks forwards, not sideways!

12. Fit the hat on the head. Turn under the edges and sew on with small stitches. Put the collar around the neck and secure at the back with a couple of small stitches.

Ready for the cuddle test.

Star Doll Sleeping Bag

The star doll looks so nice and comfy in her special little bag.

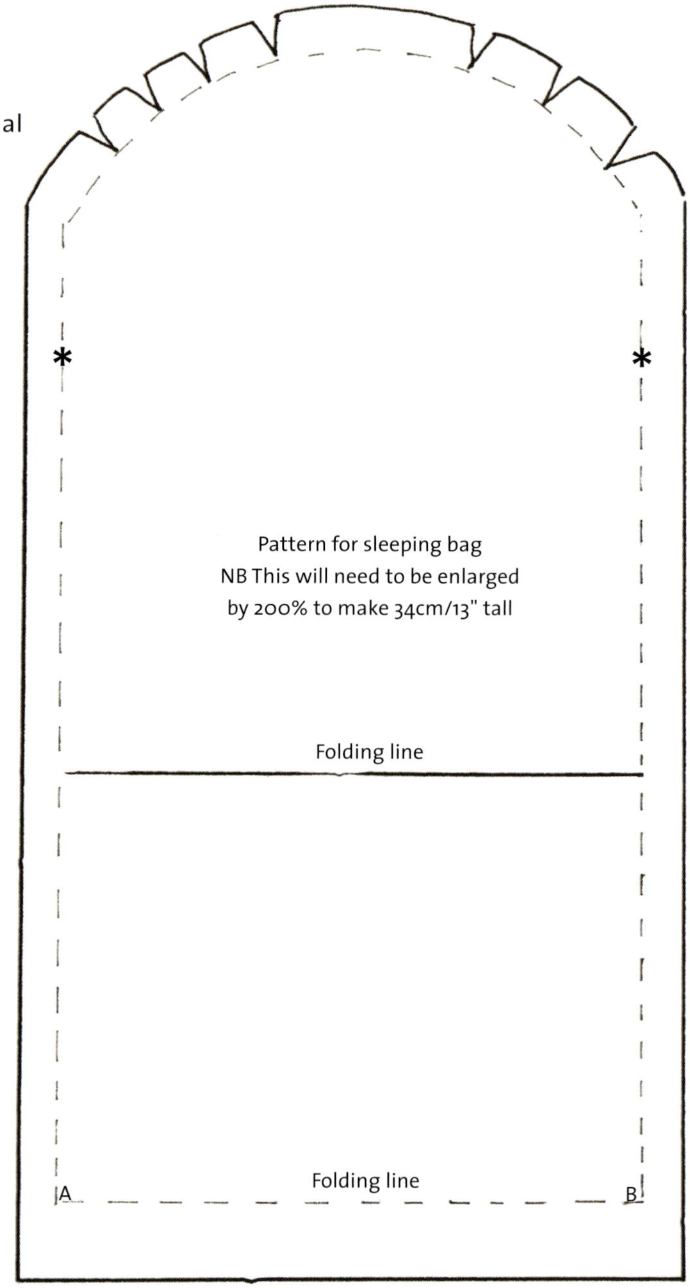

YOU WILL NEED

- Cotton fabric, about 35 x 35cm/13¾ x 13¾"
- Thin wadding, about 15 x 30cm/6 x 12"
- Thin paper for tracing and a pencil
- Sewing thread

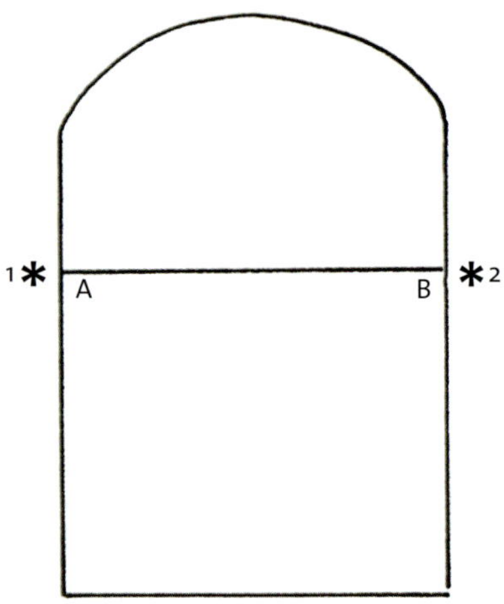

1. Having enlarged the pattern (above) by 200%, trace the pattern onto the paper and cut it out. Fold the fabric in half, right sides together. Pin the pattern on the fabric and cut out to make two pieces. Sew along the sewing lines – leave edge A to B open. Clip the edges as shown then turn it inside out before ironing it. Pin the pattern to the wadding and cut it out. Ease the wadding carefully into the bag and then fold in and sew across opening A to B.

2. Fold up corner A to 1* and B to 2* (see left) and sew up the side seams very close to the edge. You can decorate the bag by sewing on pretty braid or by embroidering it.

Time for a bedtime story.

Little Clutch Doll

Here is a beautiful, soft, cuddly little doll in an easy-to-make onesie body. For more experienced crafters to make.

YOU WILL NEED

- Tubular gauze bandage, 4cm/1½" wide, 20cm/8" long (available from craft shops, specialist chemists or online)
- Strong sewing thread or thin crochet cotton, white
- Needle
- Stockinette fabric, skin colour, 23 x 13cm/9 x 5" for head and hands
- Slightly stretchy fabric (cotton velour or finely knitted old jumper work best), 20 x 40cm/8 x 16"
- Embroidery cotton, the same colour as body
- Fleece for stuffing
- Small ball of wool, firmly wound, in any colour, for a firm base for the head
- Embroidery cotton for eyes and mouth
- Thin paper and pencil for tracing
- A few strands of wool for a fringe (optional)

1. To make the head, tie off the tubular gauze at one end and turn it inside out. Wrap up the ball of wool in a thick layer of fleece to make a larger ball and stuff it into the tub. You should end up with a firm ball about 5cm/2" diameter

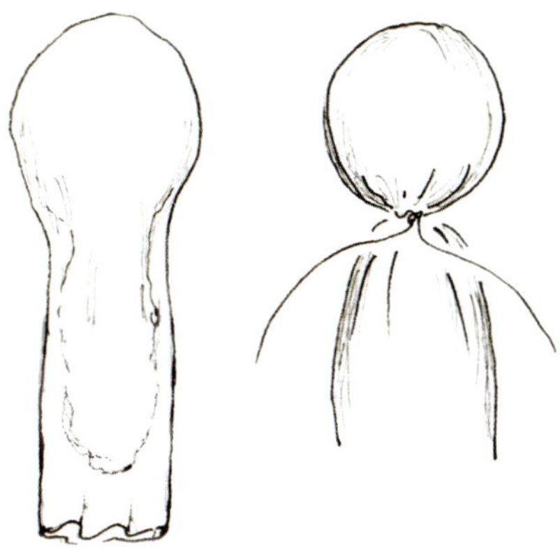

2. Tie off the tube securely just below the ball, making sure some of the fleece hangs down below the neck.

3. Use a length of strong white thread to make a stitch at the point where the ear would be – halfway down the head. Run the thread horizontally around the ball to the ear point on the other side; make a small stitch and pull tight to form a groove. Continue to run the thread around the back of the head to the first point and pull tight again. Knot the thread and cut it off. There should be a groove right around the head.

4. Pull down the back thread towards the neck whilst gently easing the fleece stuffing under it to form the back of the head.

5. Stuff more fleece into the tube below the head – it needs to be softer than the head. It should be about 9cm/3½" long. Sew up along the bottom to make a sort of torso.

6. Cut a piece of stockinette 18 x 13cm/7 x 5" to cover the head (it should be stretched horizontally around the head to follow the shape of the face closely). Make sure that the grain of the fabric runs from top to bottom. Overlap the fabric at the centre of the back of the head and pin in place. Sew around the top edge of the fabric with a running stitch, pull together and sew to the top of the head. Sew up the pinned seam on the back starting at the top.

Tie off the head under the chin and make sure the creases are at the back.

7. Sew the face fabric (stockinette) to the torso below the neck (see above). The eyes are positioned on the 'groove' created earlier and they should be equidistant from the centre and not too close together. Mark the final position with two pins pushed into the head.

Thread a long fine needle with eye colour embroidery cotton, make a knot at one end and enter on the right side of the head, coming out where the nearest pin is. Remove the pin and embroider the eye with two or three horizontal stitches. Go across the head as deeply as possible to come out where the other eye is. Remove the pin and embroider the second eye to match the first.

Push the needle through the head to come out on the left side, secure the thread firmly so the eyes cannot come undone.

8. Mark the mouth position halfway down the lower half of the head with pins. If is too low it will look grumpy! Embroider the mouth in the same way as the eyes. If you like, you could give the doll a fringe. Sew the short strands of wool securely near the crown of the head with sewing thread so that they cannot be pulled out. Most of this will all be covered by the hat.

9. To make the body and hat, trace the body and hat pattern onto paper and cut it out.

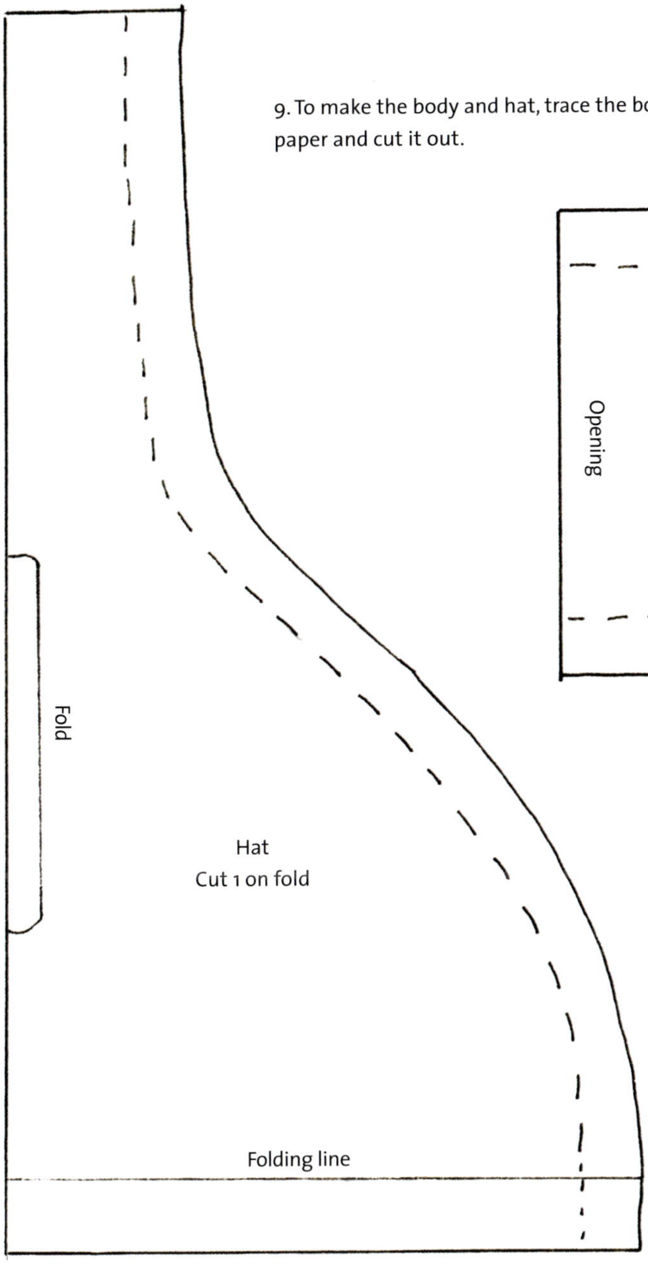

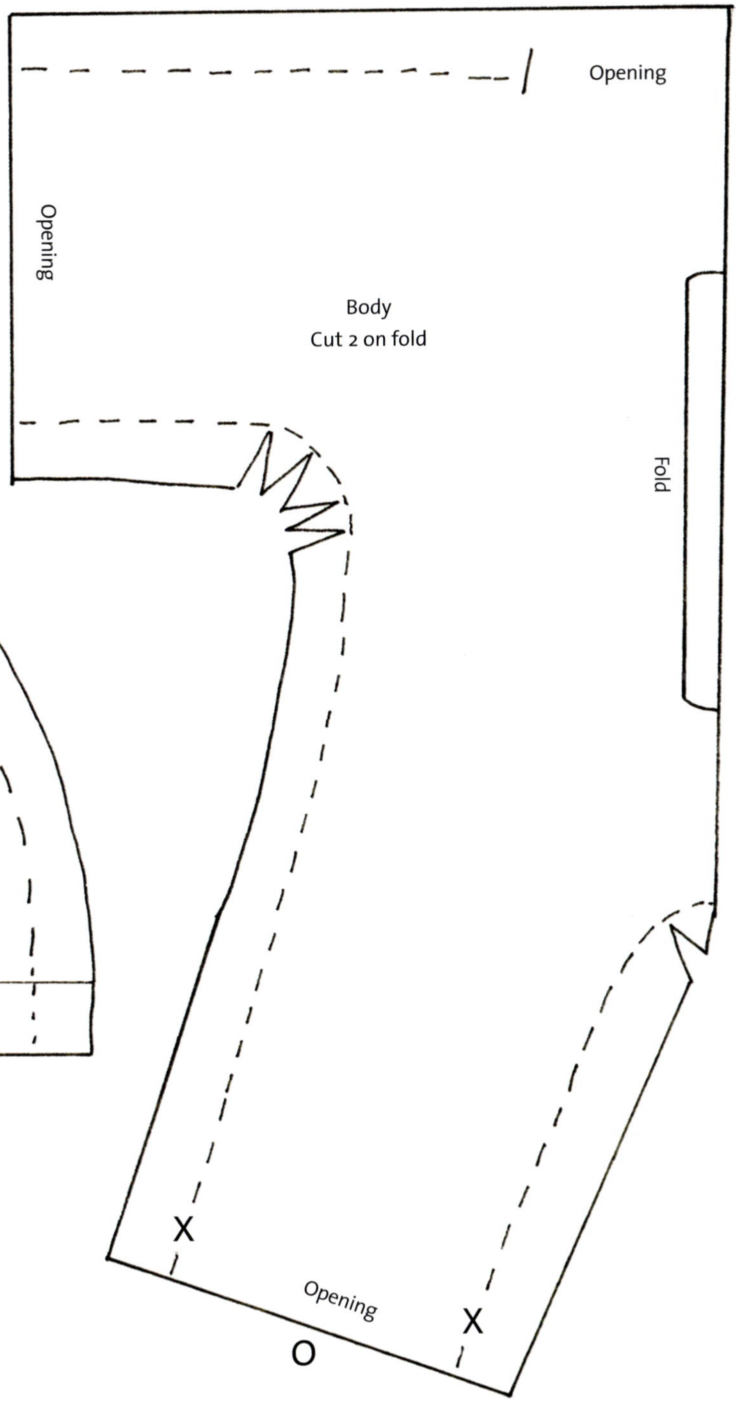

NB: These pattern pieces are actual size.

10. Fold the fabric in half, right sides together, pin the pattern onto it and cut two body pieces and one hat. Sew body pieces together along the sewing lines (if machining, use zigzag stitch to keep the stretch) and do not sew across foot, hand and neck openings.

11. Clip the fabric under the arms and crotch, as indicated on the pattern. Lay the outside and inside seam of each leg on top of each other at points X and sew across the bottom – this will make the feet point forwards: the Os will become the heels and toes of each foot.

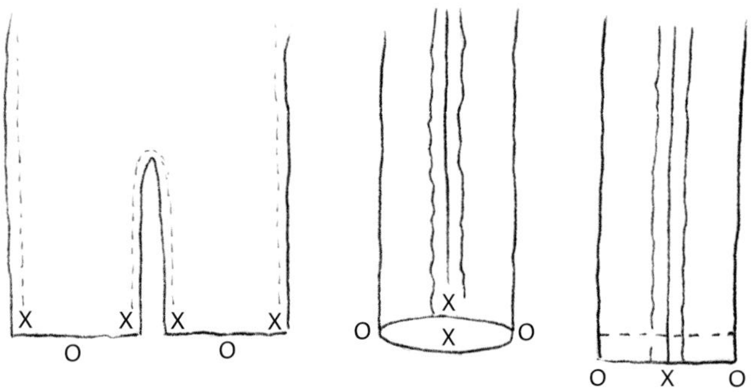

12. Turn the body inside out and stuff the feet and legs with fleece – they should feel soft. Insert the torso through the neck opening and stuff a little more wool around the body, keeping it feeling soft. Turn under the body fabric around the neck opening and gather in with a running stitch. Sew the body to the head with small stitches, using strong thread and ensure the face looks forwards, not sideways!

13. Roll some fleece into small firm balls (about the size of a marble) for the hands and place each ball in the middle of a piece of stockinette 5 x 5cm/2 x 2" and wrap them up. Tie them off with strong thread, making sure they are the same size!

14. Stuff the arms with fleece, keeping them soft, and insert the hands. Turn the edges of the sleeves under, gather fabric around the hands and secure well with small stitches. Gather each leg around the ankle about 1.5cm/½" from the bottom, with a running stitch and strong thread to form the feet.

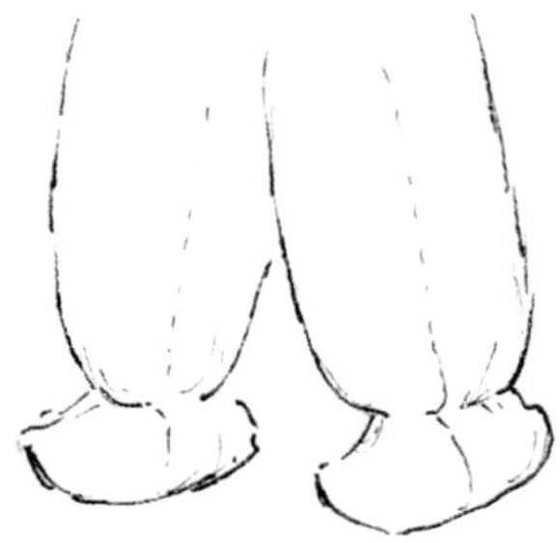

15. Sew a line of running stitch from the neck across the chest to under each arm so that the arms bend.

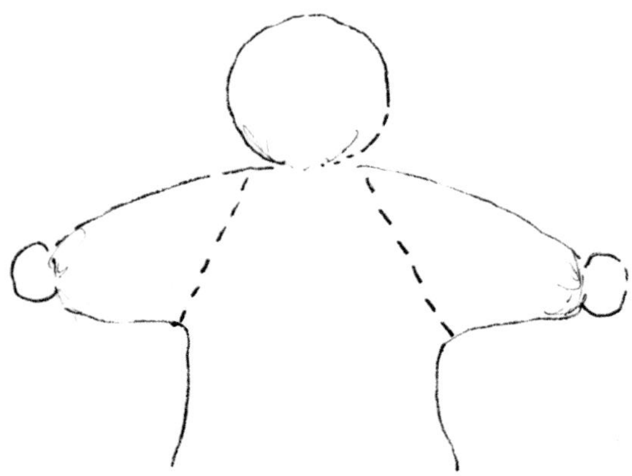

16. Sew up the hat along the sewing line and turn it inside out (a useful tip is to use a knitting needle to reach inside the top end of the hat). Make a knot near the end of the hat and fit it onto the doll's head. Turn the edges under and secure it around the face with small stitches.

He is ready for a peaceful night.

Girl and Boy

This lovely doll can be simply dressed with a pinafore dress for a girl or with a hoodie for a boy. For more experienced crafters.

YOU WILL NEED

- Tubular gauze bandage, 5 or 6cm/2 or 2½" wide, 25cm/10" long (available from craft shops, specialist chemists or online)
- Ball of wool (leftover bits), the size of a small apple
- Strong thread or thin crochet cotton, white
- Sewing needle
- Stockinette fabric, skin colour, 22 x 15cm/ 9 x 6" and 6 x 6cm/2½ x 2½"
- Slightly stretchy fabric – cotton velour or a finely knitted recycled jumper work best, 42 x 22cm/17" x 8½"
- Strong thread or embroidery cotton to match
- Fleece for stuffing, washed and carded
- Embroidery cotton for eyes and mouth
- Mohair wool or bouclé, hair colour
- Knitting needles, 4mm/US size 6
- Sewing thread to match the hair and a needle

1. Tie off the tubular gauze near one end and turn it inside out. Wrap up the ball of wool in a thick layer of fleece all round and stuff it into the tube. You should end up with a firm ball about 6.5cm/2½" diameter.

2. Tie off the tube below the ball and make sure some fleece hangs down into the 'neck'.

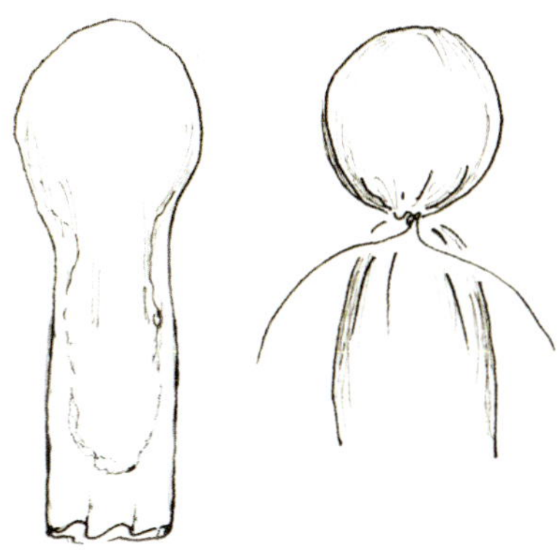

3. Use a length of strong white thread to make a stitch at the point where the ear would be (halfway down the head). Run the thread horizontally around the ball to the ear point on the other side, make a small stitch and pull tight to form a groove. Continue to run the thread around the back of the head to the first point and pull tight again. Knot the thread and cut it off. There should be a groove right around the head.

4. Continuing with the same thread, pass it through the neck (behind the chin) and up to the other ear. Stitch under the eye line at that point, go over the top of the head and back to the first ear. Pull tight and knot it, then cut the thread.

5. Pull down the back thread towards the neck whilst gently easing the fleece stuffing under it to form the back of the head.

6. Stuff more fleece into the tube below the head (it needs to be softer than the head). It should be about 11cm/4½" long. Sew up along the bottom to make a sort of torso.

7. Cover the head with stockinette fabric: it should be stretched horizontally around the head to follow the shape of the face closely. Make sure that the grain of the fabric runs from top to bottom. Overlap the fabric at the centre of the back of the head and pin in place. Sew around the top edge of the fabric with a running stitch, pull together and sew to the top of the head. Sew up the pinned seam on the back, starting at the top.

8. Tie off the head under the chin, ensuring any creases are at the back. Sew the face fabric (stockinette) to the torso below the neck (see above). The eyes are positioned on the 'groove' created earlier (they should be equidistant from the centre and not too close together). Mark the final position with two pins pushed into the head.

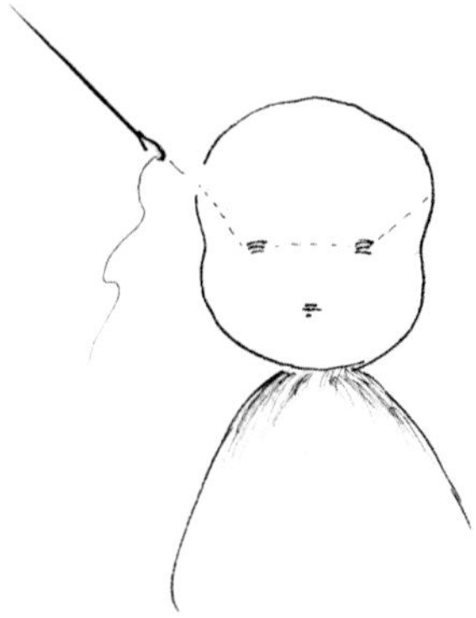

10. Fit the cap on the doll's head and sew it on, following the hairline. Add a few stitches at the crown. For a boy, the hair is the knitted cap. For a girl, add longer hair to make plaits – make a row of pins on the cap to mark the centre parting. Cover each side of the head by back-stitching strands of wool from ear to the centre parting. Take out the pins and add extra back-stitched strands for the plaits.

9. Thread a long, fine needle with eye colour embroidery cotton, make a knot at one end and enter on the right side of the head, coming out where the nearest pin is. Remove the pin and embroider the eye with three or four horizontal stitches. Go across the head as deeply as possible to come out where the other eye is; remove the pin and embroider the second eye to match the first. Push the needle through the head to come out on the left side then secure the thread firmly so the eyes cannot come undone.

Mark the mouth position halfway down the lower half of the head with pins – if is too low, it will look unhappy. Embroider the mouth in the same way as the eyes.

TO MAKE THE HAIR

Cast on 30 sts and k 6 rows st st.
Row 7: [K2 tog, k8] to end
Row 8: [P2 tog, p7] to end
Row 9: [K2 tog, k6] to end
Row 10: [P2 tog, p5] to end
Row 11: [K2 tog, k4] to end
Row 12: [P2 tog, p3] to end
Row 13: [K2 tog, k2] to end

Nine sts are left: pull the thread through the stitches and sew up side seams to make a sort of 'cap'.

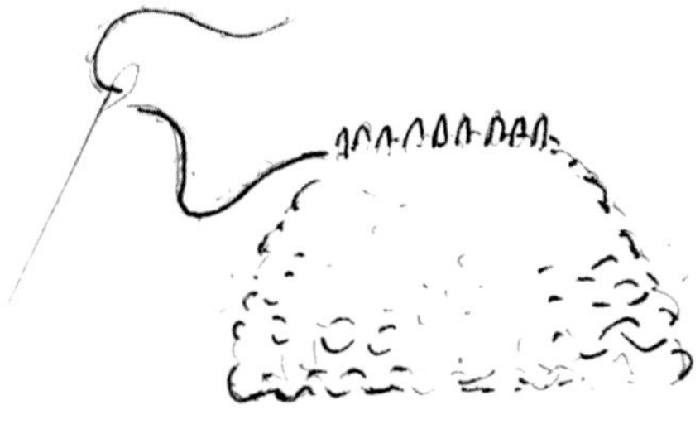

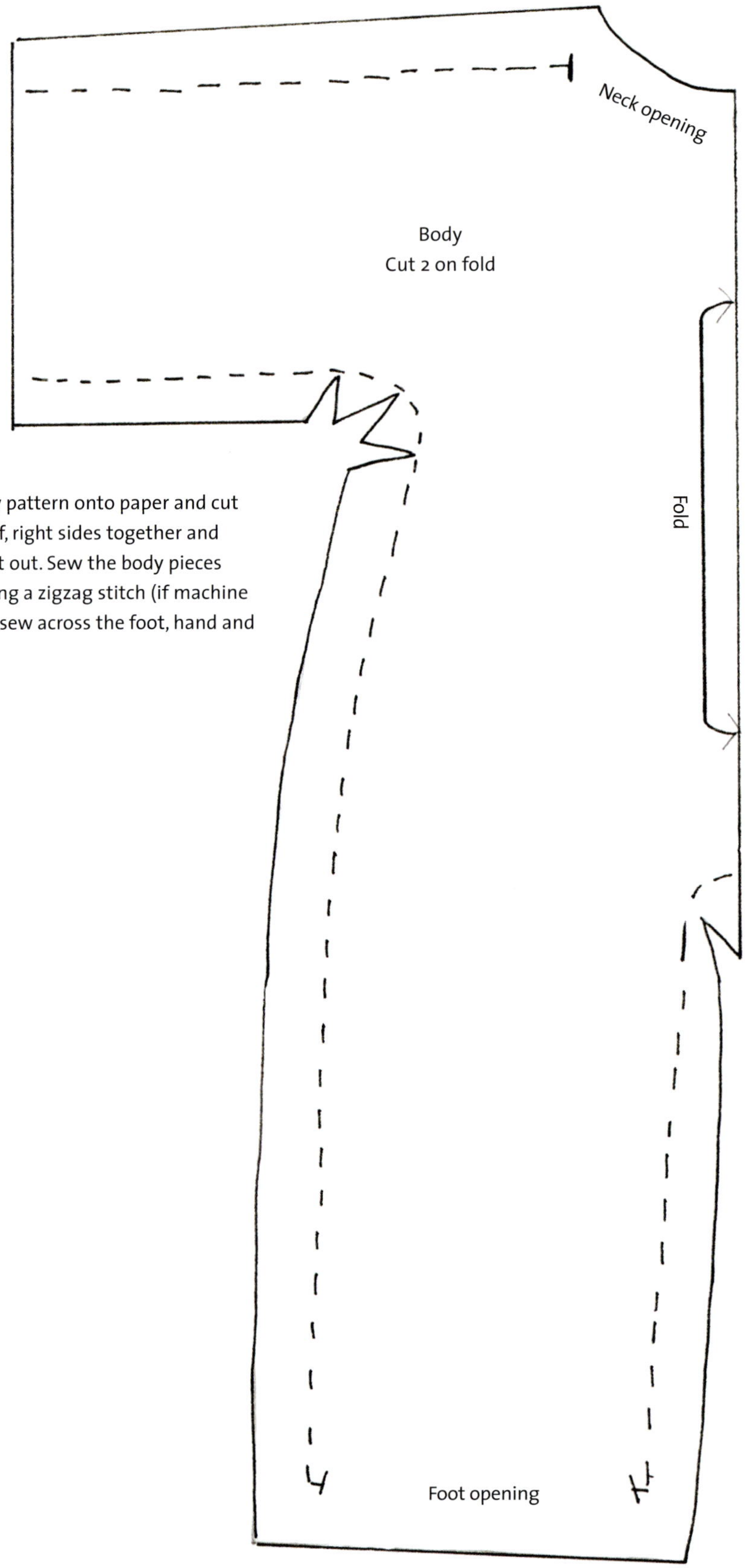

11. For the doll's body, trace the body pattern onto paper and cut it out. Fold the stretchy fabric in half, right sides together and pin the paper pattern to it and cut it out. Sew the body pieces together along the sewing lines using a zigzag stitch (if machine sewing) to keep the stretch. Do not sew across the foot, hand and neck openings.

NB: The pattern piece for the doll's body is actual size.

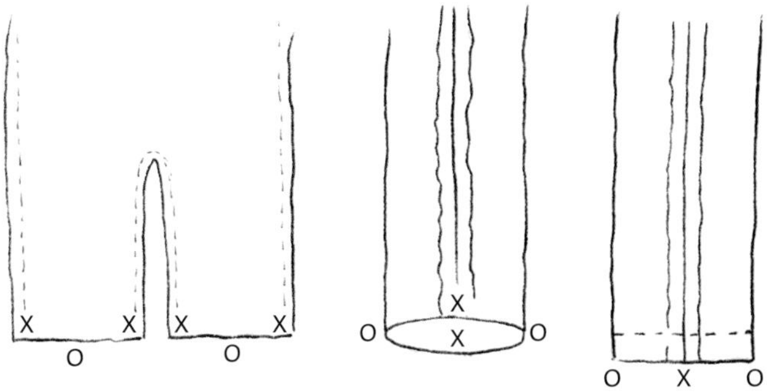

12. Lay the outside and inside seam of each leg on top of each other at points X and sew across the bottom from (O to O) to make the feet.

13. Turn the body inside out and stuff the feet and legs with fleece; they should feel soft. Insert the torso through the neck opening and stuff a little more wool around the body, keeping it feeling soft. Turn under the body fabric around the neck opening and gather in with a running stitch.

14. Sew the body to the head with small stitches using strong thread and ensure the face looks forwards, not sideways.

15. Roll some fleece into small firm balls (about the size of a marble) for the hands. Place each ball in the middle of a piece of stockinette 6 x 6cm/2½ x 2½" and wrap them up. Tie off with strong thread, making sure they are the same size.

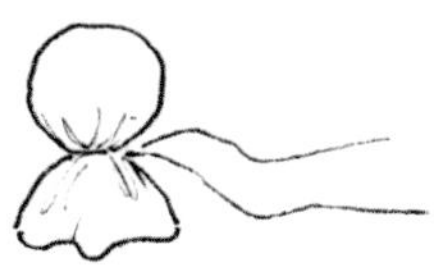

16. Stuff the arms with fleece, keeping them soft, and insert the hands. Turn the edges of the sleeves under, gather fabric around the hands and secure well with small stitches. Gather each leg around the ankle, about 1.5cm/½" from the bottom, with a running stitch and strong thread, to form the feet.

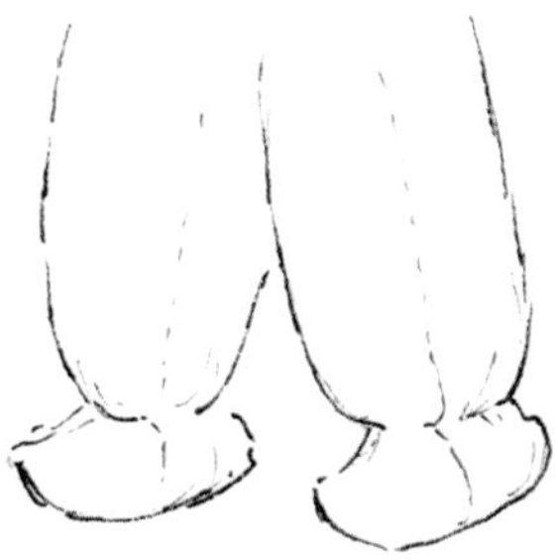

The girl doll looks great in the pinafore dress and the boy is cool in the hoodie.

Pinafore Dress for Soft Doll

This dress will make the girl soft doll look charming. The bias binding is a bit tricky to apply but the rest is very easy.

YOU WILL NEED

- Cotton fabric – 40 x 20cm/16 x 8"
- Thin paper, pencil and scissors
- Sewing cotton
- Bias binding to suit, 60cm
- Small button

1. Trace the pattern (see page 77) onto the paper and cut it out.

2. Fold fabric in half to make a square, right sides together. Pin the pattern to the fabric and cut out to make two separate sides.

3. Neaten the edges along the sewing lines, sew together both centre front seams and the shoulder seams. Fold and hem both back edges from top to bottom, sew bias binding on armholes and neck opening. Sew the button on the top right corner.

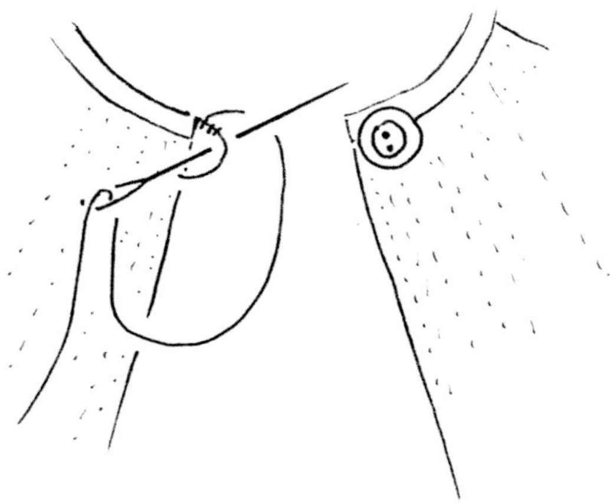

4. Sew a loop to the top left corner; strengthen it with double thread sewn around it with blanket stitch.

5. Fold and hem the bottom edge.

Ready for playtime!

NB: The pattern piece for the doll's dress is actual size.

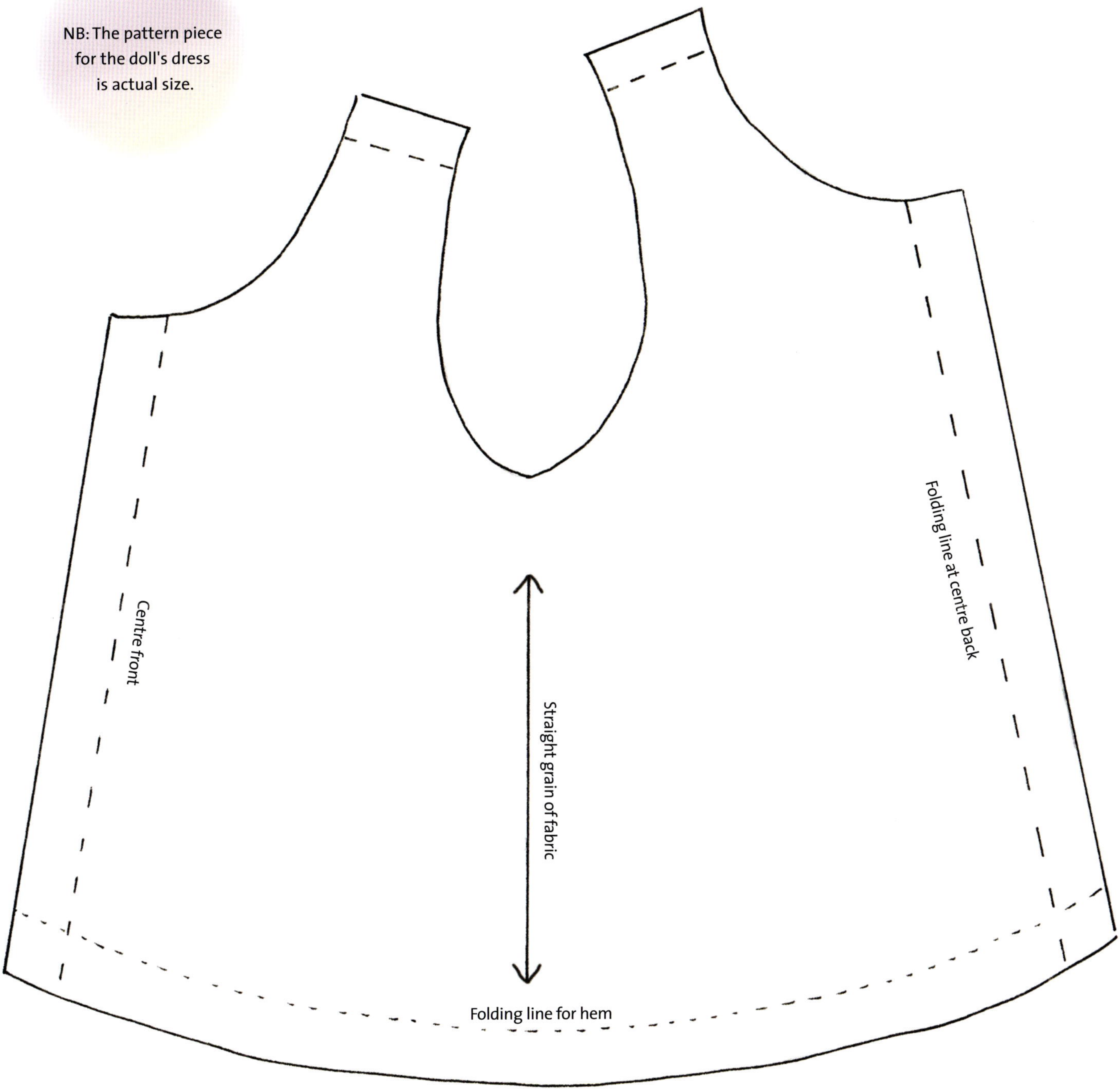

Hoodie for Soft Doll

This quick and easy jumper will finish off the boy soft doll beautifully. This is an easy knitting project.

YOU WILL NEED

- Double knitting wool, about 25 gm/1oz
- Knitting needles, 3mm/US size 2
- Stitch holder or safety pin
- Small button
- Needle and thread
- Crochet hook, 3mm/US C

1. FOR THE BODY
Cast on 24 sts
K 4 rows
Next row: P to the end
K 12 rows st st
Next row: Divide for front opening – k12, leave next 12 sts on stitch holder and continue knitting up right front
Next row: P to the end
K 9 rows st st, ending on knit row at centre front

To shape neck, cast off 3, p9 (to end of row)
Next row: K to end
Next row: Cast off 2, p7
Next row: K to end
Next row: Cast off 2, p5
Next row: K to end
Break yarn and leave 5 sts on stitch holder

Left front: Pick up 12 sts from stitch holder and k to end of row
Next row: P to end
K 8 rows st st, ending at centre front on purl row

To shape neck, cast off 3 sts, k9
Next row: P to end
Next row: Cast off 2, k7
Next row: P to end
Next row: Cast off 2, k5
Next row: P to end
Next row: K to end
Next row: P5, cast on 14, pick up 5 sts from stitch holder and p to end of row (24 sts)
K 24 rows in st st (ending on p row)
Next row: K4 rows
Cast off

2. Press work under damp cloth with iron (heat setting 'wool') then sew up side seams to point X where the front divides.

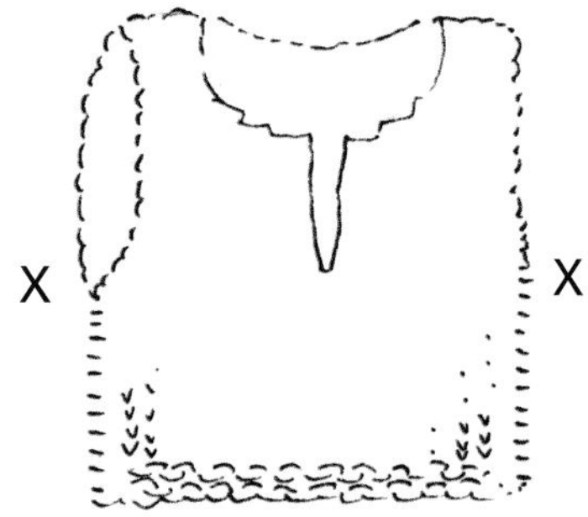

3. TO MAKE THE HOOD
Pick up 22 sts around neck opening (14 sts at the back and 4 sts each side)
K 1 row, starting on left side of neck
Next row: P to end
Next row: Inc as follows *[k1, m1] *rep to end of row (42 sts)
K 25 rows sts
Cast off

4. Fold in half the top edge of the hood and sew together then crochet around the arm holes, hood and neck edges. Sew on a button at the centre front of the neck and crochet loop to take it on the other side.

Ready for dolly's first fitting.

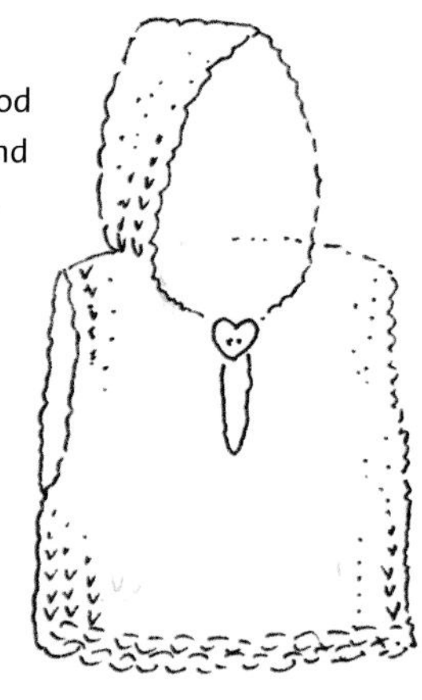

Assorted Doll's Clothes

Children love to have new clothes for their dolls. These ones are special, as they are created just for their doll. Some of these designs are so simple, older children could sew them. Use nice, bright colours.

YOU WILL NEED

- Cotton or wool fabric, 23 x 92cm/9 x 36" (1/4 yard)
- 3 buttons, press studs or poppers
- Thread to match
- Bias binding, 45cm/18" long
- Round elastic
- Sewing machine or needles for hand sewing

Onesie

This is very similar to the one to fit the doll in a onesie (page 67), except that this one is made to be removed. It will fit a doll 30cm/12" high.

1. Cut out from the pattern, following the dimensions.

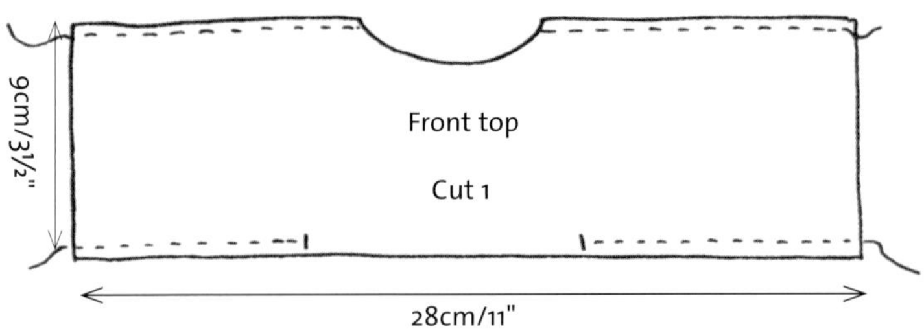

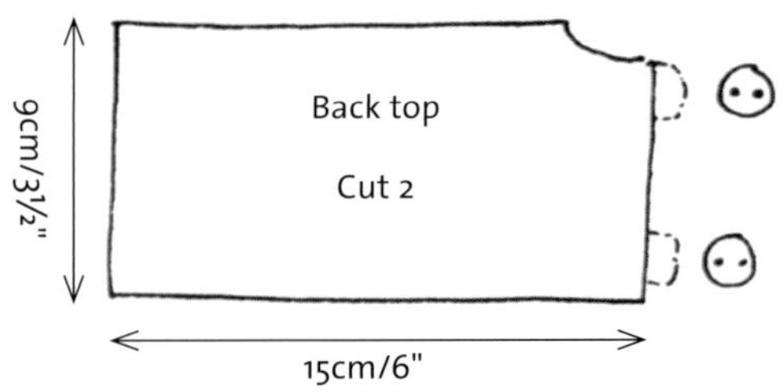

2. Pin the front, top and two back pieces, right sides together. The two back pieces will overlap in the middle. Machine a 1cm/3/8" seam on the top and bottom of the arms.

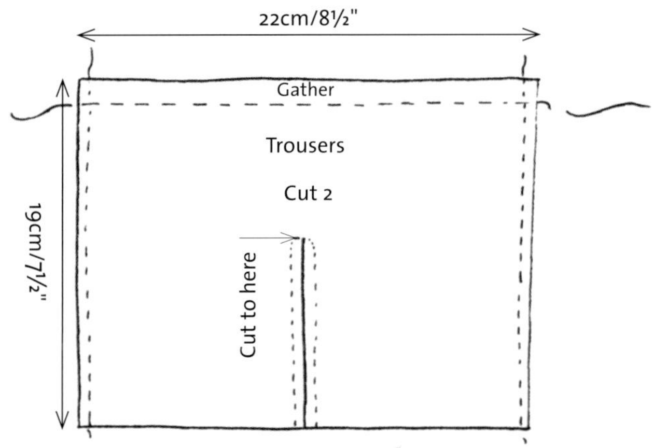

3. With the trouser pieces right sides together, machine a 1cm/3/8" seam down the outside and inside legs. Make a 5cm/2" vertical cut in the middle of the back of the trousers. Run a gathering stitch around the waist and sew the trousers to the top. Turn in the trouser bottoms and arm cuffs 1cm/3/8". Hem the seams and thread elastic through and knot it.

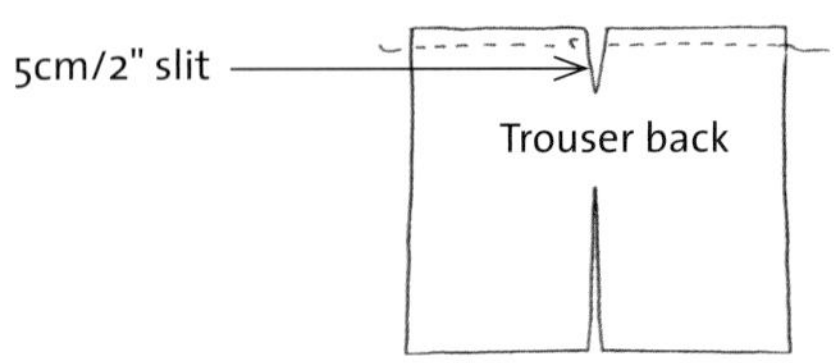

4. Lay the bias binding on the right side of the material around the neck and machine round. Turn the bias binding over and sew it to the inside of the material. Turn in the edges of the back opening twice and sew.

5. Sew on the press studs or buttons. If you use buttons you must make loops out of thin strips of material or use strong thread.

Dress

You can make a dress in exactly the same way but without cutting the material in the centre for the trousers.

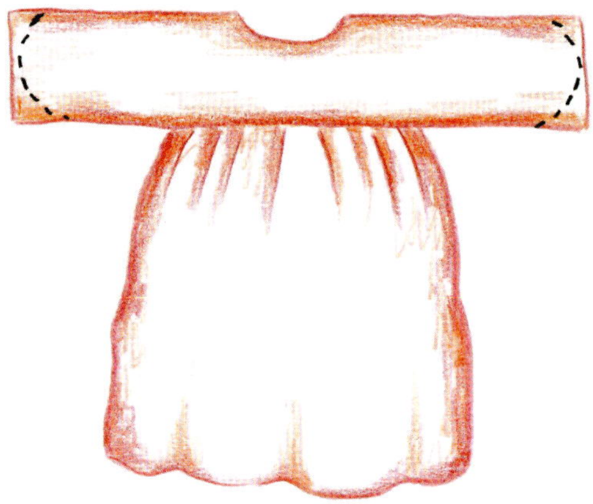

All-in-one pants and vest

YOU WILL NEED

- Old T-shirt or vest
- White tape, 50cm/20" long
- 2 press studs
- Thread

1. Measure and cut out the front and back as shown on the pattern. Machine along the shoulder seams and down each side. Turn in 1cm/3/8" and sew round the neck, back opening, armholes and leg holes.

2. Sew on the two press studs at the bottom and sew on four pieces of tape at the back.

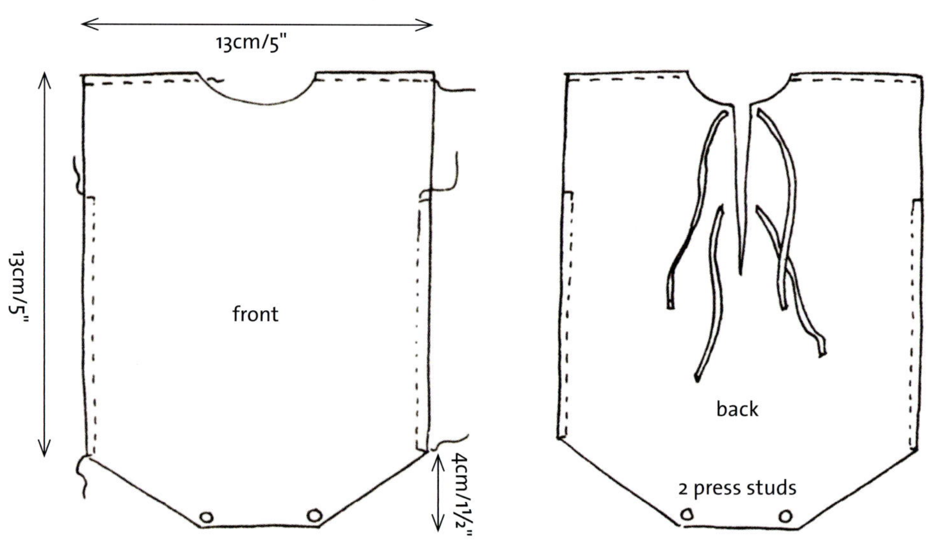

Knitted doll's pinafore

This and the following simple knitted clothes can be made by a young knitter with some experienced help.

YOU WILL NEED

- Double-pointed knitting needles 3mm/US size 3
- Small amounts of wool in clear rainbow colours

This is knitted in rounds starting from the top. The yoke-band must fit tightly around the doll's chest.

1. Cast on enough stitches so that the yoke band fits tightly around the doll's chest.
K 5 rounds in K1, P1
Next row: double the number of sts (k1, m1, k1, m1) to the end (double the number of stitches you started out with).
Knit to required length.
P the last 3 rounds
Cast off

2. Knit braces with 3 or 4 sts to the required length.
(A simple Fair Isle pattern can be used around the bottom for adventurous knitters.)

Doll's slippers

1. Cast on 12 sts.
K 14 rows in g st
K 2 tog to the end of the row (6 sts)

2. Draw stitches together and sew as seen above.

Doll's hat

1. Measure around the doll's head.

2. K 4 rows [k1, p1], which should fit tightly round the doll's head.

3. Continue in st st to the required length.
K2tog to end and draw together the leftover stitches.

4. Sew up the side seam.

Doll's waistcoat

This will look great made out of felt.

YOU WILL NEED

- Piece of felt, 15 x 25cm/6 x 10"
- Button (optional)
- Thread and embroidery thread, if you want to decorate it

1. Transfer the pattern onto the felt and cut it out.

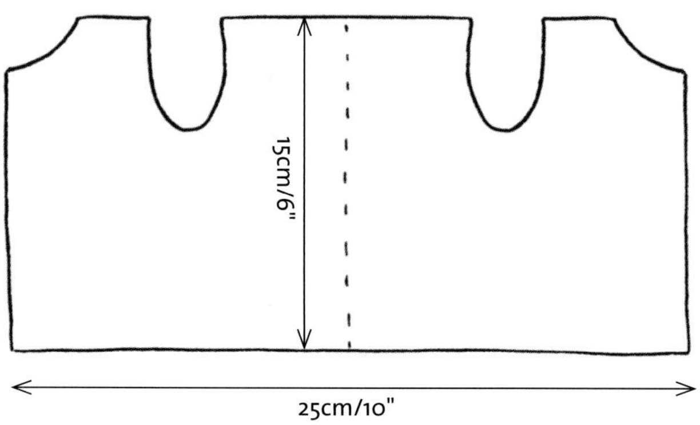

2. Sew up the shoulder seams. Add the button and decorate as you wish.

Doll's House

All children love to play with cardboard boxes, either large for hiding in or small for dolls to be in. This simple but cosy little house will invite plenty of creative play – small is beautiful! It can be made for children by older siblings or adults with plenty of help from the recipients.

YOU WILL NEED

- Cardboard box, about 30 x 23cm/12 x 9" about 25cm/10" high (not a shoe box)
- Fabrics or pale wrapping paper matching for inside and outside walls
- Felt for floor, in this case 30 x 23cm/12 x 9" (but match to the dimensions of the box)
- Ribbon and scraps of matching material for doors and windows
- Bias tape to neaten up all edges (optional)
- Sturdy scissors
- PVA craft glue or wallpaper glue
- Enough cotton material to cover the roof

1. Cut away the whole top and one broad side of the box (see shaded areas).

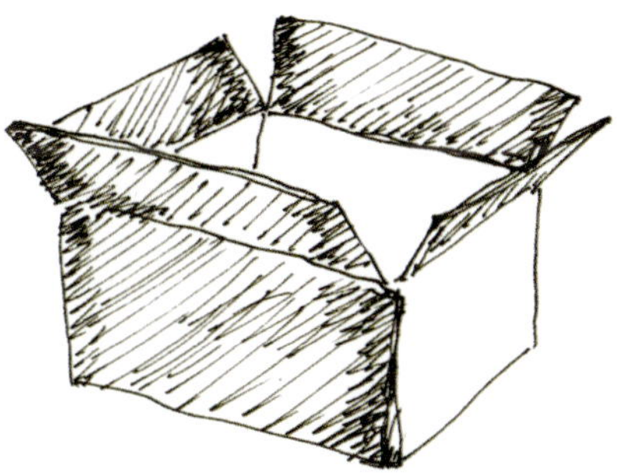

2. Cut along the bottom of the two short sides between A and B. Trim 1mm extra near B (otherwise the walls will spring open).

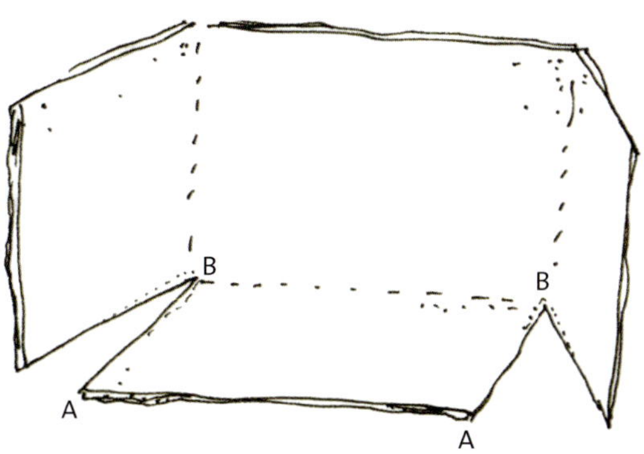

3. Cut material to fit exactly. Glue the outside wall material. Glue the inside wall material. If the floor folds, double stick some tape over it. Glue felt over the floor.

Your basic house is ready to be furnished.

4. Cover all the edges with bias tape glued on (optional). Decorate with windows and doors made from ribbon and scraps.

Doll's Bed

A matching doll's bed will complete the doll's house.

YOU WILL NEED

- Child's shoe box
- Material to cover it – quilted is a good option but not necessary
- PVA glue
- Scissors
- Scraps of material and fleece for bedding

1. Remove the lid and cut a strip of cardboard from it 5cm/2" wide and discard the rest.

2. Cover all the surfaces with material. Glue the strip into place.

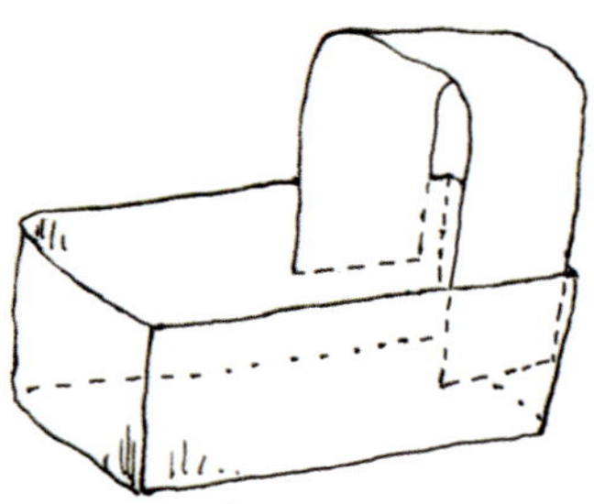

Ready for dolly's bedtime!

Glove Puppet

This is more of a toy for parents or teachers to make and then use in a puppet show for small children. A simple story with very few props and characters will have everyone enthralled.

YOU WILL NEED

- Stretchy material (eg from an old cotton vest, about 15 x 15cm/6 x 6")
- 2 pieces of stockinette, one about 15 x 15cm/6 x 6", one about 5 x 10cm/2x4"
- Small amount of wool fleece
- Thin cardboard, 7 x 7cm/3 x 3"
- Thin material, 45 x 45cm/18 x 18", which hangs well (silk is ideal)

1. For the doll, follow the instructions for the girl and boy dolls on page 71, except that when you are stuffing the under layer of cotton material you insert the piece of cardboard that has been rolled up to fit your index finger. Leave a space in the stuffing so that the cardboard roll can be pushed well up into the head. You may need assistance from somebody to tie the strong button thread around the neck. The tube is now protruding from the neck of the puppet.

2. Stitch the tube firmly to the under layer so that it is fixed to the head. Continue to make the head as for the doll, having decided what character you want the puppet to be.

3. To make the body, fold the piece of stretchy material in half so that the fold lies along the neck and shoulders of the puppet.

4. Make a hole halfway along this fold, big enough for the neck to fit into. Take it off and turn it inside out. Taper the side seams slightly inward towards the bottom. Sew the seams but leave space for hands. Hem the bottom and turn it out the right way. Sew the material onto the neck.

5. Make the hands out of stockinette big enough for you to fit your thumb and middle finger into. Sew the hands onto each end of the material.

6. Decorate your puppet according to his or her character. Look at the drawings for some suggestions.

Summer

When the sun moves to the highest point in the sky on 21 June, we celebrate midsummer. Nature has followed this upward movement with ever increasing vitality and grows and blossoms with an exuberant display of beauty. The days can be hot and seemingly endless. The magical midsummer nights are very short and with a bit of luck they can be wonderfully balmy. Barely visible flowers fill the air with their scent.

What a grand time to be outside, both day and night. If you live in a town and the local park is your only connection with the seasons, try camping in the country to reconnect with nature in perhaps a slightly uncomfortable but ever so exciting way. Choose your time and place so you don't have to wish away the clouds!

Bees buzz from flower to flower, gathering nectar and pollen. Butterflies flutter seemingly aimlessly enjoying the warm light. Even daytime can seem like a 'Midsummer Night's Dream'. But Titania and Oberon with their hosts of fairies are out to play tricks on us in this dreamy time. It is for us to stay awake.

This is the time for fires – starting with the St John's Fire on the night of 24 June. Traditionally, this is the fire we master by jumping over it!

Then we have our campfires to sit around, singing together in the flickering light that brightens up the warm darkness. We can bake potatoes in that fire (wrapped in foil) and cook soup over it. We can even bake bread over it using a thin 'sausage' of dough wrapped around a stick held over the fire. Marshmallows roasted on sticks over the fire are the best ever dessert.

From a BBQ to a picnic in the long grass, outside eating is fun for everyone. The water in the lakes and the sea is gradually warming up. How exhilarating it is jump into all that freshness! Hours can be spent damming and diverting little streams and rivulets with stones and rocks. Breach the dam and release a torrent of water and send little boats of bark and twigs racing downstream.

One is never too old to play Pooh Sticks on the bridge. Secret little fairy gardens can be created and perhaps the wee folk will show their appreciation by leaving a lovely feather, semi-precious stone or special pine cone.

On the beach we can combine sand and water to create enormous sandcastles. And if the sea is too far away, make the castles in your garden, or even inside on a very large tray, keeping the sand damp.

For the rest of our lives we will remember these blessed golden days when all life is play.

Summer Festival Table

There will be days when we want to escape the heat or (yes) the rain. So that will be the time for your nature table, but obviously it will not get quite the same amount of attention as during the other seasons. As always, you can enjoy just a simple one. But a festival table for children can be all encompassing.

When you find a beautiful natural treasure like a shell or a feather you will have a fitting place to display it. The following are suggestions that you can adapt to your situation.

For building up the background refer to nature table veils (page 15), backdrop stand (page 12), and the Colour Year (page 9).

Start by building up your background with the veils. The colours change from early/mid-summer to late summer. From a vibrant green ground and blue sky to a straw-coloured ground and a golden sky. A radiating sun can be pinned onto the background veils. Find a good spot for a deep blue crystal. In the centre you can place a glass bowl filled with water in which float a night-light and some roses. Mother Nature will look beautiful suspended from the overhead wire.

You can use a vase with summer flowers; wild ones can be stunning but remember to be careful not to pick rare species and never uproot any wildflower. Above it you can hang the fairy circle, bees and butterflies.

Any attractive natural found objects can be incorporated into the display – shells, pebbles, feathers.

As we pass the midsummer point the sun begins to take a lower path in the sky, the days start to shorten (ever so slowly) and the temperature rises. Now the ripening process starts and we can find flowering grasses. How many different ones can you collect and display?

The first pine cones come tumbling out of the trees; hops, early berries and nuts are waiting to be found. You can make a grass heart and a lavender bottle.

As with all nature tables, you take great care to build it up, so it deserves respect. Refresh the flowers regularly – wildflowers wilt extremely quickly, but some are to be found in abundance.

Simple Summer Table

When the festival time is over, change your table to a simple one using a golden yellow or orange table-mat or felt square the corners of which you can round off. Just have a vase with seasonal flowers on a golden yellow or orange table mat. Add a few seasonal nature finds, an art card, a crystal.

Remember never to leave a lit candle unattended.

Radiant Sun

Right now the sun is giving warmth and life to our surroundings. This shining sun can be suspended in your nature table. This is a quick and easy project that requires accurate scissor work.

YOU WILL NEED

- Thin paper for practice
- Shiny gold paper, 15 x 15cm/6 x 6"
- Compass and pencil
- Ruler
- Nail scissors
- Pins

1. Draw a circle with the compass on the thin paper (radius 6cm/2½"). Cut it out and fold it in half accurately, then quarters, then eighths – all with sharp edges.

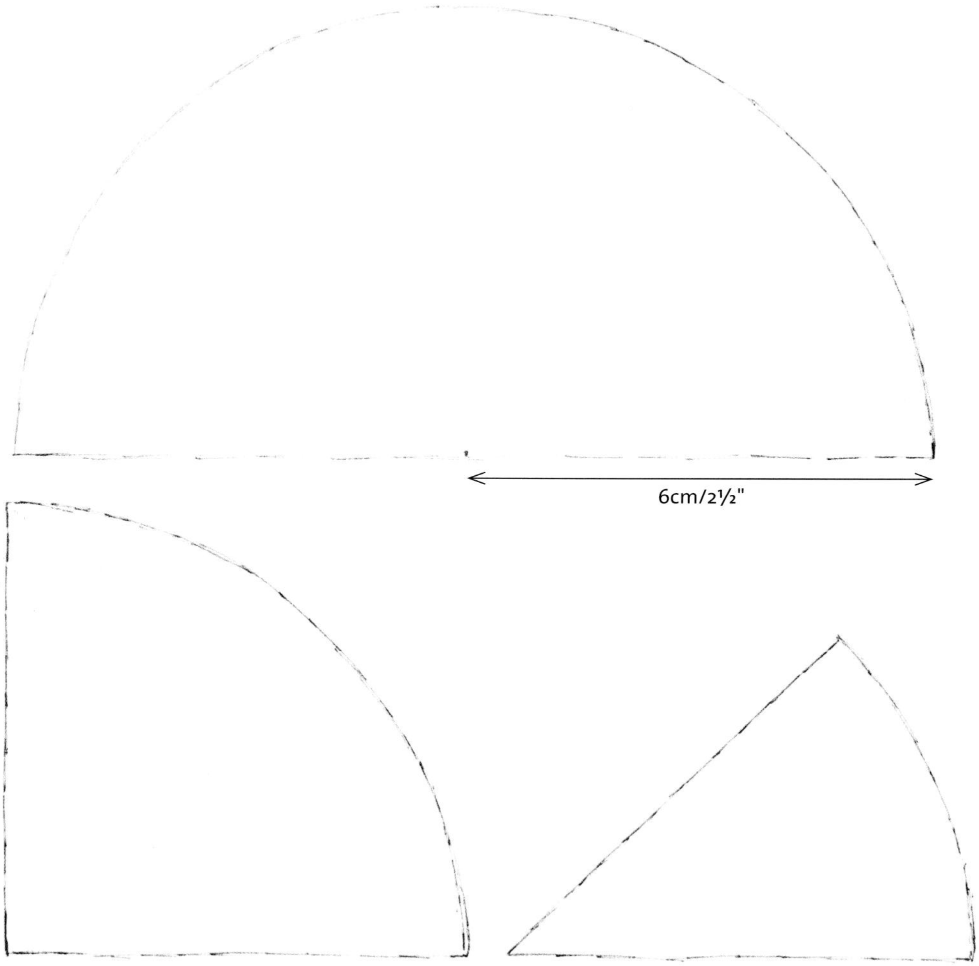

2. Draw the rays from the outer edge to halfway to the centre fold then cut them out.

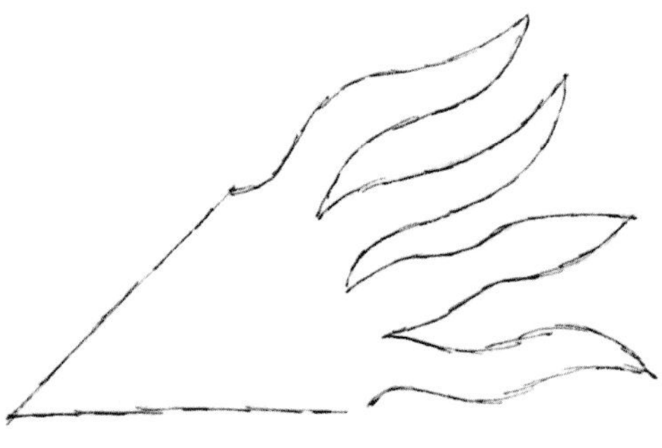

3. Unfold it carefully. If it needs adjustment, do it now – this is your practice. Now for the real thing: repeat all of the above with the shiny gold paper. Carefully unfold it and smooth out the fold lines with the back of your nail.

4. Pin it to the backdrop material on your nature table from where it can spread its bounteous warmth.

Fairy Ring

Natural silk is the most delicate of materials; its sheen is unequalled and it can absorb and reflect colour like no other fabric. In other words it is the perfect material for making fairies.

Here is a magic silk fairy ring in beautiful rainbow colours. It can be part of the summer table (page 87) or hung over a baby's cot. Either way it is delightful.

As making it is a delicate process, it is best done by teenagers and adults.

YOU WILL NEED

- White silk strip, 15 x 100cm/6 x 40", the thinnest available (the easiest way to get this is to order online; see page 21)
- Wooden ring 20cm/8" diameter
- Good quality watercolour paints in rainbow colours
- Seven small containers, such as eggcups or tiny plastic boxes
- Soft paint brush – large flat-topped
- Clean white plastic or glass work surface
- Clean jam jar of water
- Wool fleece – small quantity for heads
- Needle and white cotton thread
- Scissors

Silk tearing technique

If you have never torn silk before, practise on a small piece of old cotton.

- Make a 2cm/1" cut at the edge of the material.
- Hold the material either side of the cut.
- Quickly and firmly tear it apart. It works much better than cutting and children love watching you do it!

1. Tear the silk into a strip, 15 x 100cm/6 x 40". Gently wash the strip by hand to remove any starch. Whilst the strip is still wet, spread it out on the clean flat surface. Remove all air bubbles by gently spreading the silk out to the edges with your fingertips. Use a little water to make small quantities of paint in the containers – carmine (bluish) red, vermillion (orangey), golden yellow, lemon yellow, Prussian (greenish) blue, ultramarine (purplish) blue, violet (reddish) blue. Test it, as it should not be too strong.

2. Whilst the silk is still wet, use carmine red to paint a block roughly 15cm/6" wide across the silk. Overlap the vermillion slightly.

Follow on with the next colour in the rainbow sequence (see above). Blend the edges by using a clean, dryish brush and brush gently at right angles to the bands, thus painting a gently transitioning colour sequence.

Leave it to dry completely – it will be nice and smooth.

3. Tear it into seven roughly equal pieces. Iron out any wrinkles on a very low heat setting. Trim any threads. Then make a small fleece ball, about 12mm/½" diameter (the size of a small marble).

Place it in the middle of a silk square, twist once to form a 'neck', tie the thread around the neck and knot it securely.

4. Repeat for the rest of the fairies. Thread a needle with a 50cm/20" length of thread and tie a double knot at the end. Push the needle through the underside of the head and pull it out through the top. Repeat this for all the fairies.

5. Mark seven roughly equal spaces around the wooden ring and tie the fairies to it in rainbow order starting with the red one. Hang it roughly 8cm/3" down from the ring. Continue hanging the rest equally spaced round the ring, each one about 3cm/1¼" lower than the previous one to create a spiral.

Hang the ring over your nature table or somewhere the slightest breeze will make the fairies dance their rainbow circle dance!

Bees

The warmth of the sun now buzzes with insect life. The drone of bees collecting nectar and pollen on perfumed flowers is the epitome of summer.

Here is one made of brown woollen fleece. It is quick and easy to make but is small enough to be a bit fiddly and difficult for little fingers. Once you have made one it is very easy to make a swarm.

YOU WILL NEED

- Woollen fleece – brown
- Embroidery cotton – warm yellow
- Embroidery needle
- Scrap of cotton material or tissue paper – white
- Sewing thread – same colour as your backdrop

1. Tightly roll a bit of fleece between thumb and forefinger into the shape and size of a bean.

2. Tie off a head with the embroidery cotton.

3. Loosely wind the yellow around the abdomen to create some stripes.

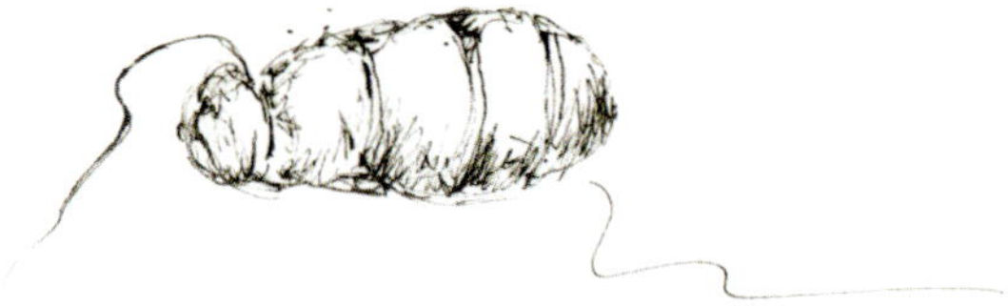

4. Using the needle, thread the two separate strands of the embroidery cotton to the front of the head, to create two antennae, and then trim.

5. Cut the wings from the white material.

6. Gather the centre of the wings with the long sewing thread and sew them onto the front of the middle part of the bee. They should face backwards.

How easy was that?

Can you find another way of making a bee? Try a tiny fir cone or even some beeswax!

Butterflies

Busy butterflies sum up the summer as they flutter from flower to flower in the warm light-filled breeze. You can hint at their quality by making them out of tissue paper. Feel free to improvise on nature by using fresh, clear colours. With a little help a kindergarten child can make this project.

YOU WILL NEED

- Pipe cleaners
- Tissue paper in at least 2 different but matching colours
- Thread for hanging the butterflies

1. Cut a square of tissue paper 7 x 7cm/3 x 3"out of each colour.

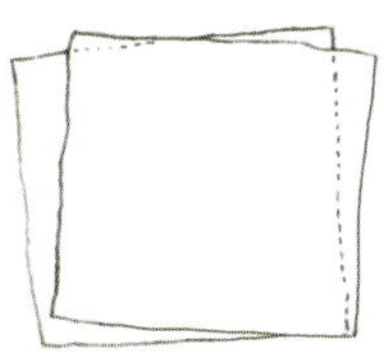

2. Place the paper squares on top of each other and fold them in half. Cut round the edges into the shape of a butterfly's wing.

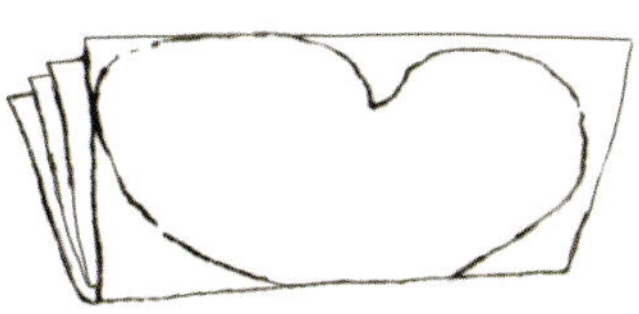

3. Fold a pipe cleaner in half and twist the folded end slightly to form the tail. Slide the tissue paper wings in between the pipe cleaner, pushing them towards the tail end to give a ruffled effect.

4. Twist the pipe cleaner at the head end, leaving the two free ends to form feelers.

5. Tie a thread to its back then hang it on a display branch or over a nature table.

Garlands

You can easily make a base for a garland with a simple plait made of straw, raffia or long-stemmed grasses, knotted together at the ends. It can be used over and over again. In spring and summer you can insert fresh flowers and leaves, and dried ones in the autumn. Once the flowers wilt you can just pull them out and remake the garland when you need it again. They make good 'crowns' for a birthday child or to wear at summer festivals.

YOU WILL NEED

- Straw or raffia about 90cm/36" lomg
- Flowers with stems, at least 10cm/4" long
- A bit of natural twine or string

1. Bind the ends together with twine and make the plait. Bring the two ends together to make a circle and secure the finished end with the same twine. Tie the knot according to the size of the head. (NB: Don't make the plait too tight or the flowers may be difficult to push in.)

Stick in as many flowers as you like – the more the merrier.

2. May garlands can be produced quickly by making a circlet of goose grass (aka catchweed or sticky willy) and sticking buttercups and daisies into it. This could be a good game for a birthday party.

Grass Heart

This project is a lovely memory of a sunny afternoon in the countryside. But it is not one for those who suffer from hay fever. Older children will enjoy making this grassy item out of nature's abundance.

YOU WILL NEED

- A bundle of long grass
- Natural twine or strong string
- Scissors
- Red ribbon, about 50cm/20" long

1. Soak the grass overnight in a bath or large sink but be careful not to snap the stalks. Whilst it is still wet but not dripping, make a sausage-shaped bundle about 1cm/½" diameter. Bind it firmly and knot it as you go; lay more grass along the bundle until it is about 60cm/24" long.

2. Fold the grass in half (the bend is the bottom point of the heart). Turn the two free ends towards each other and tie them together with string. Tie a bow of red ribbon around this point.

This is ready to be a summer gift.

Grass Mat

Summer is the time when you can find grasses going to seed along the edges of footpaths, in wild meadows, beside a stream. If you can harvest the longest grass before it goes brown, you have a wonderful crafting material. Here are two items you can make for your dining table – table mats and a bread basket.

YOU WILL NEED

- A bundle of long green grass
- Strong, natural twine
- Large embroidery needle
- Scissors

1. Soak the grass overnight in a bath or large sink (don't snap the stalks). Shake it dry. Whilst it is still damp, make a sausage-shaped bundle about 1cm/½" diameter. Bind it firmly and knot it as you go, laying more grass along the bundle until it is about 1.5m/5" long.

2. Take one end and roll it tightly to form the centre of a flat disc. Sew it as shown, with the needle and twine. Continue winding the bundle around the disc, sewing it as you go, making it as large as you want it. Cut off the excess length with a tapered cut.

Basket

YOU WILL NEED

- A bundle of long green grass
- Strong, natural twine
- Large embroidery needle
- Scissors

1. Start as if you are making a table mat but use a bundle that is a little fatter, 1.5cm/¾" diameter. When you have made the base to your chosen size, wind the bundle up over the edge of the disc to form the beginning of the side, stitching as you go.

2. Continue winding a few more layers but don't make the basket too big or it will be floppy. Finish it with a tapered cut and stitch the end to the basket edge.

Flying Streamers

This is fun for outdoors! Twirl this little bag round and round. Let go and watch it fly through the sky so high, sometimes too high ... you might have to be polite to your neighbours!

YOU WILL NEED

- 2 pieces of cotton in nice light, warm colours, 10 x 10 cm/4 x 4"
- Rice, beans or bone dry sand
- String, about 50cm/20" long
- 3 ribbons in matching bright colours, 2 x 90cm/¾ x 36"

1. Take one cotton square and lay it right side up. Place the ends of the ribbons on one corner of the square, as shown.

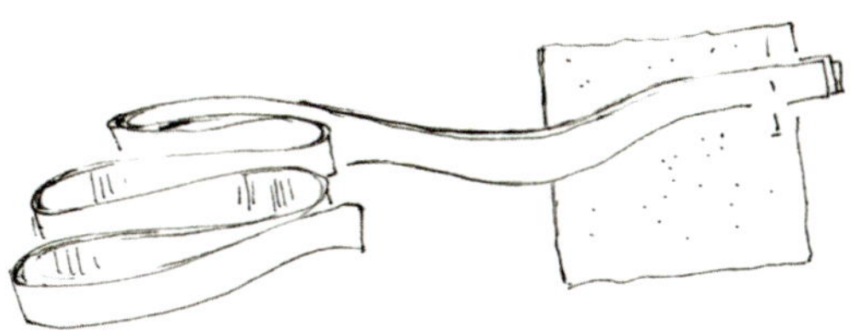

2. Lay the second square right side down on top of the first square and the ribbons. Pin together on three sides and sew as shown. Be careful not to catch the ribbons when sewing the side seams. Make *very small* stitches if you are hand sewing.

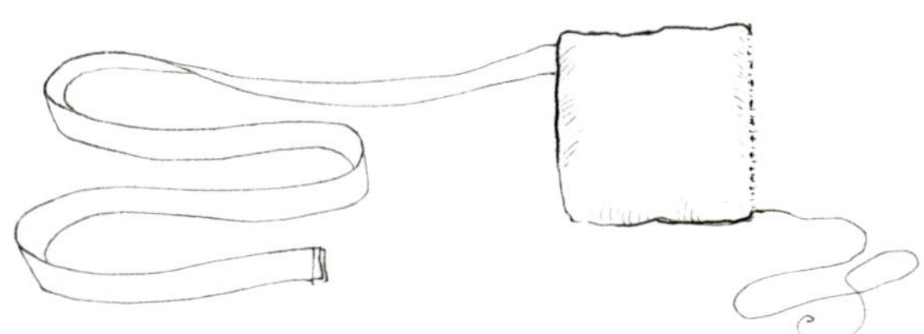

3. Turn the bag inside out and three-quarters fill with rice, beans or dry sand. Knot one end of the string and insert the knotted end into the corner diagonally opposite the ribbons. Turn in the open edges of the bag and sew together by hand, being sure to secure the string well.

4. Very young children will enjoy just throwing the bag without the string; but a lot more height and distance can be achieved when you do attach the string.

Prepare for take-off into the wide summer spaces!

Stick Streamers

You can twirl it round, make big circles, swoop figures of eight or even write your name in the air! Or just run around stirring up the air.

YOU WILL NEED

- 3 ribbons in matching bright colours, 2 x90cm/³⁄₄ x 36"
- Dowel, 2cm/³⁄₄" diameter and 60cm/24" long
- Glue and 2 tacks

Glue and tack the ribbons to the end of the dowel. Wait an hour for the glue to really dry.

Beanbag Frog

This frog likes to be thrown from one person to another, or from one hand to the other, or he just sits on a shelf with his legs dangling down.

YOU WILL NEED

- Smooth cotton fabric (not thick), about 40 x 23cm/16 x 9" – it doesn't have to be a realistic colour
- 2 beads for eyes
- Dried beans or rice for stuffing, about 180gm/7oz
- Tracing paper and pencil
- Scissors
- Sewing machine or needle and thread

1. Trace the outline (shown on page 102). Cut it out to make a pattern, fold the material in half, right sides together, and pin the pattern on to one side. Cut round it to make two similar pieces.

2. Remove the pattern, tack the two pieces together (leaving a 3mm/1/8" seam), going almost right round the frog but leaving enough room to get the stuffing in.

3. Sew it, then cut towards the stitching as shown by the arrows (shown overleaf). Turn it inside out and put the stuffing in. Finish it off by hand and sew the two beads onto the head for eyes.

He is ready for the long jump!

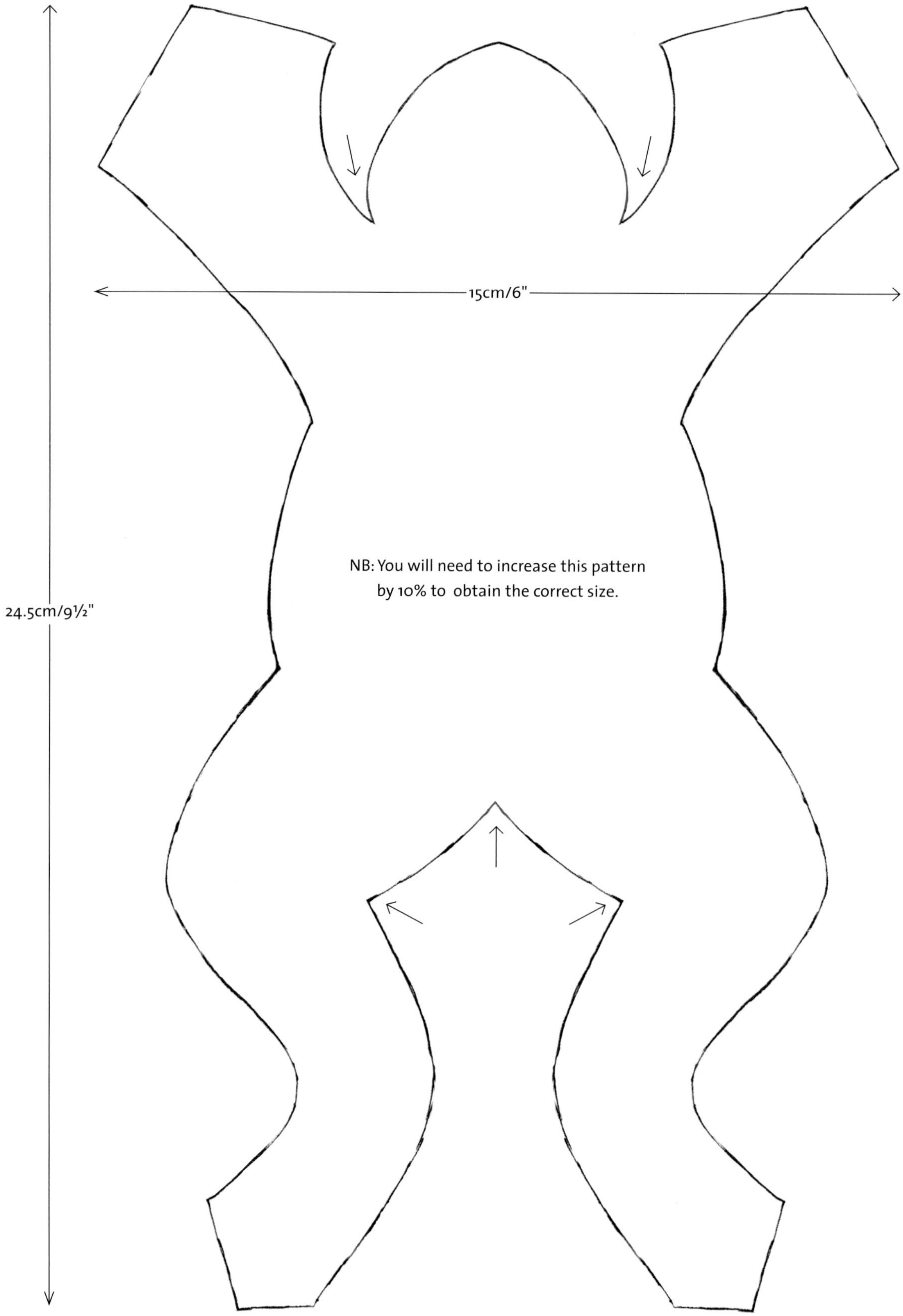
15cm/6"
24.5cm/9½"
NB: You will need to increase this pattern
by 10% to obtain the correct size.

Cup 'n' Ball

Children can easily make this paper cup themselves. It can be used for a traditional game of cup 'n' ball. It can also be a beaker if the paper is strong enough.

YOU WILL NEED

- Piece of paper, 20 x 20cm/8 x 8"
- String, about 40cm/16" long
- Darning needle
- Wooden bead, about 2cm/¾" diameter

1. Fold your square of paper in half diagonally.

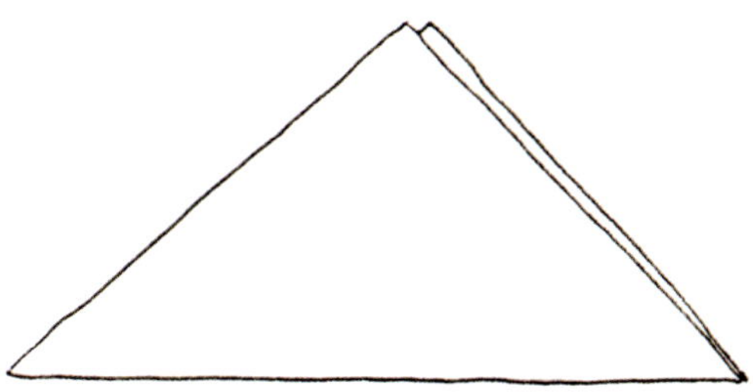

2. Fold both corners across as shown.

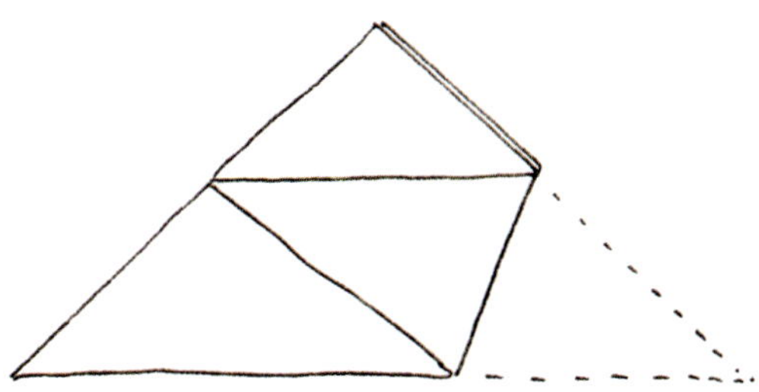

3. Fold down the triangles at the top, one at the front and one at the back.

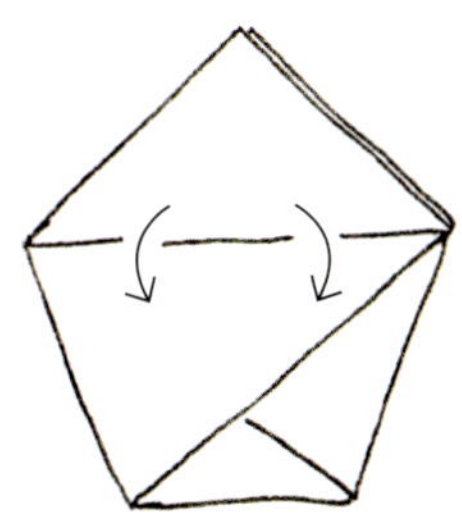

4. Open the top and flatten the two main creases to form a cup shape. Fix the string to one corner by threading the string through a needle and pushing it through the paper. Tie a knot in the string inside the cup. Fix the bead at the other end of the string with a knot on each side to prevent it slipping.

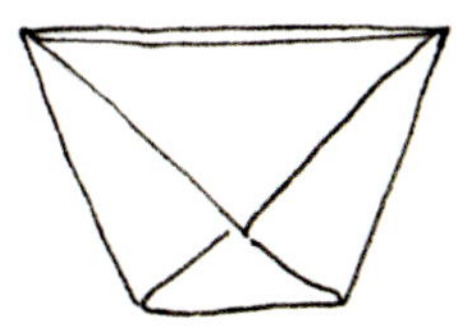

Time to practise your cup tennis.

Flowerpot Bells

You can create an interesting musical instrument if you make several of these flowerpot bells in different sizes. They can be hung in a row from a low branch of a tree or from a broomstick fixed between two chairs. This project can be made by anyone who can tie a simple knot.

YOU WILL NEED

This will make one bell

- 1 clay flowerpot (not cracked) – for a deep sound use a large one, for a high sound use a small one
- 1 bead, larger than the hole in the base of the pot
- Very strong string or natural twine – twice as long as your pot is high

1. Firmly knot the bead to the end of the string.

2. Thread the string through the hole in the base of the flowerpot so that the bead is inside.

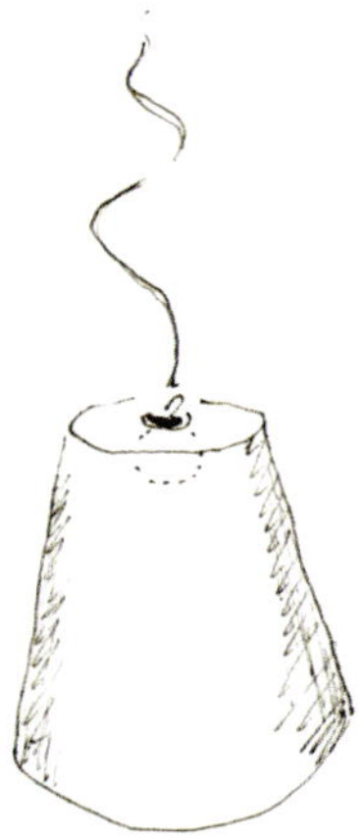

3. Make a loop at the top end of the string and hang up the pot.

4. Find a stick that is nice to hold. Tap the pot on the rim, or waggle the stick from side to side inside. Ring that bell! A cluster of different sized pots can give you enough notes to play a simple tune.

Prepare to play the flowerpot concerto.

Lavender Bottle

Lavender has a strong evocative scent, the smell of high summer. Right through the centuries it has been used medicinally and also as a sweet-smelling moth-proofer.

The stems can be quite brittle so pick them in the morning when the flowers have just come into bloom and use them the same day.

YOU WILL NEED

- 19 lavender stems, freshly cut and as long as possible
- Ribbon, about 7mm/¼" wide and 100cm/40" long, colour to match.

1. Tie the ribbon round the bundle just below the flowers so that the ribbon ends are unequal lengths, about 65 and 25cm (26 and 10") for an open weave.

2. Carefully bend each stem back onto itself so that the flowers are completely surrounded and covered by the stems. Lay the shorter end of the ribbon down the centre of the bundle.

3. Take the long ribbon and start weaving it 'over and under' the stems, turning the bottle as you go to form a gentle spiral. Continue weaving the next row, which will be 'under and over' because there is an uneven number of stems. Make sure you keep the stems in place.

4. Keep turning the bottle, working with an open weave, until you reach the bottom of the flowers, about 4 turns for an open weave, or more for a tight one. Wind the long ribbon once round the bundle and finish with a knotted bow using both ribbons. Trim the bottom of the stems.

Place the bottle where it will fill the air with its calming scent.

Hairband

There are such pretty ribbons for sale. Just a bit of one of these can make a beautiful hairband. This is a very easy project.

YOU WILL NEED

- Ribbon, 1cm/½" wide and 45cm/18" long
- Elastic, 1cm/½ wide and 7cm/3" long
- Needle and thread or a sewing machine

1. Sew the elastic to one end of the ribbon.

2. Measure and adjust the elastic length to fit the head. Sew the other ends together.
Ready!

Scrunchie Hairband for Fairies

This scrunchie is a beautiful hairband that can double up as a fairy crown. And with a veil it can create a wonderful headdress for a princess. Basic sewing machine skills are needed for this – it is ideal for learners.

YOU WILL NEED

- 1 piece of lightweight natural fabric, 'fairy' colour, 130 x 8cm/51 x 3" or 2 pieces 65 x 8cm/26 x 3" joined together to make the above
- Sewing thread to match
- Elastic, 12mm/½" wide and 53cm/21" long
- Safety pin
- 3 or 4 ribbons (optional), matching colours, 7mm/¼" wide, 40cm/16" long
- Pale felt for flower (optional), matching 4 x 2cm/1½ x ¾"
- 1 button to match

1. Fold under 1cm/½" on each long side and iron flat.

2. Fold in half, wrong sides together and iron flat.

3. Top stitch 2mm/⅛" from the top then top stitch 2mm/⅛" from the bottom. Now you will have a long tube.

Fix the safety pin to one end of the elastic and push it through the tube – make sure the other end does not disappear inside. With both ends of the elastic exposed, remove the safety pin.

4. Place the elastic round your fairy's head with the ends overlapping. It should fit comfortably but not tightly. Sew the overlapping ends together (but not the fabric). If you are using ribbons, sew them together then sew them to the elastic next to the joint on a single layer of elastic.

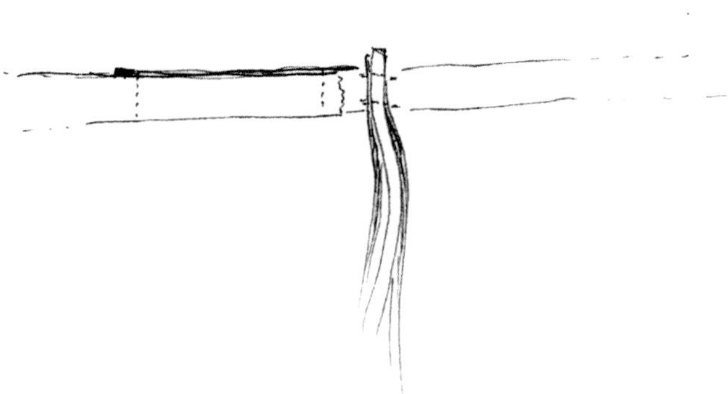

5. Fold the two ends of the fabric back into the tube and bring them together and leave the ribbons to hang free. Sew the seam by hand.

If you're making the flower, trace the pattern (below) on thin paper.

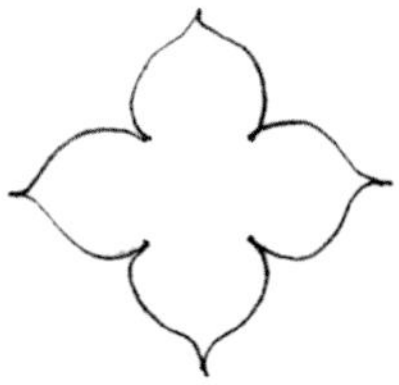

6. Cut out two flowers using the pattern and put one on top of the other at 90°. Sew the button in the middle.

7. Sew the flower onto the hairband just above the ribbon.

Ready for your fairy or princess!

Bee House

The sound of bees buzzing around the garden flowers is the essence of summer. Honeybees and bumblebees are gathering pollen and nectar and flying back to the hive to join the rest of their colony.

Not all the bees we see are the same, however: there are many solitary bees. They too go from flower to flower and pollinate our plants. They make their homes and raise their offspring entirely on their own and they make their nests by burrowing in the ground, in soft rock and in old wood.

Sadly, many towns today are hard landscaped, and quiet corners of decay are 'cleared up' so the bees cannot always find a place for their home. We can help them by making and erecting a special bee house.

Bumblebees will not use it – they are not solitary and live in colonies in holes in the ground or clumps of long grass.

There are several points to bear in mind about a bee house. It should:

- be dry – bees survive cold but not damp
- be firmly fixed
- have a range of hole sizes so that all bee types can move in
- face south or south east to get full sunshine
- be in a peaceful part of your garden away from playing children and bonfires
- have a clear 'flight path' to the entrances
- not be treated with chemicals or paint

This project can be made by teenagers with some woodwork experience.

YOU WILL NEED

- 1 plank of untreated 2cm/¾" thick wood, 20cm/8" wide and 30cm/12" long
- 1 plank 15cm/6" wide and 90cm/36" long (don't use plywood or MDF – both are full of chemicals which are not bee-friendly)
- Assorted lumps of untreated wood – firewood logs are good
- 1 bamboo cane (optional)
- Saw
- Wood screws, about 4cm/1½" long
- 2 mirror plates, medium/large
- Drill (electric makes it a lot easier) and a range of bits from 2 to 10mm/$^1/_{16}$ to $^3/_8$"

1. Cut the planks to make a roof, two sides and a bottom roughly to the sizes below.

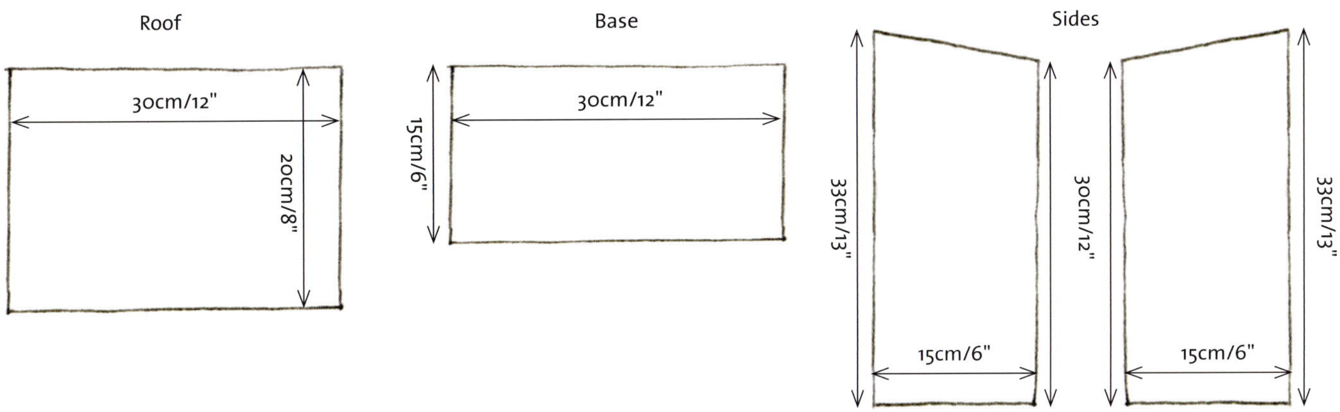

2. Drill and screw all 4 pieces together to make an open box (NB: the roof should hang over the front). Cut the assorted lumps of wood to about 12cm/5" long.

3. Drill holes in the ends of the lumps using all the different drill bits, about 2cm/¾" apart. This may need supervision.

4. Stack the lumps of timber in the box so that they cannot be easily dislodged. To fill the gaps, you can use short bamboo lengths with their holes cleaned out.

5. Fix the house to the wall or fence using the mirror plates. If you want to mount it on a post you must put a back on it. Use more of the same planks that you used for the walls.

Watch out for the new tenants – from a distance!

Felt Flower

It is amazing how such an easy-to-make flower can be so luscious. It can be made singly or in sets of three fixed onto leaves. They can adorn hats, jackets, bags – you name it. When made of thin card they can be glued onto wrapping paper on a present.

You can make them in different sizes but I have found this one is a good starter.

YOU WILL NEED

- Pink felt, not too thick, 15 x 15cm/6 x 6" (for 1 flower)
- Green felt (thick), 10 x 6cm/4 x 2½" (for 1 leaf only)
- Thin paper for a pattern
- Pencil
- Scissors
- Pins, needle and thread

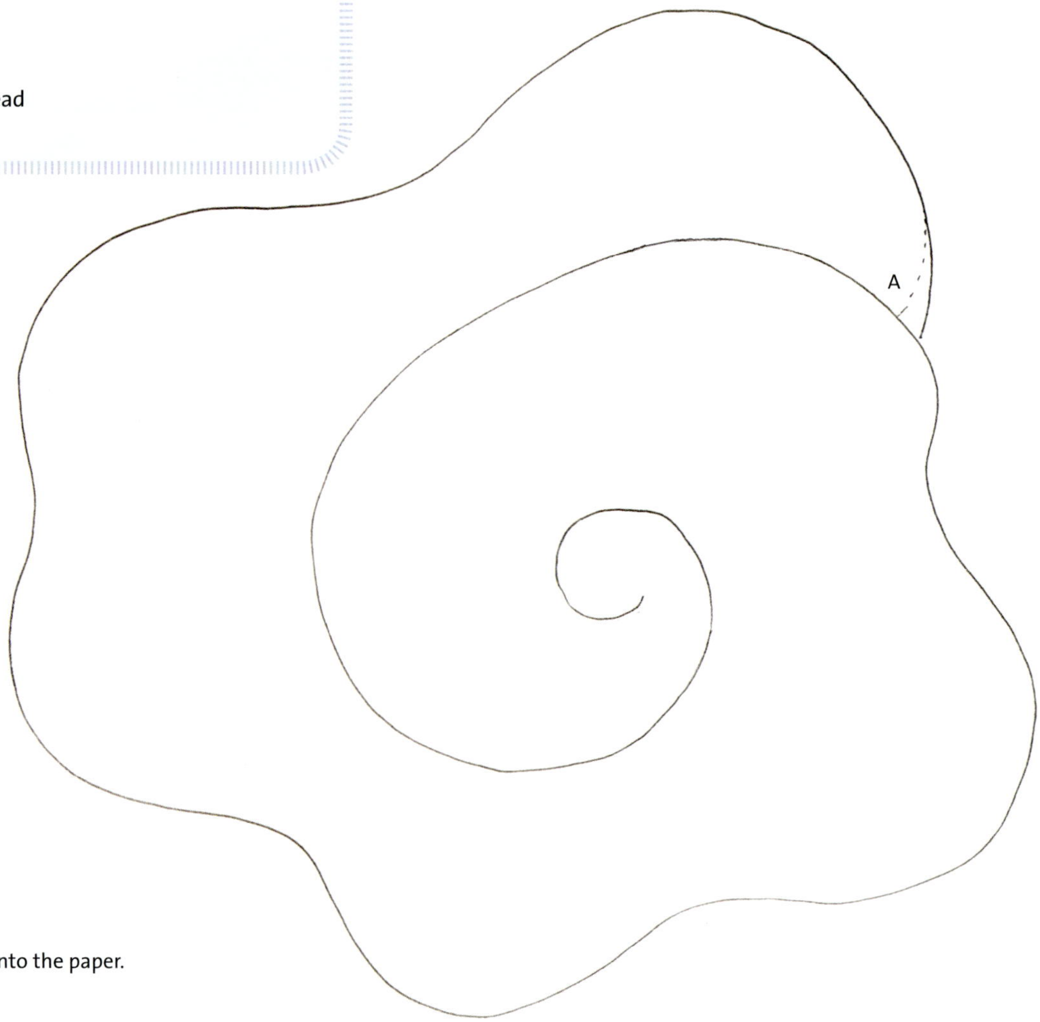

NB: All pattern pieces for the flower are actual size.

Trace the flower pattern onto the paper.

1. Cut it out and pin it onto the felt. Cut around the shape then cut off the sharp corner at A.

Start rolling the felt at A (it may feel counter-intuitive that this will be the flower's heart) – roll firmly but not too tightly. Make sure you keep the bottom line level, especially just before the end. Hold it all together temporarily with two pins stuck at right angles through the lower part.

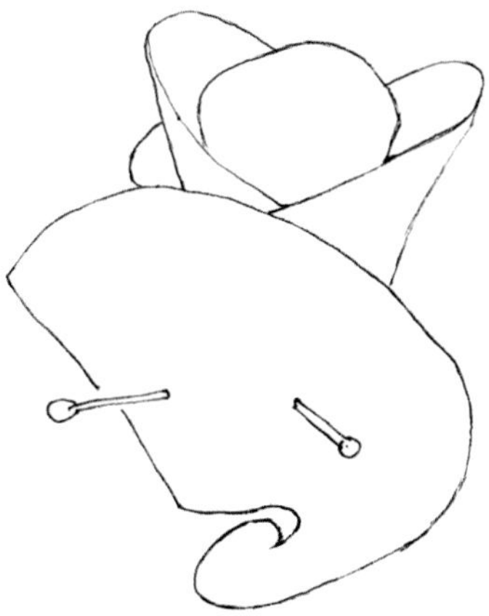

2. Firmly sew the bottom edge of the roll together but leave the curly bit. Fold the curly bit underneath the roll to give it a flat base and sew it securely.

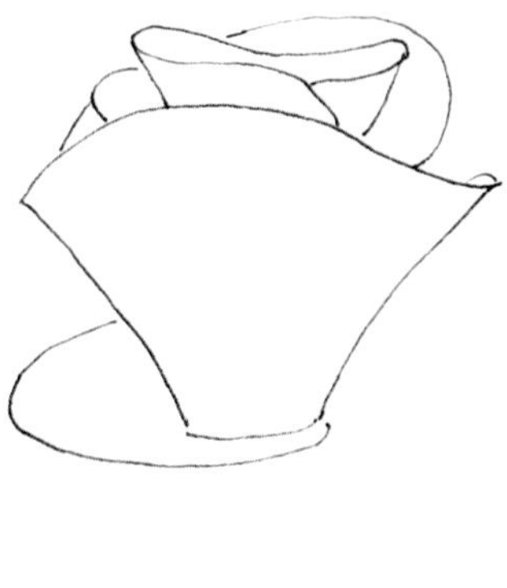

3. Trace the leaf pattern onto the paper – two of these go under three flowers

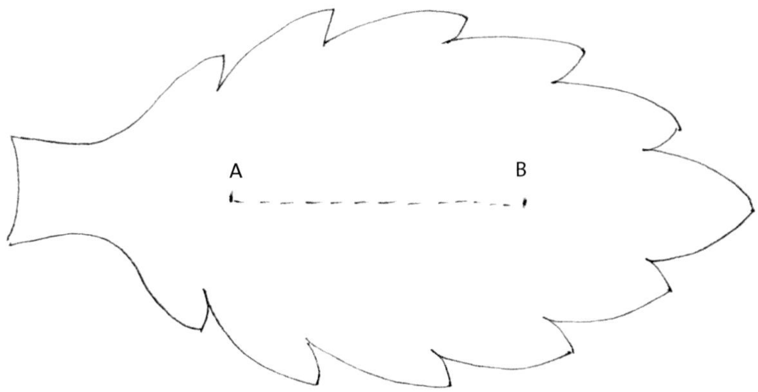

4. Cut out the pattern and pin onto the felt. Cut around the shape. Fold the one leaf in half and sew neatly between A and B with small blanket stitches (see page 49).

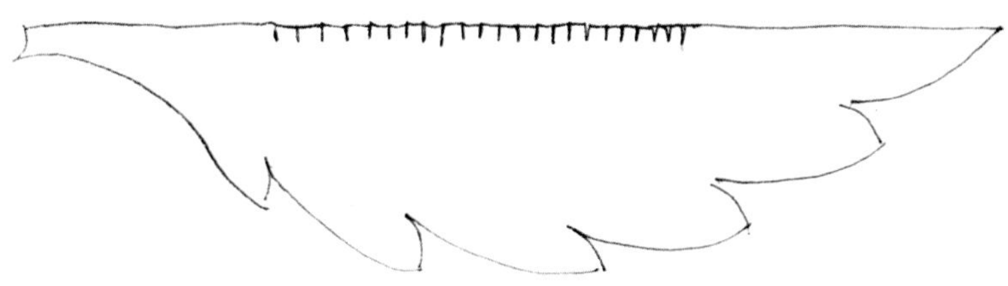

5. Open up the leaf and you have an indication of the vein. Stitch the two leaves together then sew the flowers in a bunch on top of the leaves near the stem.

Mob Cap

Here is a traditional country hat. It is equally great for dressing up as it is a sun hat. It does not take long to make and is an easy project for machine sewing. This size will fit a two- to five-year-old.

YOU WILL NEED

- Cotton fabric, 45 x 45cm/18 x 18"
- Bias binding, 250cm/100", in a contrasting or matching colour
- Elastic, 6mm/¼" wide, 52cm/21" long
- Pencil or tailor's chalk
- Scissors
- Sewing machine and thread
- Safety pin

1. To make a paper pattern circle, see Mother Nature (page 22). Now cut a circle out of the fabric (diameter 45cm/18"). Draw another circle, on the wrong side, 6cm/2½" inside the first circle, using a pencil or tailor's chalk.

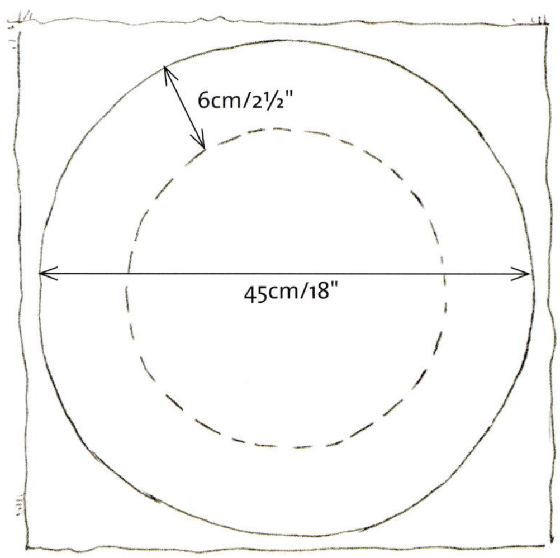

2. Centre the bias binding on the second circle. Pin in place and stitch the edges, folding the ends under. This is the casing for the elastic.

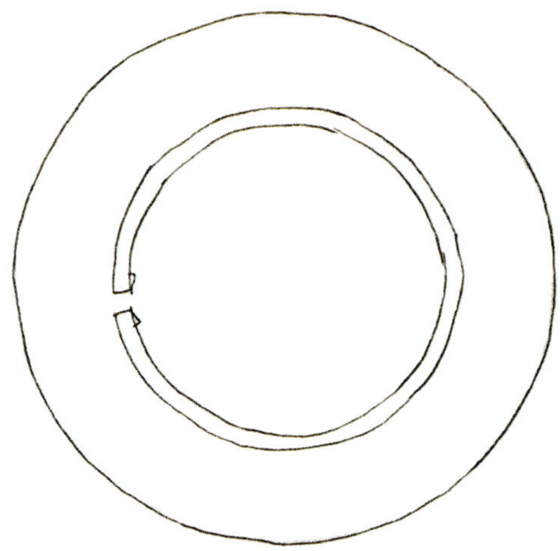

3. Finish the outer edge of the circle by folding the bias binding around the edge. Pin and sew. Insert the safety pin through the elastic and thread it through the casing (see scrunchie hairband, page 106).

4. Overlap the ends by 1cm/3/8" and stitch together securely.

Ready for the play!

Orange Oil Lamp

These glowing little lanterns are ideal mood-setters for a summer evening party in your garden. The darker the night the more these little lights glow. To be made by adults only.

YOU WILL NEED

- 1 orange, thick-skinned
- Narrow candlewick, 5cm/2" long
- 1 drawing pin
- Sunflower oil or other vegetable cooking oil
- Sharp knife
- Grapefruit knife or sharp teaspoon

1. Cut the orange in half horizontally. Remove the flesh with the grapefruit knife or scoop out the flesh with the spoon, taking great care not to puncture the skin. Cut an opening in the middle of one half (2½cm/1" in diameter). This is the lid.

2. Tie a knot in the wick and push the drawing pin into it so it acts as a little weight.

3. Place the drawing pin and wick into the centre of the bottom half of the orange and stand it on a saucer. Half fill it with oil. Light the wick and when it is burning place the lid on top of the bottom half.

4. The glowing orange will look best in a shady corner – a few together will look better still.

Please note: Never leave a lit flame unattended.

Baby's Rainbow Ball

All the colours of the rainbow (and a few extra) come into this pretty little woolly ball. It is an ideal gift for a small baby who is just discovering how to grasp things. It is soft and easy to hold, only 6cm/2½" in diameter. You can put a bell inside to make it even more attractive if you like.

This is an excellent little project for learners, as it places equal weight on strips of garter stitch (simply knit every row) and stockinette stitch (knit one row and purl one row). It does require alertness with the swapping of the stitches and colours.

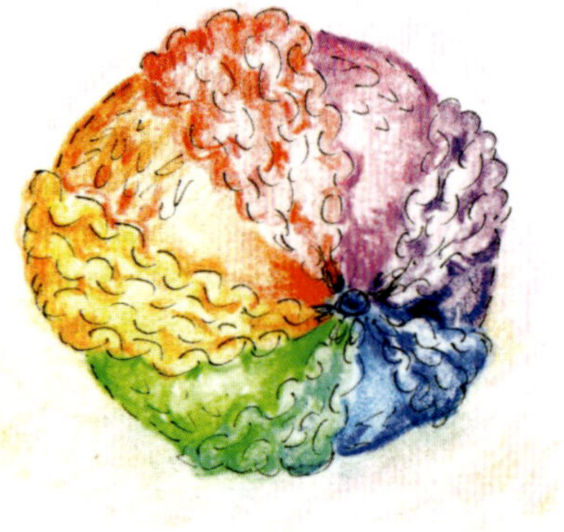

YOU WILL NEED

- 2 knitting needles, 3.5mm/US size 3
- Small amount of fleece for stuffing
- DK wool, 2.5m/8' long in each of the following shades:

  lemon yellow for the garter stitch (8 rows)
  golden yellow for the stocking stitch (6 rows)
  orange for the garter stitch (8 rows)
  orange-red for the stocking stitch (6 rows)
  wine red for the garter stitch (8 rows)
  purple for the stocking stitch (6 rows)
  purple-blue for the garter stitch (8 rows)
  green-blue for the stocking stitch (6 rows)
  green for the garter stitch (8 rows)
  yellow-green for the stocking stitch (6 rows)
  You should have 10 colours altogether.

(NB: The colours above are only a suggestion. Vary them according to what you have available. You may want to consider using embroidery wool for smaller quantities of any missing colours.)

The important point is that the first colour and the last colour should blend to complete a full colour circle when the ball is made up.

1. Cast on 15 sts in the first colour
K 8 rows (garter stitch)
Change to second colour and work 6 rows in st st (k one row, p the next)
Repeat this sequence of stitches with the remaining colours in the order given (left).

Cast off

You now have an oblong 'scarf' of rainbow colours.

2. Sew the lemon yellow edge to the yellow-green edge to make a continuous band. Then gather together one side, only picking up the st st strips on the first time around. Pull tight and secure. Now gather together the garter stitch strips on the second round, pull tight and secure.

3. Fill the ball with the stuffing (including the bell if you wish) but do not over-stuff. Gather together the other side in the same way then pull tight and secure.

Ready to delight both young and old.

The Camp

For years the camp has been one of the most favourite toys for imaginative play for our children and grandchildren. It provides the walls for the children's playhouse. Veils, tablecloths, sheets or the plank (page 117) can all be used to make the roof of this easy-to-erect secret corner.

Last but not least, although it is fairly large when in use, it folds up and hardly takes up any storage space.

For an experienced woodworker and skilled sewer.

Please note: Not all wood suppliers stock the same range of *planed* timber sizes. Sizes shown are the *minimum* suitable for this project – you may have to use a slightly larger size depending on what is available.

YOU WILL NEED

- 10 pieces of planed wood, *minimum actual* size 2.7 x 2.2cm/1¹/₈ x 1", length 80cm/32" for the uprights
- 10 pieces of planed wood *minimum actual* size 2.7 x 2.2cm/1¹/₈ x 1", length 50cm/20" for the cross bars
- Saw
- Hammer and chisel
- 20 screws, 3.5mm/size 6, 20mm/³/₄" long
- PVA wood glue
- Sandpaper, fine to medium
- Webbing (suitable for upholstery), about 4cm/1½" wide
- Tacks 20mm/³/₄"
- Strong glue
- 5 pieces of fabric, each 95 x 50cm/37 x 20", preferably in golden yellow or pink

1. To make the wood frames cut the wood to length and make the 20 joints as indicated (see right).

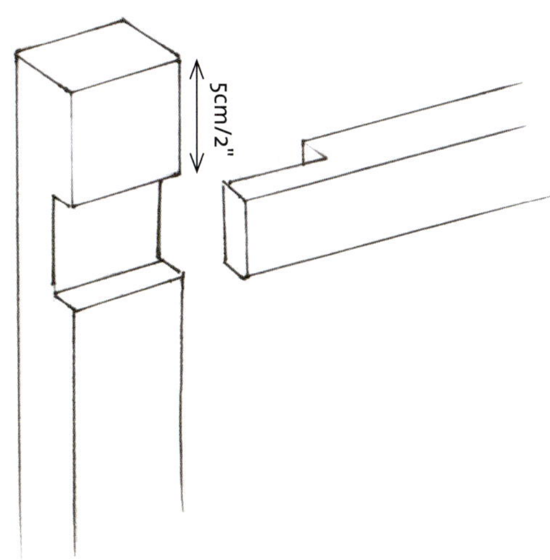

2. Sand down the edges until smooth. Assemble each frame 'dry' and adjust as required. When everything fits together tightly, number each joint and pull apart again. Keep the wood for each frame separate.

3. Drill and countersink a hole at each end of the crossbars. Assemble two crossbars and one upright, glue and screw them together and put aside to dry. Repeat this for the other four frames.

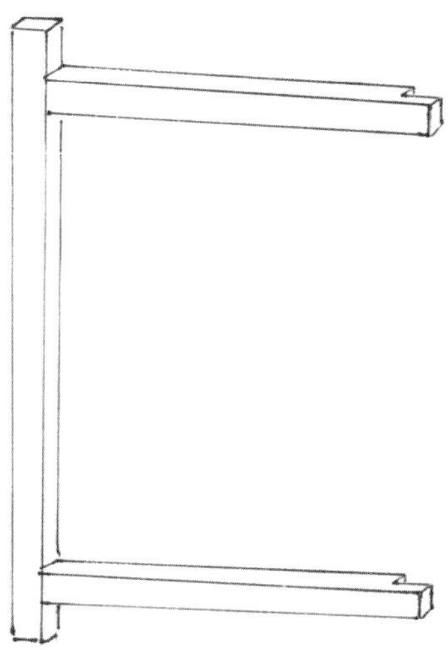

4. To make the fabric panels, cut the fabric into five equal pieces, as indicated. Neaten the sides and fold under approximately 2cm/¾" at the top and bottom, and make seams wide enough for the horizontal slats to slide through.

5. Slide the crossbar of one frame carefully through the seams. Assemble dry the second upright and see if the fabric fits tightly on the frame. If it is too slack, remove it and adjust the seam depth or take up the fabric in a ruffle at the top.

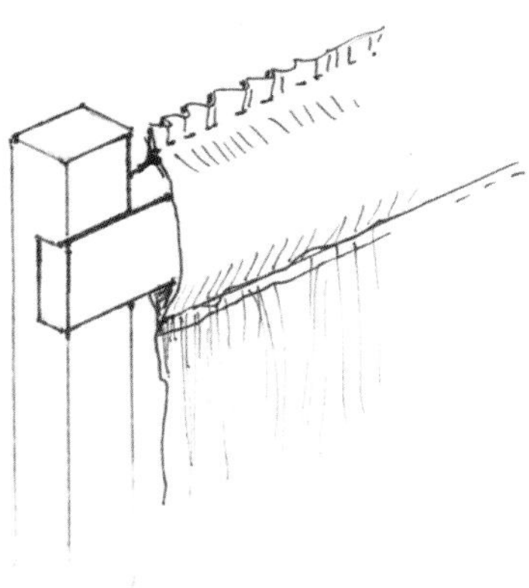

6. After testing each frame and its fabric panel, glue and screw the second upright in place. Join all five frames together by gluing and tacking the two pieces of webbing, one above the other, as shown. On frame A top joint: fix webbing on front of A and on back of frame B. Just below this, fix the second piece of webbing on back of A and front of B. Repeat this for frame A bottom joint. Then repeat both stages for all remaining frames

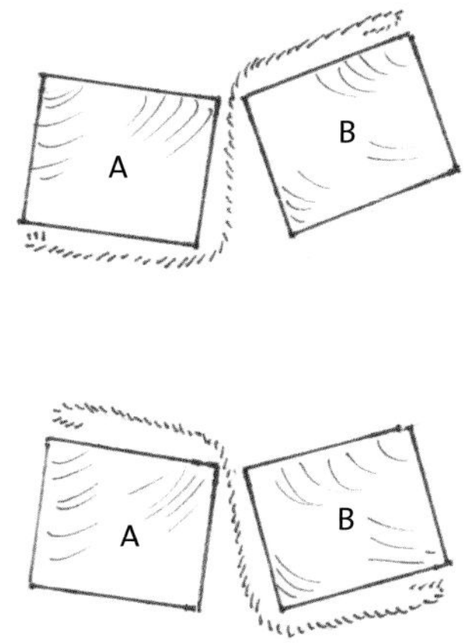

7. Add a roof to your camp with a piece of fabric or bed sheet dyed to match the sides (150 x 150cm/60 x 60"). Drape it over when the sides are erected.

The Plank

In our family, the plank has been the simplest and, at the same time, the most versatile plaything around the house and garden for years. It can be played with as a slide, a see-saw and a bridge.

YOU WILL NEED

- Wood (reasonable quality pine, building quality mahogany with as few knots as possible), roughly 200 x 23 x 2cm/84 x9 x ¾". If you use prepared timber try to get the full thickness shown. 2cm/¾" is the minimum unless you use oak.
- Rasp – could be a plane
- Sandpaper, medium and fine, and sanding block (could be an orbital sander)
- 4 strips of wood 18 x 4 x 2cm/7 x 2 x ¾"
- 8 screws, 32 x 3.5mm/1¼" x 8
- PVA wood glue
- Oil – Danish, teak or linseed
- Old rags

Please note small children will need supervision with all this. Make a clear mark where little children are not to place their hands when see-sawing.

The children can put the plank between a climbing frame and a work bench.

It can be part of a building, part of a roof with veils or sheets covering it. It makes an ideal companion to the camp (page 115).

And when the children are past building their playhouses, the plank can be used as a bench or a shelf. For an adult to make and for use by kindergarten upwards.

1. Round off the edges and the ends very thoroughly with the rasp. The goal is a child-friendly plaything! Sand the wood on all sides, using the roughest sandpaper first and finishing with the finest. Use your fingers to test for smoothness and keep going until it feels like silk.

2. Screw and glue the four wood strips to the plank. The middle pair should be about 30cm/12" apart; the end ones are about 5cm/2" from the ends. Apply several thin coats of oil and allow to dry properly after each coat. You may need four or five coats until it is shiny and very smooth.

The wood will take a lot of wear and weather so varnish is not appropriate (it will crack and allow water to seep in and rot the wood). Oil will soak into the wood and can easily be re-done where necessary.

The two middle wood strips steady the plank when it lies across a tree trunk or low fence rail when it is used as a see-saw. The two end ones stop it falling off a higher fence rail when it is used as a slide or a bridge.

You may like to fix a batten on the top of an old table in the house so that you can hook one end of the plank over it to make an indoor slide.

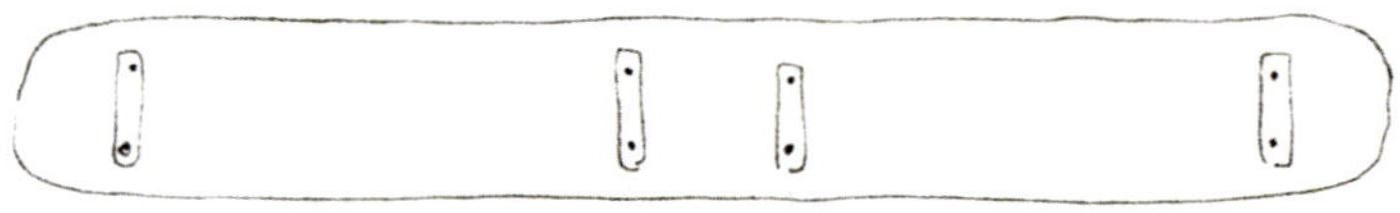

Needle Case

This is another project for a child who has just learned to knit. The knitting can be done in various colours or just one, and it is quick and simple. It makes a nice present for anyone who uses needles and pins.

YOU WILL NEED

- Scraps of matching DK wool
- Pair of 3.5mm/US 4 knitting needles
- 2 pieces of felt about 12 x 8cm/5 x 3" (the colours should match the wool)

1. Cast on 20 stitches
K 60 rows in garter stitch
Cast off and sew in threads
Lay the two pieces of felt on top of the knitted piece and sew down the middle, using a running stitch.

2. Attach a short cord (see page 120) to the middle of each side of the knitted piece so that the case can be tied and closed. Fill the 'book pages' with pins and sewing needles.

Cords

Lengths of cord are among the playthings that children always need most. When they build camps they need cords to tie sticks and bits of cloth together. When playing horse or other animal games, they need the cords to be reins or leads. For dressing up they need belts. The edges of rivers and lakes can be indicated with a cord.

Cords are quite easy to make – and cord-making in itself is a well-loved activity of many children. They can be made in many colours and with thick or thin wool, cotton or string.

Besides crocheting cords with a crochet hook, there are other ways of making them.

Twisted cord

This project makes a colourful, strong cord that can be used in many ways – basket handles, bootee laces, horse reins, etc. Different projects will need different lengths and thicknesses. The thicker your yarn, the thicker the finished cord. You can use one or many colours.

Children, some quite young (five years), love making cords like this.

YOU WILL NEED

- 2 or more lengths of yarn (wool, string, thread, twine), which are two- and-a-half times the required length of the finished cord
- Pencil or knitting needle (optional)
- A weight with a loop or a handle on it, eg a bunch of keys
- Scissors

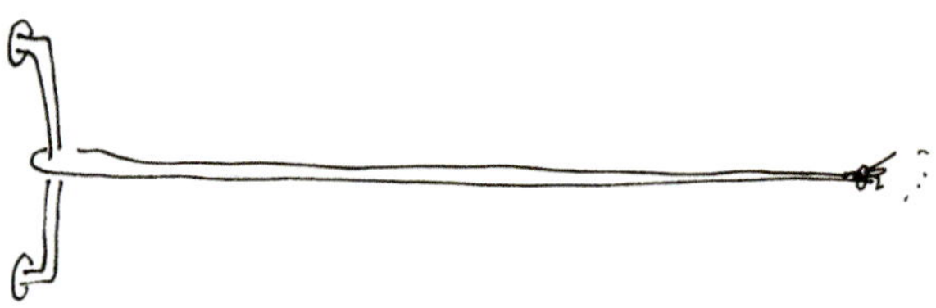

1. Find a fixed object – a door handle is ideal, but you could use a coat hook or a window catch (our granddaughter uses her big toe!) – and tie or loop one end of each of your lengths of yarn onto it. Hold the other ends so that the yarns are all stretched tight and then tie them in a knot.

2. Insert a pencil, a knitting needle or just your index finger into the end you are holding and start twisting (only in one direction), whilst keeping it tight with the other hand

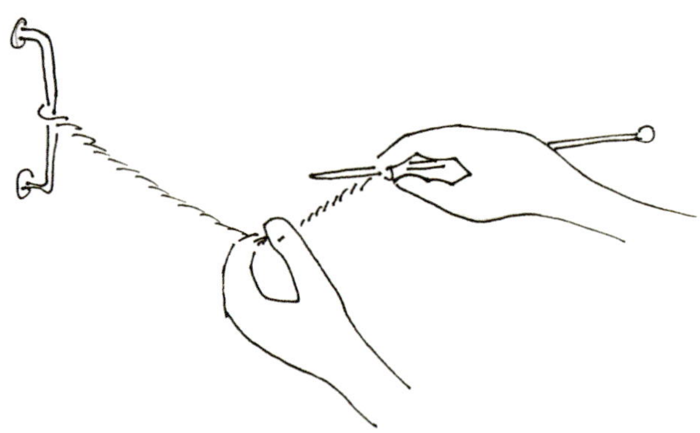

3. When the cord starts to twist on itself, hold it tight and remove the pencil, needle or finger. Thread the weight along the cord so it hangs in the middle of it for a tight cord. Or just hold onto the middle for a looser cord.

4. Unloop or untie the cord from the door handle (or toe). Carefully bring the two ends together with the weight still at the midpoint. Hold up the ends together so that the weight can spin freely. Allow it to twist but stop it when it starts to go in the other direction.

5. Cut the cord so you can remove the weight and knot that end straight away.

Your twisted cord is ready for action.

Finger-knitted cord

1. For an easy start, use thick wool. Make a slipknot in the middle of a long piece of wool. A slipknot is the first stitch you put on the knitting needle when casting on stitches.

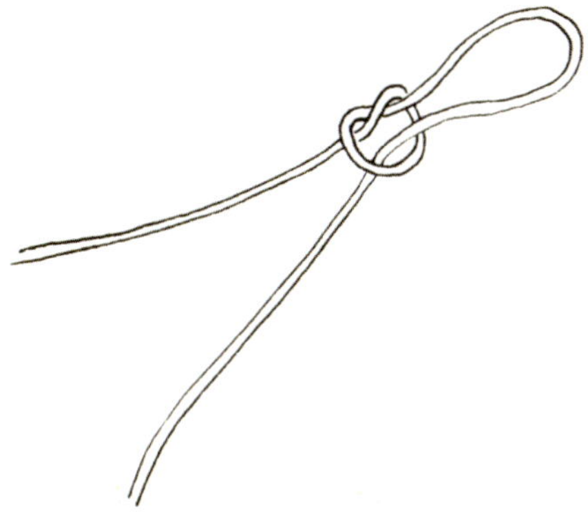

2. Put the loop over the index finger of your right hand and hold the knot below the loop between the thumb and middle finger of your right hand.

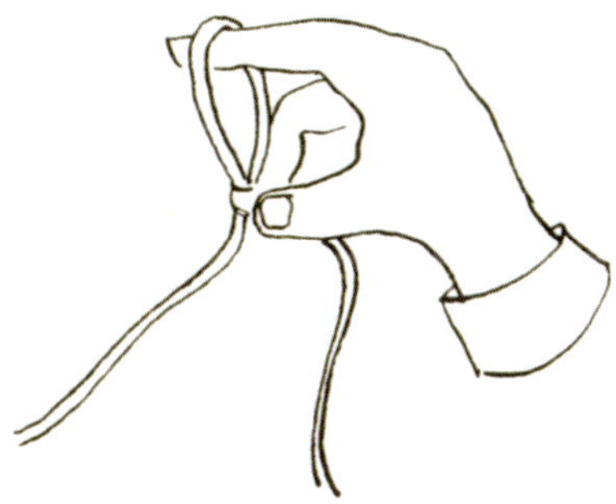

3. Put the index finger of your left hand through the loop and pull out a second loop, having the strand of wool on the left.

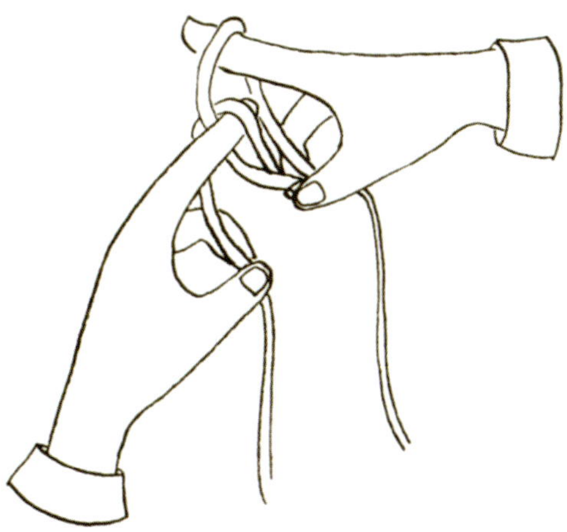

4. Move the knot you are holding with your right hand over and hold it with the thumb and middle finger of your left hand.

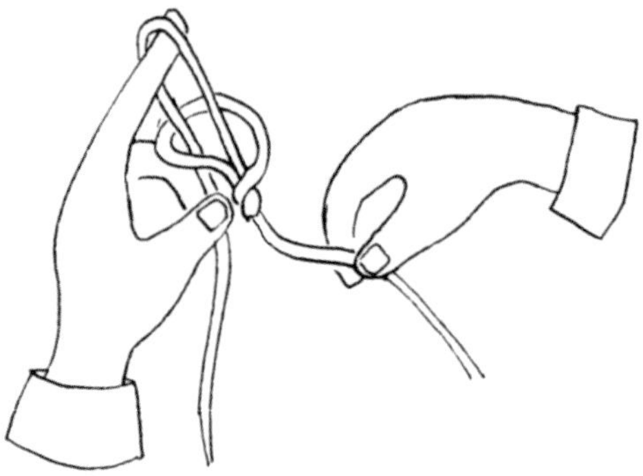

5. The right hand pulls its end of wool tight. Now put the index finger of your right hand through the second loop, have the wool on the right and pull out a third loop.

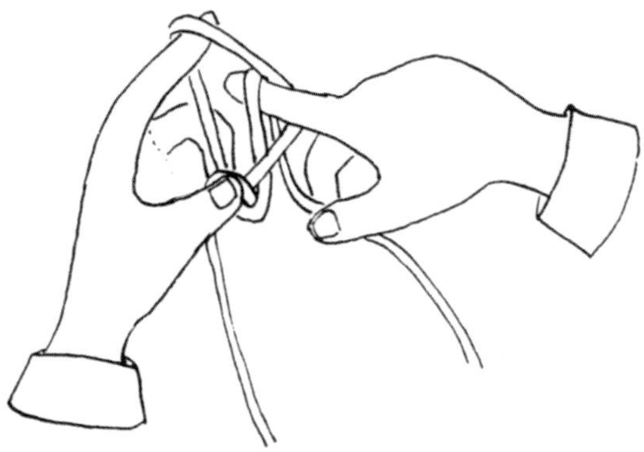

6. Let go of the knot you are holding with your left hand and take hold of the knot with the thumb and middle finger of your right hand – your left hand pulls its end of wool tight. Continue to make loops over and over again using the left and right hand alternately.

Baby's Bonnet

This pretty little bonnet is very practical because it really covers baby's ears! For a winter baby knit it in wool, and for a summer baby use thin cotton or silk. The size given is for about 6 to 12 months. For a smaller size use 3mm/ US size 3 knitting needles. Easy knitting.

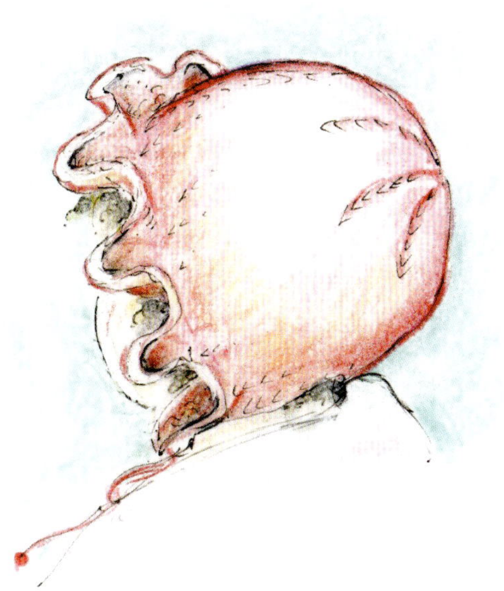

YOU WILL NEED

- 4 ply wool, cotton or silk, 30gm/1oz
- Pair 3.5mm/US size 6 knitting needles
- Crochet hook, 3mm

1. FOR THE FRILL
Cast on 160 sts
K 8 rows (garter stitch)
Next row: [k2 tog] until the end of the row (80 sts)
Continue knitting in st st until work measures 12½cm/5", including the frill
Next right side row start to decrease:
1st row: [Sl 1, k1, psso, k8], repeat to the end of the row (72 sts)
2nd and every alternate row: purl
3rd row: [Sl 1, k1, psso, k7], rep to end
5th row: [Sl 1, k1 psso, k6], rep to end
7th row: [Sl 1, k1, psso, k5] rep to end
9th row: [Sl 1, k1, psso, k4] rep to end
11th row: [Sl 1, k1, psso, k3] rep to end
13th row: [Sl 1, k1, psso, k2] rep to end
15th row: [Sl 1, k1, psso, k1] rep to end
17th row: [Sl 1, k1, psso] rep to end
You now have 8 sts left.

2. Break the thread and gather the 8 sts on a needle and pull the thread through the stitches. Your 8 sts will now form a beautifully spiralling star at the back of the bonnet. Sew 9cm/3½" of the back seams together.

3. As the cotton yarn tends to stretch a bit when the bonnet is in use, you may find it necessary to weave a length of elastic thread through the front of the bonnet just behind the frill – this stops the bonnet from slipping. Crochet two strings about 25cm/10" long and sew one on each side of the bonnet just behind the frill.

What a lovely present this will make!

Hip Horse

All children love to play with cardboard boxes – they are so full of potential for creative play.

Here is one made into a variation of the traditional hobby horse.

YOU WILL NEED

- A cardboard box, 30 x 40 x 30cm/12 x 16 x 12" high
- Stiff card or bits of another cardboard box, about 75 x 50cm/30 x 20"
- Ribbon, string, strong cord or light rope, about 3.6m/12' long
- 2 sheets of paper, about A3 size
- Ruler and pencil
- Cutting knife and cutting board
- Glue – UHU or glue gun
- Watercolour paints (optional)

1. Cut the flaps off the top of the box. Turn it upside down and cut out a piece of the bottom that goes right across the box and leaves 10cm at each end. The hole should be big enough to fit over your child's head and shoulders. Glue another piece of cardboard along the top of the sides to stiffen them.

2. Cut away a scallop on each side of the box to suggest the horse's belly and legs, as shown in the colour illustration.

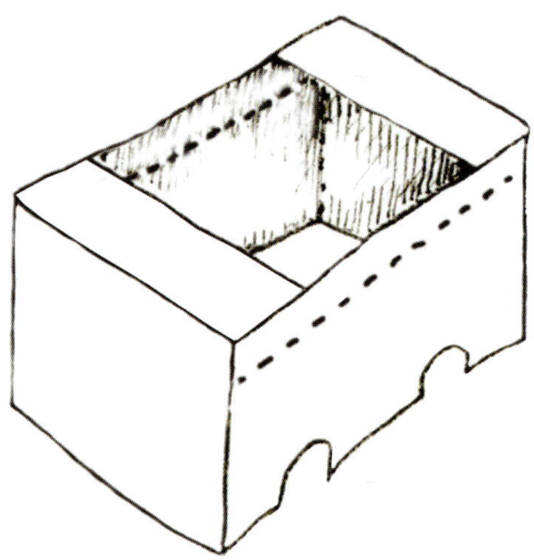

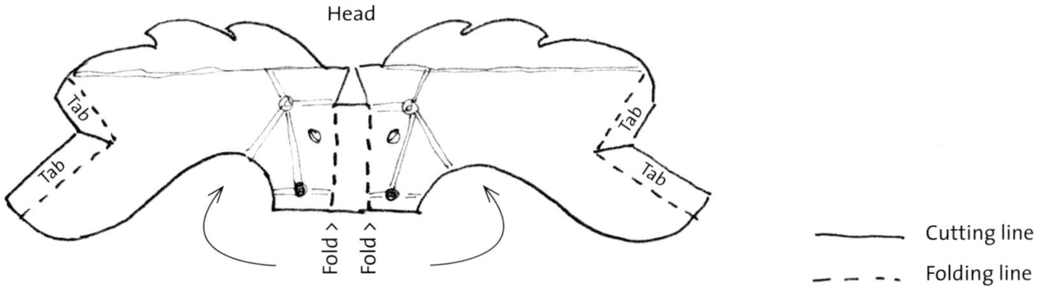

3. Draw one head on the paper and adjust it till it looks right. Cut it out to make a template. Place it on the thick card, leaving space for the tabs and the other half as shown – you may want to fix it with masking tape. Draw around it and then add the tabs and the centre strip. Turn over the template, place it next to the centre strip, draw around it and add the tabs.

4. Cut out the heads, centre strip and the tabs all in one piece. Score and fold, as shown. Glue (and staple if necessary) the tabs of the head to the cardboard box.

5. Repeat the process above for the tails with a paper template etc.

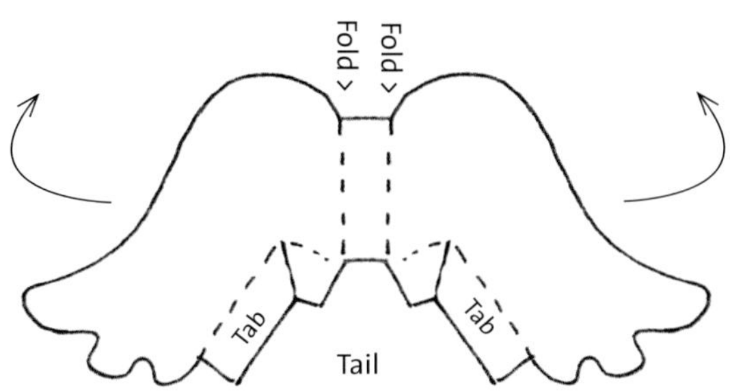

6. Glue the tabs of the tail to the box. If you want to, paint your horse with some thick paint.

7. Make a hole on opposite sides of the lower part of the head near the mouth, insert a length of ribbon through both holes and tie the ends together to make the reins.

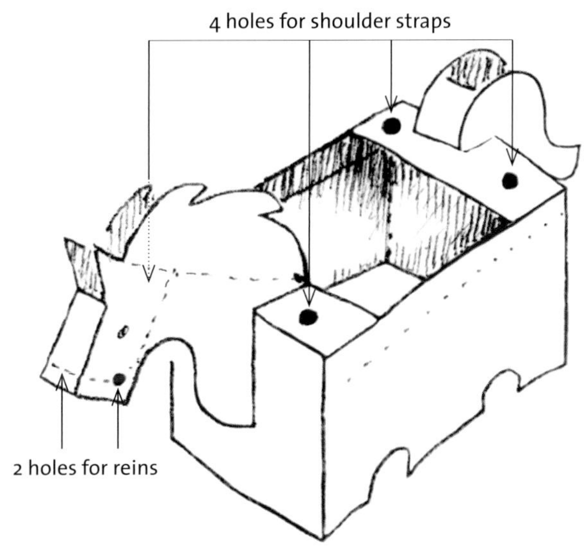

8. Make a hole in the top of the box on either side of the horse's head, and either side of its tail (see above) for the shoulder straps.

9. Find the rough length of the shoulder straps by measuring your child from shoulder to waist – cut two pieces of cord, allowing extra for adjustment. Thread each shoulder strap through one hole at the front and one at the back and tie large knots.

Try the horse on the rider – you may have to add a short cross strap behind the shoulders.

Your horse and rider are ready to gallop away.

Popover Apron

This pretty little apron has no strings attached! It slips easily over a toddler's head and will fit little ones from about 18 months to two years. You can always enlarge it for older children if you like.

You will need some machining sewing skills to sew the bias tape neatly around various corners.

YOU WILL NEED

- Cotton fabric 64 x 90cm/25 x 36"
- Bias binding in a contrasting colour, 345cm/11' 4"
- Scissors
- Sewing machine and thread

1. Enlarge the pattern till you have the height you want – at least 5 times (500%).

2. Cut it out of paper and pin it onto the fabric before cutting it out. Allow a seam of 1.5cm/5/8" at C and A–B. Neaten edges A–B and C as preferred (see sewing tips, page 16).

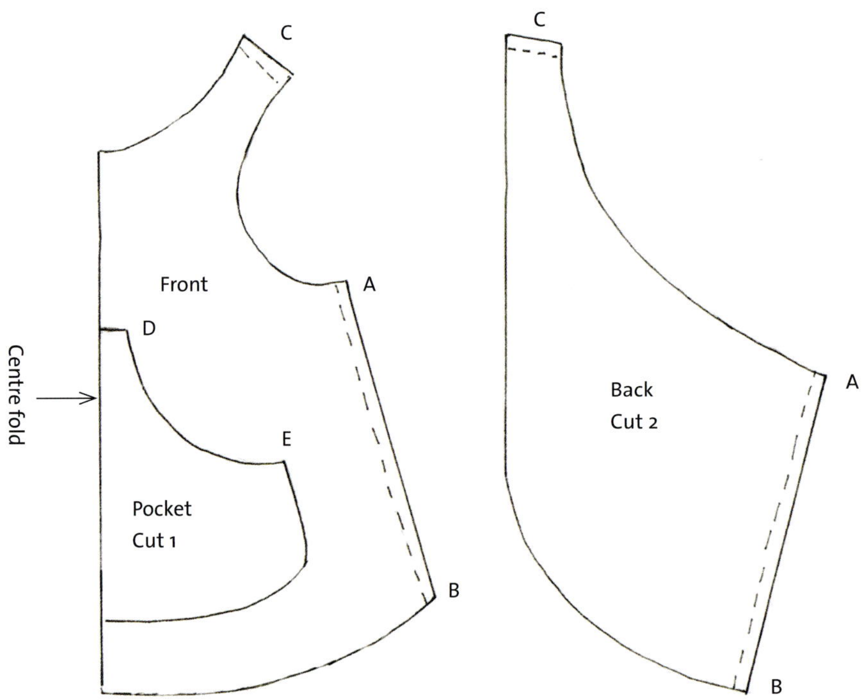

3. Bind the edge of the pocket all the way round with bias binding starting at D. Pin the pocket into position on the front of the apron and topstitch, leaving D–E open on both sides.

4. Join side seams A–B with right sides together. With wrong sides facing, cross the two back sections. Join shoulder seams C with right sides together.

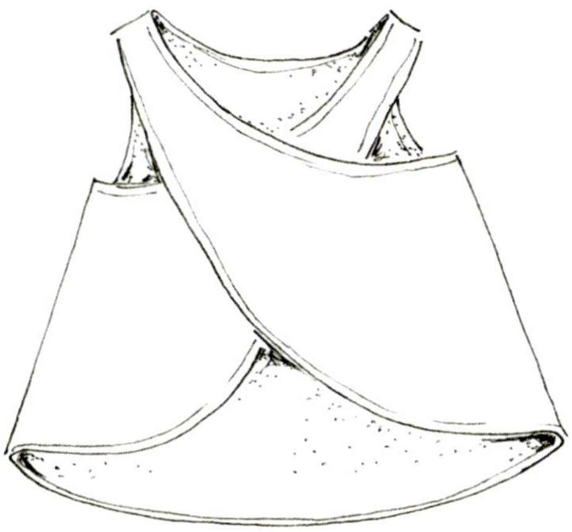

5. Press the seams towards the back then bind the edge with one continuous piece of bias binding, starting under one arm at A.

Roll up the little baker's sleeves and start baking.

Lavender Bags

Towards late summer lavender perfumes the air. You can take a bit of summer well into the autumn and winter by collecting lavender seeds and filling little bags with them. Place them amongst your linen and wardrobe for a lovely evocative scent. Ideal for teenagers and adults to make.

YOU WILL NEED

- 2 pieces of cotton or linen, 10 x 10cm/4 x 4"
- Lavender stalks with seeds
- Sewing cotton

1. Dry the lavender by loosely tying about eight stems together and pull the heads to different positions so that they do not touch one another. Hang in a warm dark place for about two weeks. Pull the dry seeds from the stems and gather them in a bowl.

2. Whilst the seeds are drying you can make the bag. A very plain bit of fabric can be turned into a sophisticated design by simply leaf printing onto it (see page 146). Choose the leaves and print your fabric (you only need to print one piece of fabric for each bag).

3. When the print is dry, iron the back to fix the paint before making the bag. Pin the two pieces – right sides together – and sew the four sides but leave a 5cm/2" gap on one side for filling.

4. Cut the corners to the stitching and turn inside out. Iron flat. Then fill with dry lavender seeds and sew up the gap.

5. Place the bag in your wardrobe. When the scent diminishes just give the bag a little squeeze and summer returns.

Jack in the Box

Surprise, surprise! This is an easy project.

YOU WILL NEED

- A matchbox
- Scraps of coloured paper
- Stick-on stars or dots
- Strong cotton – like button thread
- Glue
- Scissors
- Needle
- Scrap of tissue paper or plain fabric
- Little bit of sheep's fleece

1. Cover the matchbox with the coloured paper and glue the edges well. The stars and moon can be stuck onto the front and side. Line the inside of the box with coloured paper.

2. Roll the fleece into a little head shape and cover it with tissue or fabric. Tie a piece of cotton around the neck.

3. Draw on the eyes and mouth and stick some fleece on his head for hair. Glue him into the box.

4. Leave the box out of the cover then thread the cotton right through the front and the back of the cover with the needle. Tie the ends at the bottom.

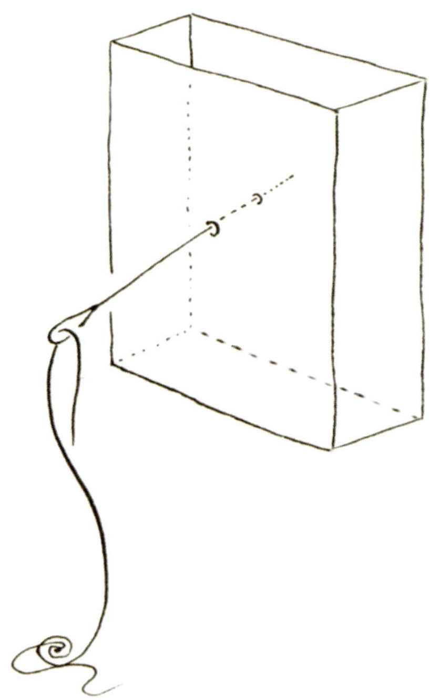

5. Slide Jack's box into the cover and pull the thread – Jack comes out of the box!

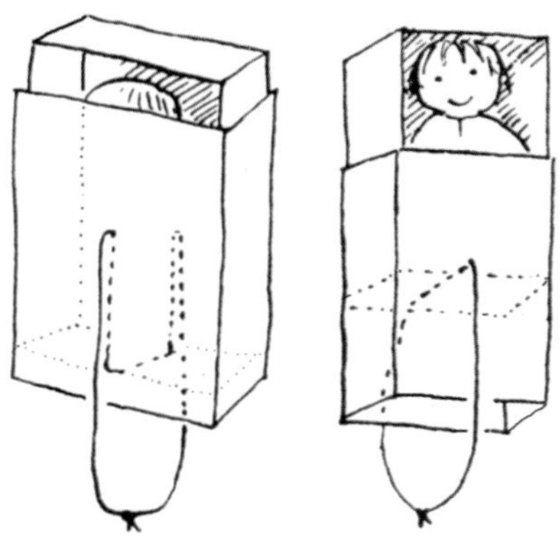

Autumn

The change of the seasons is a gradual, steady process. After the sun has reached its highest point in the sky and the days are at their longest, the temperature rises. It seems like the summer will last forever.

But soon the nights get longer and gradually cooler. Towards autumn there is a distinct damp feel in the air. Whereas we were treated to an abundant floral display in summer's out-breathing into the wide expanse of the blue heavens, with the autumn's in-breath the days draw in and Nature concentrates itself into brightly coloured round little fruits and seeds. The summer sun seems to have been soaked up by them.

The watery greens and blues disappear from the leaves and they turn fiery red and golden yellow then glorious russet browns are seen everywhere. Mushrooms appear in the dank undergrowth – better leave them for the gnomes. Fruit and leaves fall and float down onto the still warm Mother Earth.

It is great fun to outwit the wind by raking and gathering enormous piles of leaves for the waiting compost bin.

This is the time of harvest thanksgiving. With the equinox comes wind, rain, increasing cold and darkness. This can be a difficult time for some people but also a great one for new beginnings. Schools have started again, colleges hold open days to display new courses, new initiatives abound. This is the time to resist the dying down of Nature with courage and energy.

Traditionally St Michael and St George are seen as the embodiment of this mood: keeping the Dragon of Darkness in its place. Right across the world there are light festivals addressing this deep human need. Halloween can show us what we are made of!

We balance this autumnal downward movement with the sowing of seeds and the planting of bulbs in anticipation of Nature's abundance next year.

Autumn Festival Table

It is wonderful to create a large display for little children to enjoy and be involved with. Start with the background, which sets the autumn mood. Drape a large, strong red veil or cloth over the backdrop stand (see page 12) and arrange an orange transparent veil over part of it (see page 14 for veils).

The autumn flowers, leaves and berries seem to have soaked up all the summer sunshine and show rich, velvety warm colours. These can be arranged into a joyous central display. There is plenty of space for a little bright orange pumpkin, conkers (horse chestnuts), acorns, sweet chestnuts, sycamore seeds, etc and a small bowl with red apples. A corn dolly can be pinned to the backdrop.

Can you find a little old tree root on your walk in the woods? Dry it in the sun for a day or two to give its inhabitants a chance to relocate – then place it towards the back of the table. Brightly coloured leaves can be pressed so they will not curl up and lose their colour quite so quickly, and then pinned to the backdrop.

Just as in the summer table (page 88) the fairies looked after the flowers, so now is the time that gnomes take over and care for all the seeds, roots, minerals and crystals. They can be placed with their treasures in the shadowy hollow of the tree root or the folds of the veils. Mice come to gather their share of the seeds. Spiders start to weave their webs and you can make one too and add it to the table.

Spiky chestnut shells (careful!) can be placed in a line and made into a dragon; or you can make a bread one. Teasel hedgehogs show off their prickly character. A candle or a lantern can light up your wonderfully colourful table.

Like all tables, they only look good and inspirational if they are cared for. Things can be moved to an even better place, and played with – but should be removed when they start wilting and look tired.

Gradually the whole display can be made much simpler and a simple table may even start to suggest the sleep of winter to come – this can make the arrival of the winter table that much more exciting.

Simple Autumn Table

A simple, small autumn table can be created by using a little red place or table mat or a square of bright red felt the corners of which you can round off.

Add a vase with brightly coloured berries, hips, fruits or autumn flowers like heleniums, marigolds or Japanese lanterns arranged around strongly coloured leaves, such as maple.

You can add an art postcard showing light and dark or St Michael or St George fighting the dragon, a candle, a crystal and some pine cones, acorns or beech nuts. A few red apples or a small pumpkin will finish off the table beautifully.

If there is space it can be a feature on the dining table; otherwise find a place on the sideboard, shelf or windowsill. It will look great if it is regularly refreshed.

Please note: Never leave a lit candle unattended.

About Gnomes

Oh dear! What a shame that the garden gnome was ever invented! It has put a bad spell on our real friend. When people still had a strong connection to nature, gnomes were seen in quite a different way – look at all the fairy tales and folklore.

Here they are immensely wise and understand deeply nature's rhythmic laws. Hence they are portrayed with large heads and a bulbous nose, a pointed hat (towards the light) and long white hair and straggly beard.

We see them being busy caring for the Earth with all summer's golden treasures (seeds, roots and crystals) and they therefore have long arms and large hands and feet.

They help the searcher but laugh about the arrogant intellectual and they can be very rude or tricky. They don't understand human love, but are in awe of Snow White's innocence.

We dress gnomes in the colours of their environment – warm, earthy tones with bright red (fruit and new growth), the green of the Earth's mantle, or purple and blue, caring for the Earth's crystals.

Children and animals know their presence but, oh, how they would love to be recognised by adults!

Easy Felt Gnome

This little fellow is very easy and quick to make, but is not any less beguiling.

YOU WILL NEED

- Thin paper to trace pattern
- 1 piece of felt – orangey red or green – 10 x 10cm/4 x 4"
- Contrasting embroidery cotton
- A scrap of well-carded fleece

1. Trace the pattern onto the paper and cut it out.

2. Pin it onto the felt and cut it out.

3. Then sew a running stitch from A to B and fold in half vertically. Sew the top slanting edge X to Z – either overstitch or use blanket stitch (see page 49). Sew the vertical front seams AC and BC then stuff the hat and the body with the fleece.

4. Pull the gathering thread AB to create the head, neck and body. Gently pull the fleece into place and pull some out to make a straggly beard. Adjust the amount of fleece in the body if necessary.

As this was so quick and easy, what is to stop you from making a lot of these wee folk in various autumn colours?

NB: The pattern piece for the gnome is actual size.

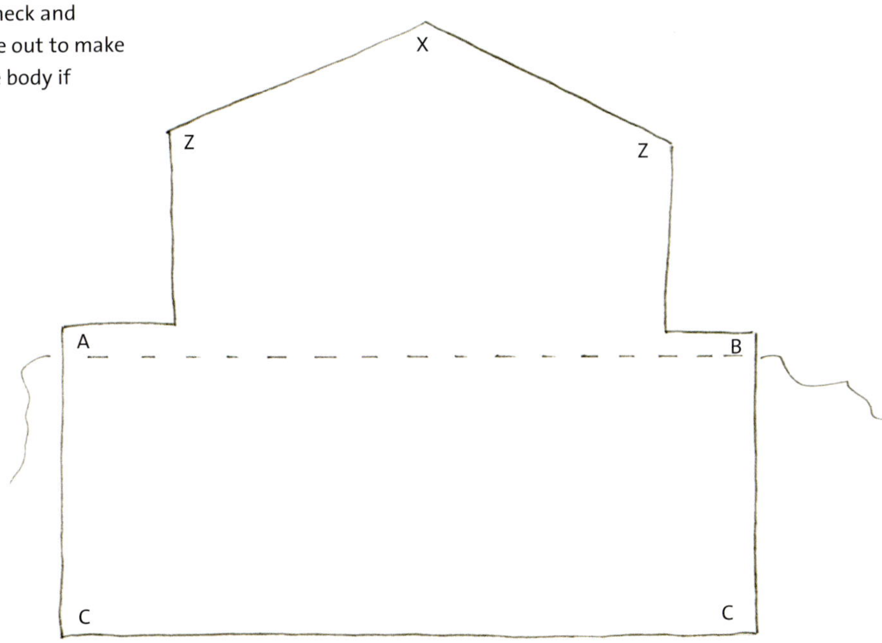

Boot Gnome

Everyone can have their own boot gnome to look after their wellies! This gorgeous little gnome is easy to make and can be made in a very short time. Use different colours for each pair of boots – rich greens, yellows, reds.

YOU WILL NEED

- Wooden clothes peg, old-fashioned style
- Piece of felt 7 x 6cm/3 x 2½"
- Embroidery thread, matching or contrasting

1. Trace the gnome pattern and transfer it to the felt.

2. Cut it out of the felt and sew from C to D with a running stitch as shown, leaving a piece of thread about 2½cm/1" long at each end.

3. Fold along the line A to X with wrong side together. Sew from A to B to make the hood, using blanket stitch. Put the hood over the peg 'head' and draw the thread from C to D together at the neck. Make a knot and tie with a little bow.

No more boot confusion (or arguments)!

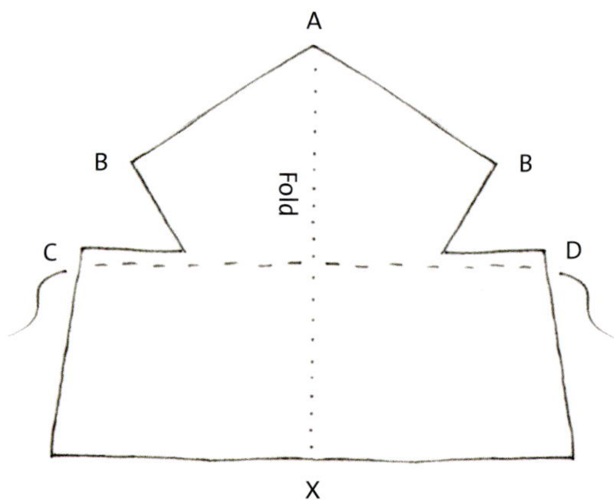

NB: The pattern piece for the boot gnome is actual size.

The Old Gnome

This wise old gnome shows his affinity to the Earth, roots and seeds in his appearance! He consists of small knitted pieces that can be made by young knitters. The assembly and final finishing can be helped by a more experienced knitter.

You can change the colours if you like – use any rich autumn tones or blues and purples if you want to put him next to crystals on your autumn table.

YOU WILL NEED

- DK wool or a thicker yarn for a slightly larger gnome. I suggest the following colours:

  greyish beige for old skin colour (not pink) – about 10gm/⅓ oz

  warm orange-red for body and arms – about 15gm/½ oz

  golden yellow for hat – about 10gm/⅓ oz

  dark brown for boots – about 10gm/⅓ oz

- A bit of thin, white mohair for hair
- A little embroidery cotton for the face
- Wool fleece – washed and well carded – 15gm/½ oz
- Darning needle

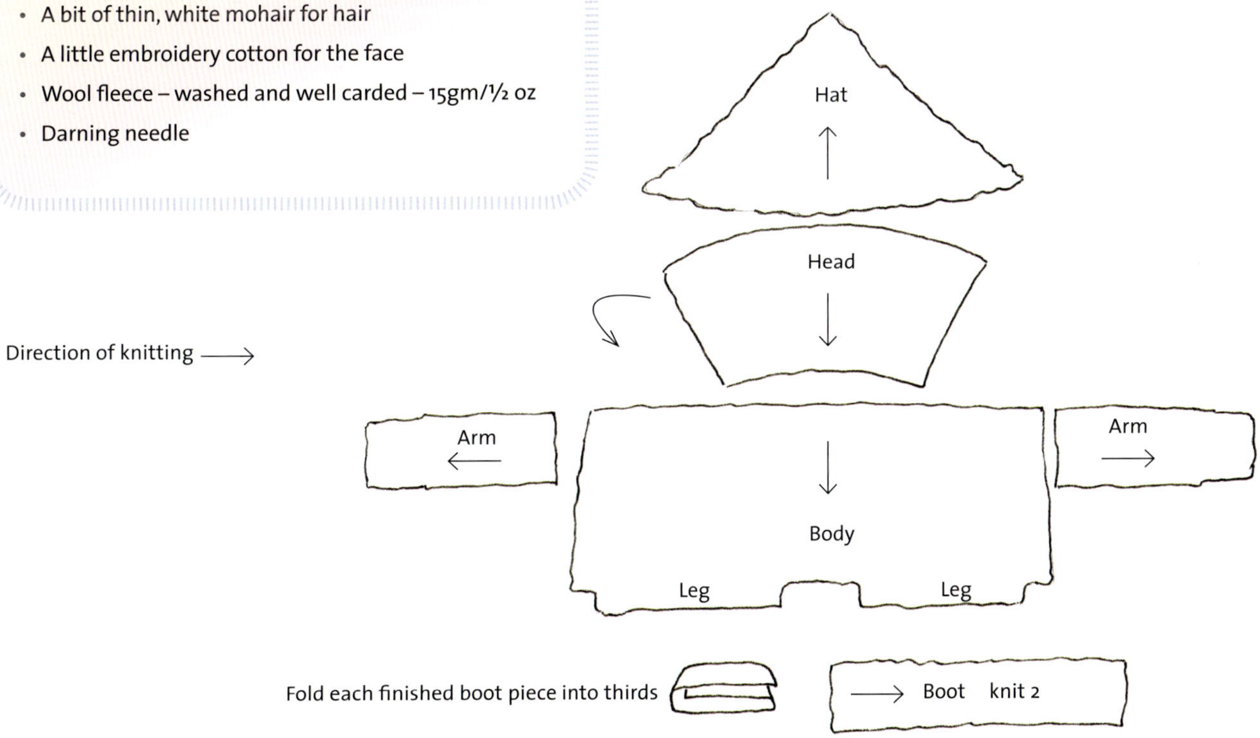

1. TO MAKE THE BODY

This is knitted from the neck towards the legs.
Cast on 28 stitches in the orange-red.
K 8 rows
9th row: K7, m1, k14, m1, k7 (30 sts)
10th row: K to end
11th row: K7, m1, k16, m1, k7 (32 sts)
12th row: K to end
13th row: K7, m1, k18, m1, k7 (34 sts)
14th row: K to end
K 8 rows
23rd row: Cast off 3, k to the end
24th row: Cast off 3, k to the end

2. TO MAKE THE LEGS

Knit 14 stitches for leg 1, cast off 4 stitches, knit 14 stitches for leg 2
This is the beginning of 2 legs so knit each leg with 4 more rows
Cast off
Knit the other leg as above.

3. Sew up the back seam on the body, then sew up the inside seam and crotch on the legs and stuff with fleece. Sew up the body's top seam and leave the bottom of the legs to be sewn to the boots.

4. TO MAKE THE BOOTS

Cast on 6 stitches with the dark brown wool
K 40 rows
Cast off
Fold into thirds and sew the back and sides. There's no need to stuff it (see diagram on page 137)
Repeat for second boot and sew both onto the legs.

5. TO MAKE THE HEAD: (KNITTED FROM THE TOP DOWN)

Cast on 28 stitches with the skin colour and use stocking stitch (k1, p1) for 16 rows ending with a purl row
Row 17: [K1, k2tog] rep to last stitch, k1
Row 18: P to end
Row 19: [Kk2tog, k1] rep till 14 stitches left
Row 20: P to end

6. Cut the yarn, leaving enough to sew the seams. Gather up the remaining stitches with the needle and pull tightly closed. Sew up the back seam, stuff with fleece then sew up the top.

7. TO MAKE THE HAT

Cast on 30 stitches with the golden yellow
K 4 rows
5th row: *[K1, k2tog], *rep till last 3 stitches, k2tog, k1
6th row: P to end
Repeat 5th and 6th rows until 4 sts remain
P 1 row
Cast off
Cut the yarn, leaving enough to sew the back seam.

8. TO MAKE THE ARMS

Cast on 8 stitches using body colour
K 22 rows
Change to skin colour
K 1 row, p 1 row for 6 rows
Cast off and repeat for the second arm.

9. Sew the side seams and pull the yarn through the inside of the palm to half close the hands but don't stuff.

10. To assemble the pieces together, place the head in front of the top of the body – not on top of the body. This creates the characteristic, slightly hunched gesture of the gnome. Sew in place with a few stitches.

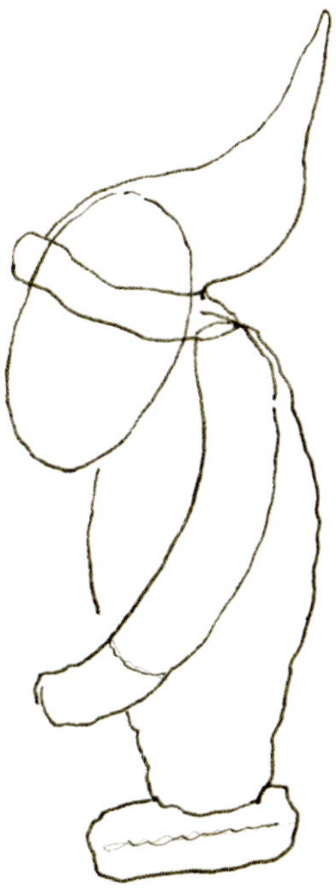

11. Pull the hat over the head till it touches the back and sits well at the front. Securely stitch it on. Then attach the arms to the sides of the top of the body and pull them slightly forward by running thread through the inside. Pull it and fix.

12. For the hair, sew loops of mohair around the face, running under the hat and over the chin and knot these in place as you go along. The gnome's characteristic facial features are wide-apart eyes halfway down from the top, and a wide mouth low down. Embroider these in place.

Now he can take the central place in the nature table and oversee the rich autumn scene.

Corn Dollies

Towards the end of the summer the wheat fields glow with their golden crop. Just a few of their stalks can make a beautiful corn dolly. These dollies hark back to ancient harvest traditions. They are just a bit more tricky to make than plaiting hair.

If you know a farmer, ask him or her well before harvesting time if you can have about twenty long stalks with ears (failing that, you can get straw for craft work online). The straw needs to be hollow or it will be too stiff to plait.

YOU WILL NEED

- 3 whole stalks of wheat
- Beige thread
- Red ribbon

Simple dolly

YOU WILL NEED
- 3 whole stalks
- Beige thread
- Red ribbon

1. Strip off the loose outer leaves and soak the stalks in hot water for about forty minutes until they are pliable, then wrap them in a damp towel. Remember – hard straws will snap and will be useless. Tie the three straws together with the thread, just below the ears.

2. Plait the straws from the top – towards the bottom they will get thicker and more difficult to plait. Stop after about 25cm/10" and firmly tie with thread. Make a loop and tie with red ribbon then trim the stalks at the back.

Straw heart

YOU WILL NEED
- 6 stalks
- Beige thread
- Red ribbon

1. Make two separate simple dollies, as described (left), but do not make a full loop. Tie the six heads together with the thread, just under the ears. Bend the two halves into a heart shape and tie at the crossover point – you may need an extra pair of hands here. Tie the ribbon into place. Trim the stalks.

2. Pin your dolly onto the backdrop of your autumn table or put it somewhere in your house where it will remind you of the golden summer.

Conker Web

What an amazing sight it is when the sun lights up a busy spider's woven web! Here is a colourful version to make for the autumn table.

A very easy project for careful little fingers.

YOU WILL NEED

- 1 conker
- 8 cocktail sticks
- Scraps of brightly coloured knitting wool, preferably in part of a rainbow sequence
- An awl (sharp spike) – a bradawl is not so good, but would do
- Pliers
- Scissors
- Glue
- Needle (optional)

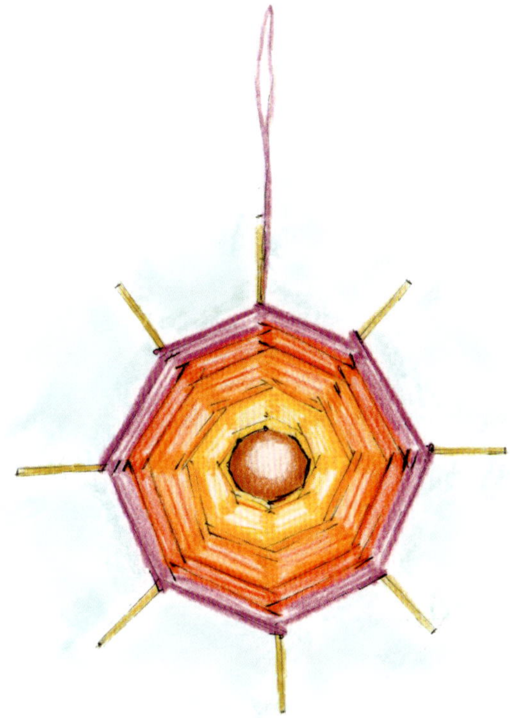

2. Take the lightest coloured wool and tie it to one of the cocktail sticks. Wrap it once around the next stick.

1. Please note that these first three points need adult help. Make eight small holes with the awl around the circumference of the conker. Glue the cocktail sticks into the holes and leave till the glue is properly dry. Cut off the sharp pointed ends with the pliers.

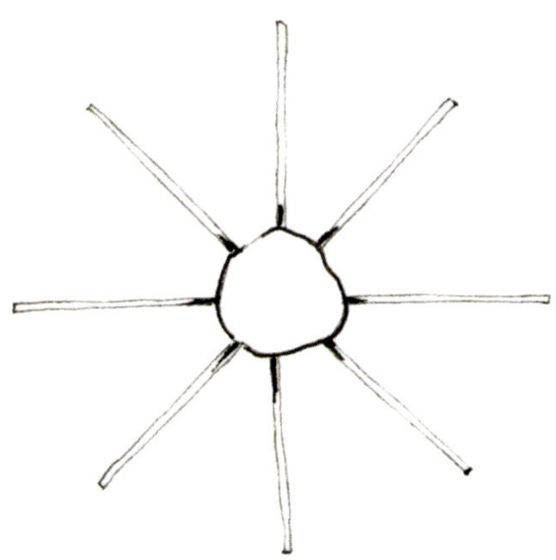

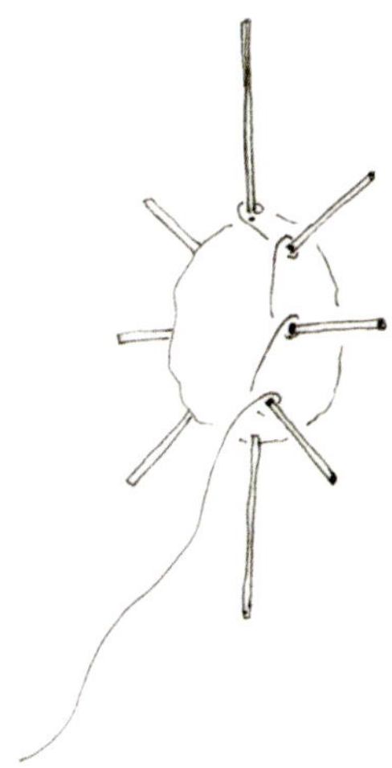

3. Continue doing this, pushing the wool together (unlike a spider's web) to make a continual weaving without gaps. After about ½cm/¼" of weaving, tie a different colour to the thread and make sure the knot is at the back or you can use a needle to secure the thread. Continue weaving with different colours until the web has filled up between the cocktail sticks to about 2cm/¾" from the ends. Make a firm knot around the last cocktail stick and leave about 30cm/12" of wool to hang the web on the nature table backdrop.

Pressed Leaves

The strong, low slanting sunlight adds drama to autumn's colourful tree display. Golden yellows, orange, red and rich browns stand out against the purple clouds. Soon the damp autumn wind hurls the leaves down until the ground is covered with a rich carpet.

When we bring these leaves indoors they quickly curl up, crumble and fade. But we can press them to preserve both their shape and their colour.

A lovely activity for young and old.

YOU WILL NEED

- Coloured leaves – freshly collected ones are best
- Old newspapers
- A few big, heavy books

1. Cut or tear the newspaper to make sheets about the same size as your books. Find a quiet corner where you can leave this project alone for some time. Lay a wodge of newspaper on a book and spread some leaves on them, taking care not to let them overlap. Place another wodge of newspaper on the leaves and then another book on top. Put the rest of the books on the pile

2. Then leave it for at least ten days. Unwrap the pile and check the leaves – they must be absolutely dry. If they are still damp, remake the pile with fresh sheets of newspaper and leave for a few more days.

When the leaves are ready you can add them to your autumn table, either pinned to the backdrop or scattered on the ground. You can stick any leftovers to thin card to make greetings cards.

Mice

Where there are seeds and nuts there are mice! The first one we spot is a cute little foraging grey felt one.

Felt mouse

This one is easy to make with a few basic sewing skills.

1. Trace the patterns below.

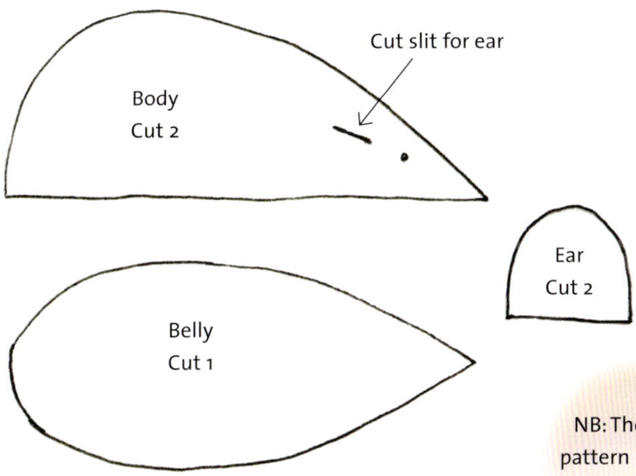

NB: The mouse pattern pieces are actual size.

2. Split a strand of the embroidery cotton in two.
Sew the top of the back together with blanket stitch (see page 49), starting at the back. Make a few knots where the nose is.

3. Pin one side of the back to the underbelly and sew it. Stuff with the fleece and sew the other side.

4. Embroider a few knots for the eyes.

5. Cut out the ears, fold in half and sew along the bottom. Sew in place (see diagram) and open them up.

6. For the tail crochet 10cm/4" of unsplit embroidery cotton or sew the chunky knitting wool in place.

YOU WILL NEED

- Pale grey felt 10 x 10cm/4 x 4"
- Pale grey embroidery cotton
- Embroidery needle
- Thin paper for tracing
- Very small amount of fleece
- Pale grey chunky knitting wool, 10cm/4" long

As this is quick and easy, why not make a few more in different sizes and colours?

Quickest-ever mouse

To make this little fluffy fellow, follow the instructions for the quickest-ever Easter hare (page 32) but use the diagram below. Again, this one is very easy to make.

YOU WILL NEED

- Thin card (cereal packet is ideal) and scissors
- Pale grey wool roving, about 25g/almost 1oz
- Pale grey felt, 5 x 5cm/2 x 2"
- Pale grey embroidery cotton
- Pale grey chunky knitting wool for the tail, 15cm/6" long
- Black felt pen

1. Make a woollen ball, following the instructions on page 32 but using the pattern on this page:

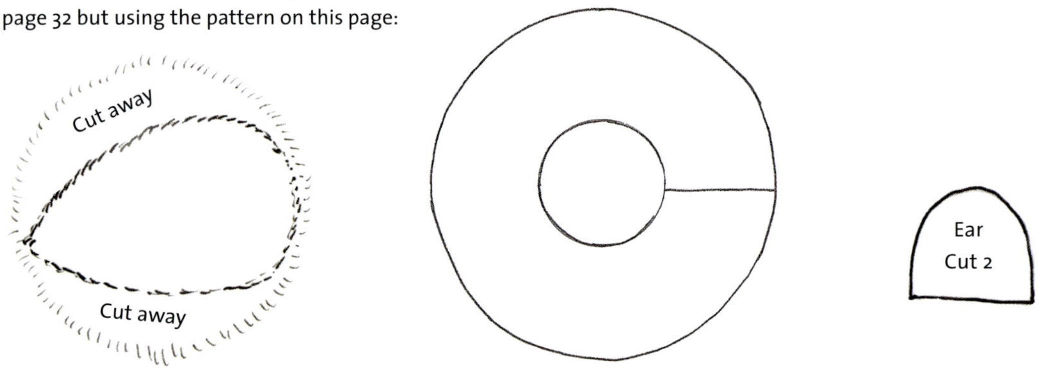

2. Make sure you tie the wool very tightly round the centre of the pompom. Rough up your pompom a little then snip a level base to form the underside. Snip the mouse into shape by flattening out the sides of the head to make a pointed nose. Remember you can't put it back once you have cut it off.

3. Cut out the ears, fold them in half and sew the bottom halves together. Sew them in place and open them up. Draw the eyes with a felt pen.

4. Sew the chunky knitting wool tail in place or crochet 10cm/4" of embroidery cotton to make a tail and sew it on.

When the mice have gathered all the nuts and seeds they hide them under an old tree root (dried) on your nature table. The gnomes approve of these goings on ...

Teasel Hedgehog

Are you lucky enough to hear the contented grunting of a foraging hedgehog in the night? If not, can you help him by providing a little easy access to your garden (provided you have one of course), which is small enough to keep out the hunting fox and badger.

Although this hedgehog is quick and easy to make, his prickles are considerable and not suitable for little children to play with.

YOU WILL NEED

- A teasel seed head
- Sharp nail scissors
- Thick gardening gloves
- 3 black-headed map pins

1. Hold the teasel seed head with your gloved hand and snip off the stem and the long spiky bracts (thin curling 'leaves' at the base).

2. Lay it on its side and cut off enough prickles to flatten the 'tummy'.

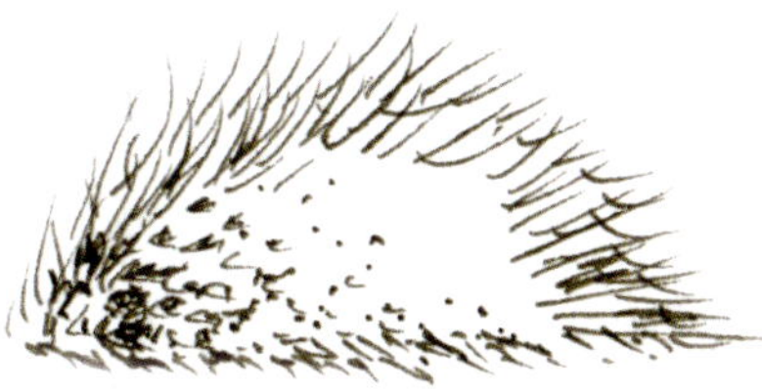

3. Cut away some prickles around point A to form a snout and also cut away a few just above each eye.

4. Insert the pins to make the nose and two eyes.

Your hedgehog is ready to snuffle about in your nature table.

Leaf Printing

You can easily recognise a plant by its flowers but experienced gardeners can recognise a plant by its leaves. They are either single or in clusters in two, three or more. Smooth, serrated, rounded, pointed, oval, indented – oh, so many shapes! We can use Nature's designs for leaf printing. It takes a little practice to avoid smearing paint all over, so start simply.

For teenagers and adults – children will love to watch and have a go as well!

1. Cover your work surface with newspaper and put on the apron – it is likely to get messy! Then put a little paint in the saucer but don't add water. Put a leaf on the newspaper and paint it. Cover it well but do not leave blobs. Carefully pick it up and gently place it paint-side down on the cartridge paper.

2. Carefully cover it with a single sheet of kitchen paper and press down firmly onto the leaf. Remove the kitchen paper and, very carefully, lift the leaf – there maybe some little smudges but that is fine. Repeat the process making rows or patterns. Now you are ready to print on cards, wrapping paper and paper crowns. You can use a good sturdy leaf over and over again.

YOU WILL NEED

- Small leaves with a little stem – firm, not floppy. Something like small rose leaves are ideal – no shiny ones
- Poster paint
- Old saucer for a palette
- Brush
- Jar of water for cleaning
- Old newspapers
- Good quality cartridge paper for printing on
- Old apron
- Kitchen paper towels

Leaf printing on fabric

Follow the instructions above but use fabric paint on cotton or linen. When your design has dried, iron on the back of the fabric to fix the paint. This is ideal for decorating napkins, tablecloths and bags.

Autumn Lantern

When the nights are drawing in and the vast dark skies are damp and cold, it is time to make our own little lights. At Martinmas (11 November) in Continental Europe, children take their lanterns outside in a procession, singing as they go. The best way to challenge the darkness!

This is a good project for teenagers and adults to make.

YOU WILL NEED

- Dark blue card, weight 220gsm, 46 x 40cm/18 x 16"
- Sharp cutting knife and sturdy cutting board or mat
- Ruler and pencil
- Kite or tissue paper in pale yellow, orange and red
- UHU and Pritt Stick
- Wire for handle, 30cm/12"
- Tea light
- Blu-Tack

1. Draw up the pattern as shown.

2. Now cut out the windows. Score the fold lines with the back of the knife and cut out the rest.

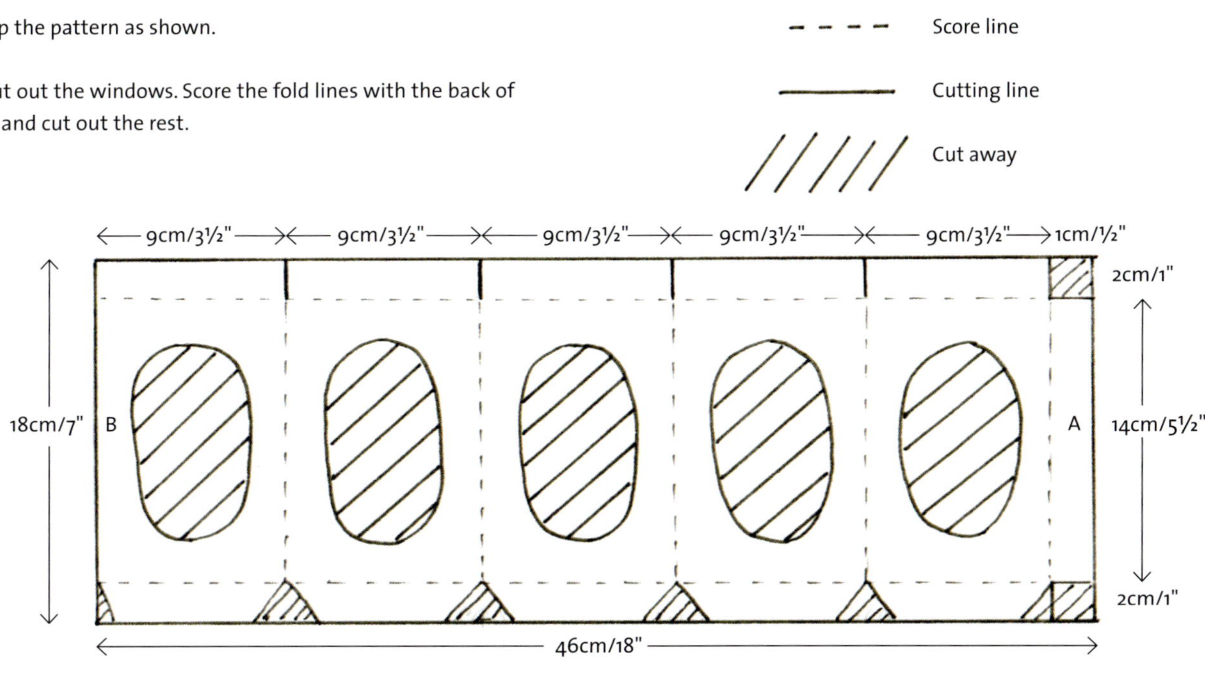

3. Cut out the pentagon for the bottom. You can draw a pentagon using a compass with a pencil and a protractor, following the diagram below:

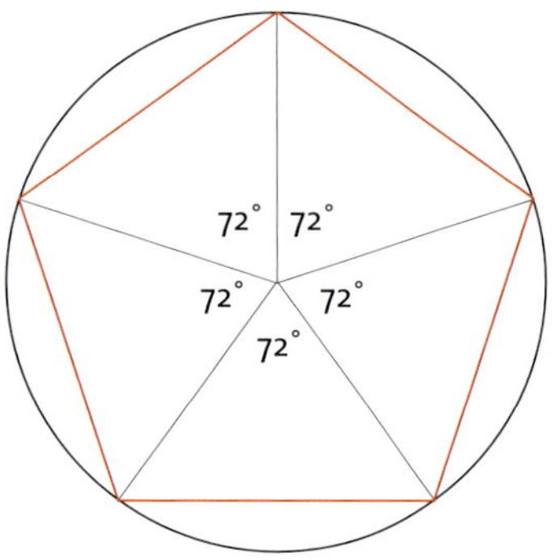

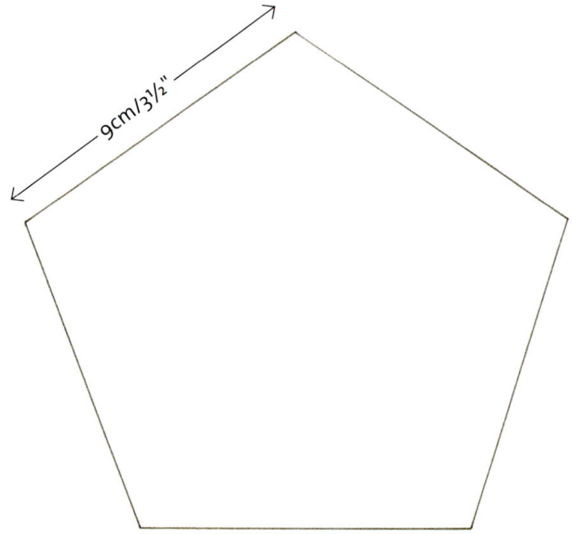

4. To make the windows, turn the card over and glue the pale yellow all over the window; then add a warm yellow around the outside, leaving the centre free; then use orange and lastly red for the general pattern. The more colours you use the richer the effect, but the lantern will give less light – so go easy! (See transparencies on page 206.)

5. Trim and glue all loose bits in place then glue tab A under B and fold in the top tabs; overlap and glue the corners. Fold under the bottom tabs and glue them onto the pentagon base. Make two small holes through the top tabs on opposite sides and insert the wire to make the handle. Fix the tea light to the centre of the base with a small amount of Blu-Tack. Ready for the cold dark night!

Please note: Never leave a lit candle unattended.

Tissue Paper Lanterns

Lantern processions light up the darkest autumn night with great cheer. These cane and tissue paper beauties can take on just about any shape or size – even butterfly, bee, human or angel forms. Shown here are three beginners' shapes – but feel free to use your own imagination. Bear in mind that these are for use in the dark and that simple shapes can work very well.

Use pale-coloured tissue to cover the shape so that the lights inside can shine out well.

For teenagers and adults to make, with decorating help from younger ones.

YOU WILL NEED

You may not need everything on this list – it all depends on your chosen shape.

- Hedgerow canes or twigs – long, bendy and smooth – from willow, dogwood or maple. If necessary buy willow canes about 150cm/5' long from a craft shop
- Sturdy bamboo bean pole for the main support stick
- Secateurs
- Strong tape (parcel tape, electrical tape or gaffer tape)
- Clingfilm
- White tissue paper to cover the whole surface
- Pale-coloured tissue paper, yellow or orange to make a warm glow
- PVA glue diluted 50/50 with water
- Brush
- Several battery-powered fairy lights – the more the merrier

1. Soak the twigs or canes (not the bamboo) in the bath overnight – they must all be bendy before you start – and wipe them dry. Decide how long the main bamboo should be and allow for the lantern carrier's height plus the lantern shape. Cut the bamboo.

2. Decide on the lantern shape and cut some canes to suit. Trim off the side shoots from the twigs. If some canes are too short, join two by overlapping the ends and wrapping a lot of tape around them.

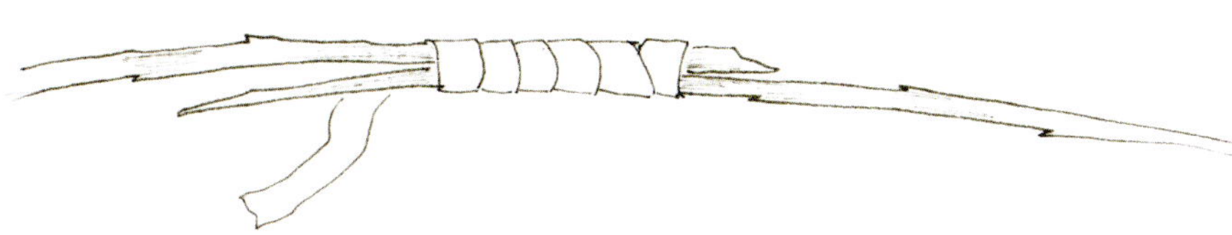

Here are three lantern shapes in more detail.

Five-pointed star

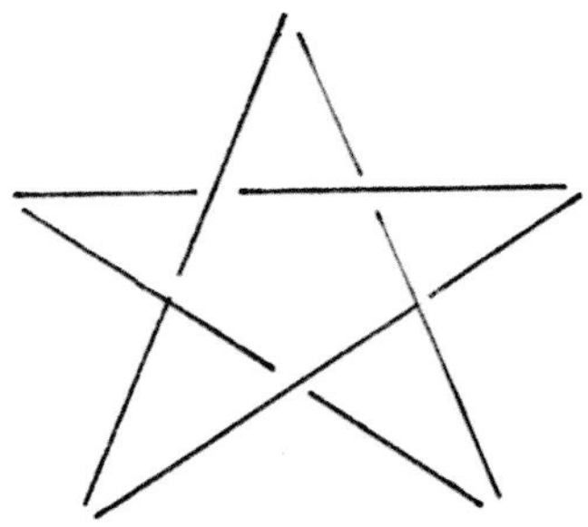

1. Cut 10 canes to the same length, say 60cm/24". Lay five pieces into a star shape.

2. Firmly join the five crossing points. See drawing (right).

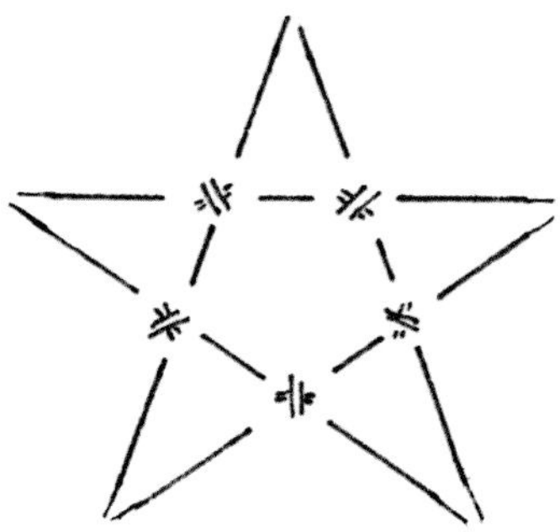

3. Repeat with the other five pieces. Cut five sturdy pieces, about 8cm/3" long, depending on your own design. These are spacers to give volume to the star. Firmly fix these at right angles to the two stars at the five crossing points.

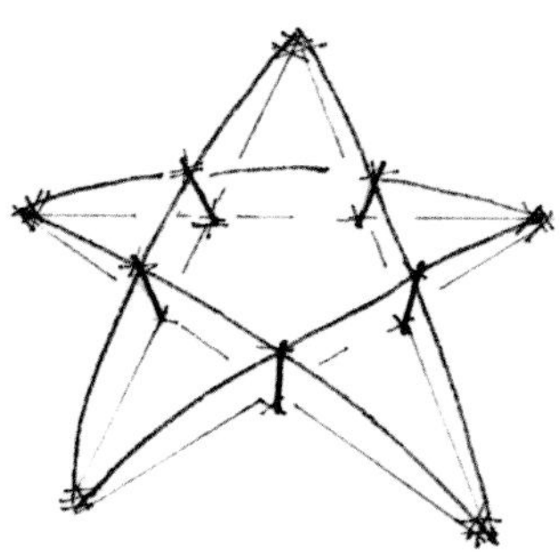

Any cross joint needs to be firmly fixed by winding lots of tape diagonally around it:

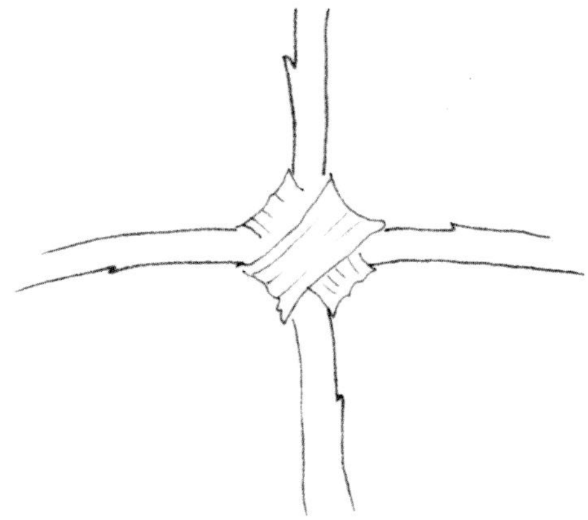

4. Pull together each pair of the five tips of the stars and firmly join together to make a hollow framework. Arrange the lights inside and fix them in place, including the battery.

5. Cover the star with clingfilm and leave a hole to enable you to switch on the lights. Stick white tissue paper directly onto the clingfilm (leaving the hole open) using the diluted glue generously. You may want to test the star in a dark room to see that it works well before proceeding.

6. Glue on pale yellow or pale orange tissue paper and check progress in a dark room as you go. Tie some string at the top to make a handle for carrying it or to attach it to the end of the bamboo pole.

Sun lantern

1. Cut six canes, soak them and bend four of them to make four same-size circles by joining the ends firmly together.

2. Take three circles and space them equally to form a sphere, taping all the joints firmly.

3. Place the fourth circle around the sphere to form the horizontal 'equator' and tape it firmly in place.

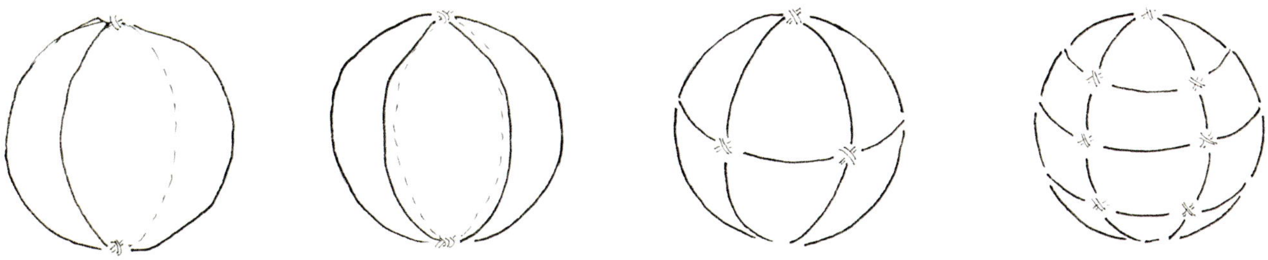

4. Use the two remaining canes to form smaller circles and fix these above and below the 'equator'. Arrange the lights and battery inside and secure in place, allowing access to the switch. Cover the sun with clingfilm and tissue paper as with the star.

5. Attach the sun firmly to the carrying bamboo.

Easy sun lantern

Use a spherical paper lampshade, add the lights, decorate with tissue paper and fix it to the bamboo.

Cone or Christmas tree lantern

1. Make a large base, circle (A). Join two pieces of cane with tape to form a cross to fix across circle A. Firmly fix A to the support bamboo about a quarter way up from the bottom. Make a smaller circle (B) with a cross and fix it about a quarter of the way down from the top of the bamboo.

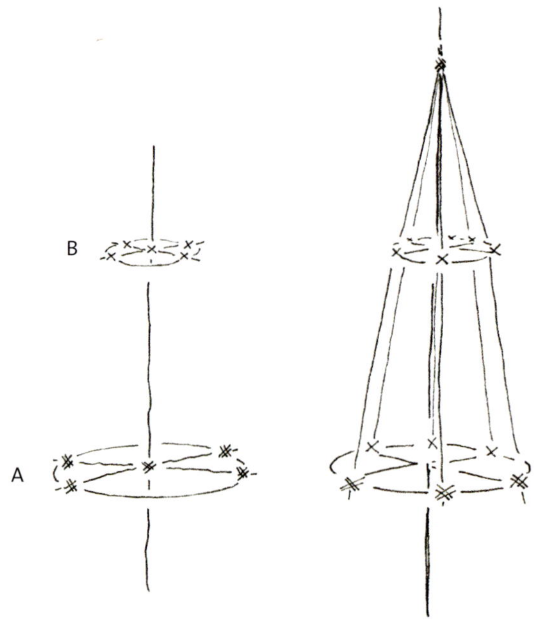

2. Cut about six long twigs to run from the top of the bamboo, via circle B to circle A. Space them equally around the cone and firmly fix them to the tip and both circles.

3. Arrange the lights inside and fix them in place, including the battery. Cover with clingfilm and tissue paper – leave all or part of the bottom open so you can switch on the lights and test in a dark room. Cover with pale, warm-coloured tissue paper.

4. Make two small equal triangles and join them together to form a six-pointed star.

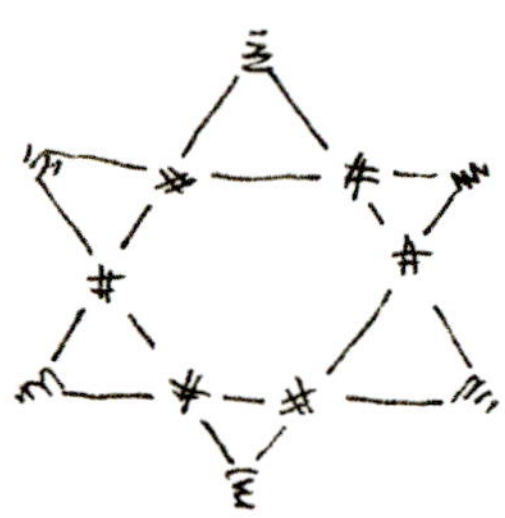

5. Cover the star and fix it firmly to the very top of the bamboo.

Put on your thick coats and join the lantern procession in the dark!

Climbing Gnome

Children love to make the gnome climb quickly to the top by pulling first one string and then the other. It's even more fun to watch the gnome rush down again the moment the strings are slackened.

This toy can also be made with different climbers (even animals) so long as the essential feature is there, which is a hole drilled at an angle at the end of each arm. This is a toy to be made for a child.

YOU WILL NEED

- 2 pieces of dowel 10cm/4" long and 12mm/½" diameter
- Drill and 3mm/⅛" drill bit
- 2.1m/7' thin string – must be smooth
- 5 small, round wooden beads
- Cotton fabric 24 x 17cm/9 x 7"
- Teaspoon of dry sand
- Skin-coloured stockinette, 7 x 7cm/3 x 3"
- Small piece of fleece
- Needle and thread

1. Make up the pattern for gnome, pin the pieces to the material and cut out all the pieces.

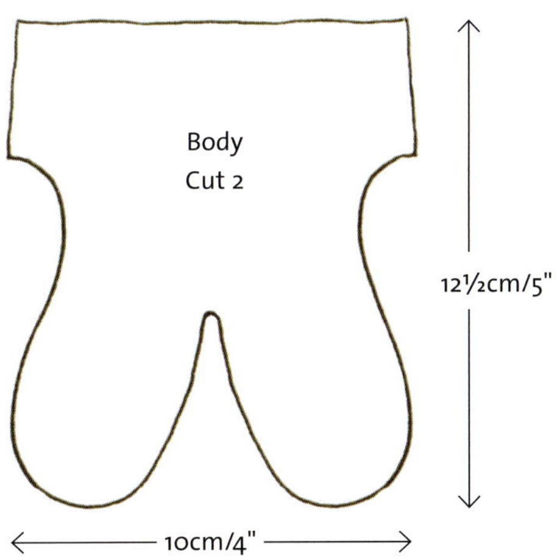

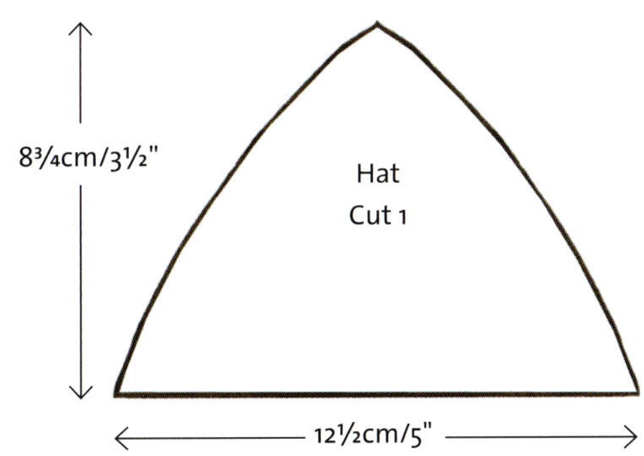

2. With right sides together, sew around the edge of the gnome's body (A to B) leaving the top edge and armholes open.

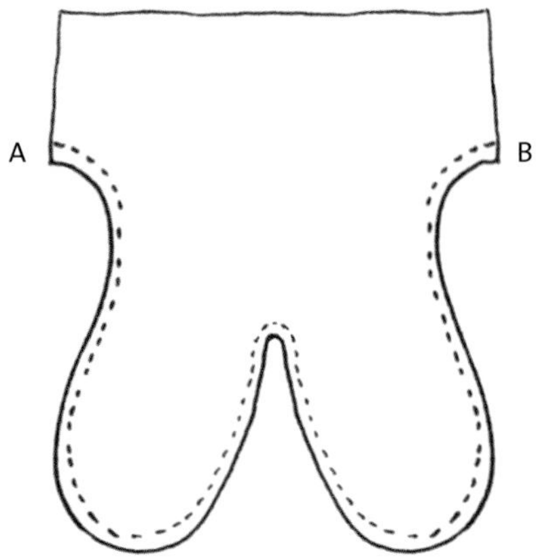

3. Fold the hat in half and sew up the back seam with right sides together. Clip the curves, especially round the legs of the body piece, and turn both hat and body the right way out.

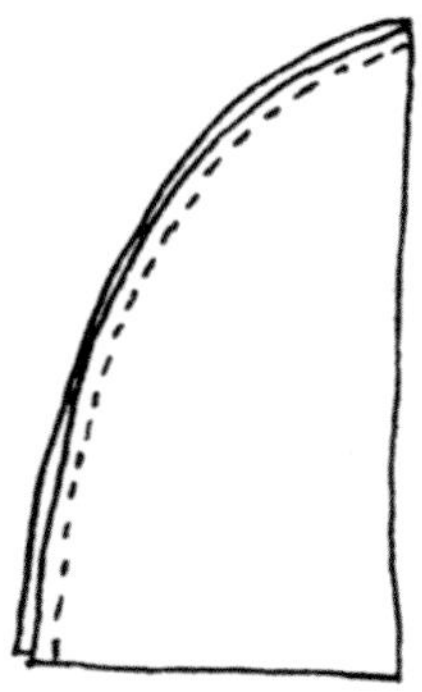

4. Drill three holes into one of the pieces of dowel, which will be used for hanging up the gnome.

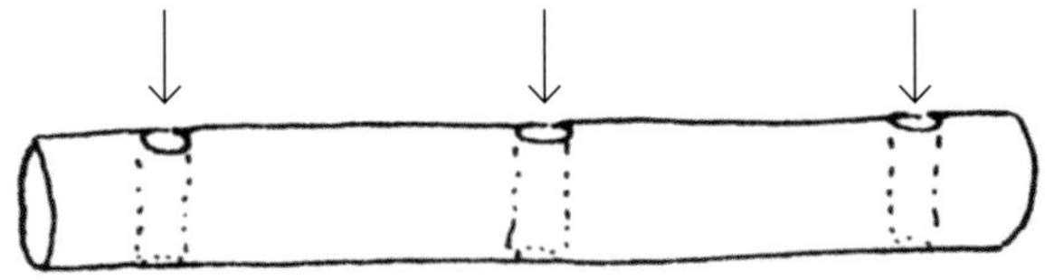

5. Drill two holes into the other piece of dowel for the gnome's arms. It is very important that they are at an angle.

6. Make a small ball of fleece or cotton wool, diameter 3cm/1¼". Tie the stockinette around this ball.

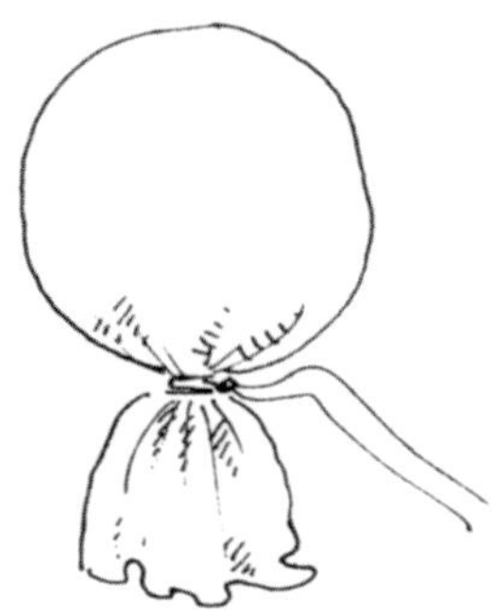

7. Sew some fleece around the head for hair and a beard. Fold in the bottom edge of the hat and secure the hat on the gnome's head with a few stitches.

8. Put the half teaspoon of sand into each leg of the body. Carefully centre the head and arrange the folds of the cloth (below the neck) around the back and the front of the arm-stick.

9. Sew the body piece around the arm-stick, folding in all edges and securing the head firmly in the middle.

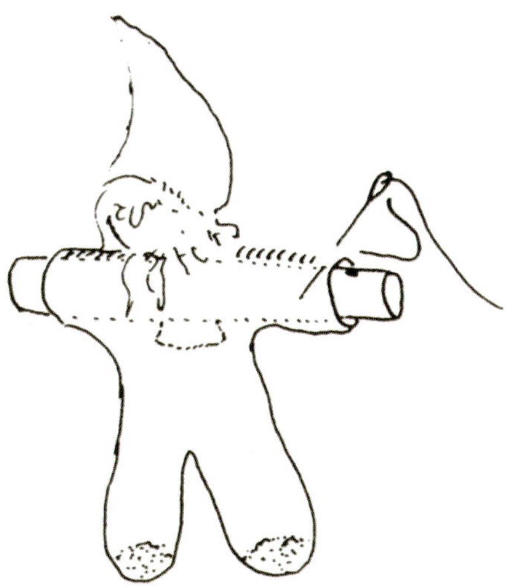

10. To hang up the gnome, thread the strings though the holes of the dowel and secure with beads as shown.

Make him climb by first pulling on one string then on the other. Watch out! If you let the strings go loose he will drop straight back to the bottom again.

Woven Pencil Case

This can be a lovely present for Mum or Dad, or a good friend. It is simple to make and very rewarding.

YOU WILL NEED

- Firm card 25 x 10cm/10 x 4"
- Sharp scissors or a craft knife
- Small scraps (leftovers) of wool in matching colours
- Small amount of thinner wool
- Extra-strong wool, such as rug-making wool, for the warp
- Large embroidery needle

1. Cut teeth out of the card on both narrow sides, as shown.

2. Put the warp on, as shown, covering front and back.

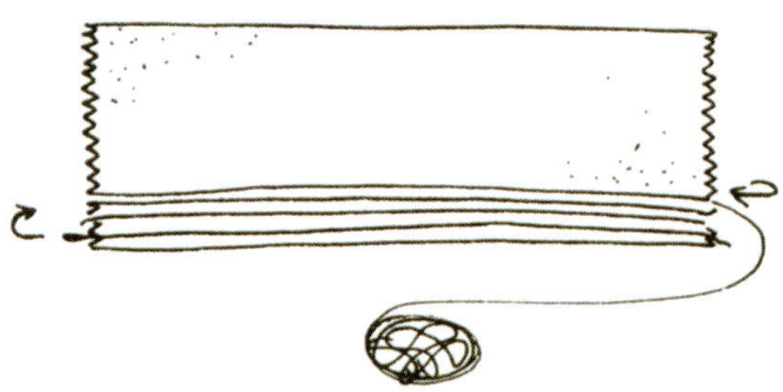

3. Start the weaving with a few rows of thin wool to prevent the end from fraying. Begin 3cm/1½" away from the end.

4. Continue to weave on the front and the back. This is unusual, but necessary to make a tube. Your first row is on the front, then turn over the card and continue to weave on the back. Turn it over again for the second row on the front. Always weave under-over in one row followed by over-under in the next. Continue weaving like this, while pushing the weaving firmly together so that it makes a firm piece of cloth. Stop when you have about 17cm/7" of weaving.

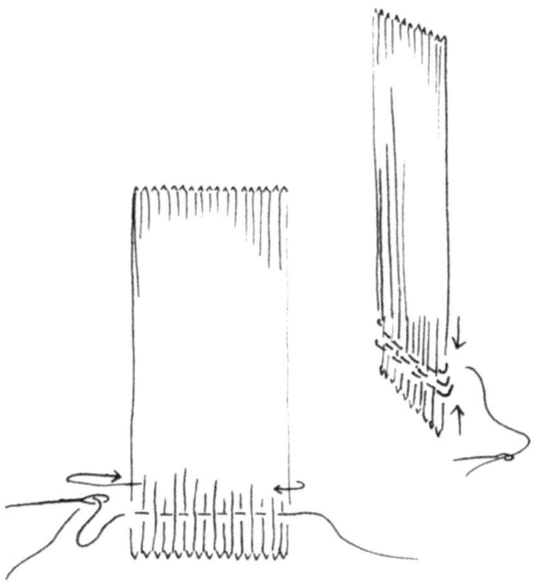

5. Now you're only going to weave on the back. Do this for another 3cm/1½". This is the flap.

Cut the warp furthest away from the weaving.

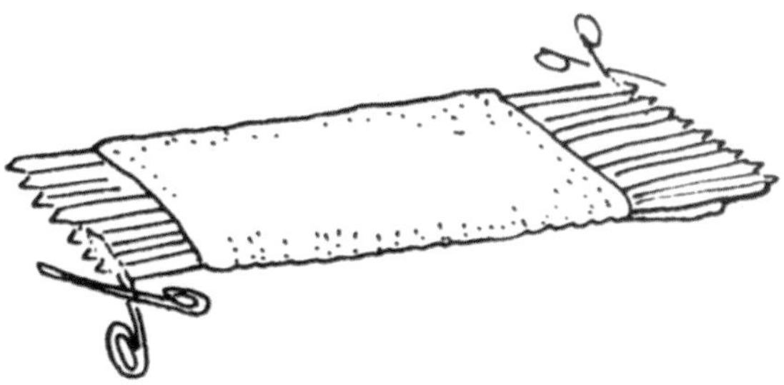

6. Knot the warp as shown. You can sew the warp back in if you like, or you can leave it.

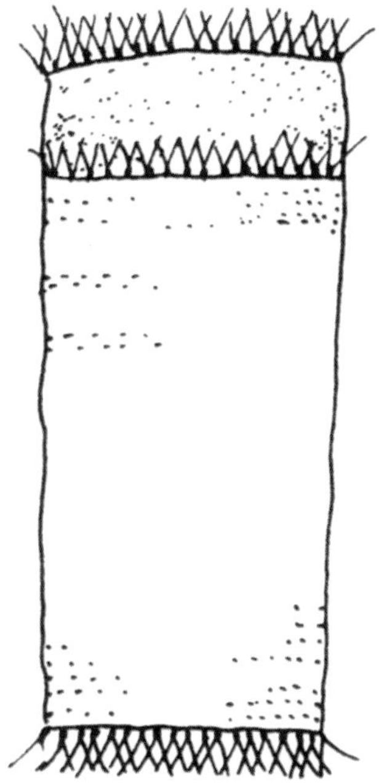

7. Fold the flap over and make a loop. Sew a button on to the case to hold the loop.

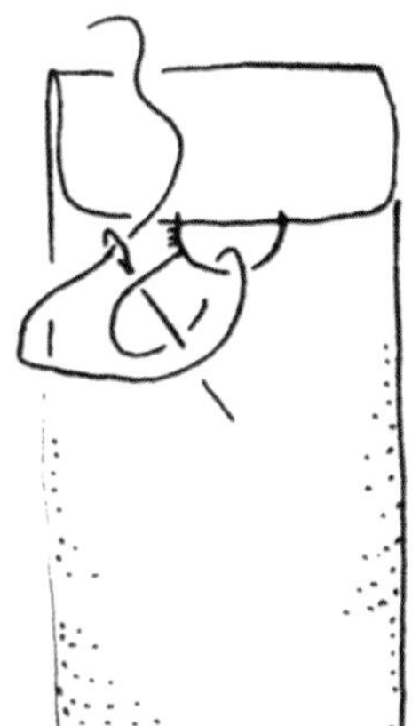

Exotic Belt

This exotic belt is all about plaiting and gives a pleasing result. A harmonious colour combination is essential. Ideal for young teens who love to plait.

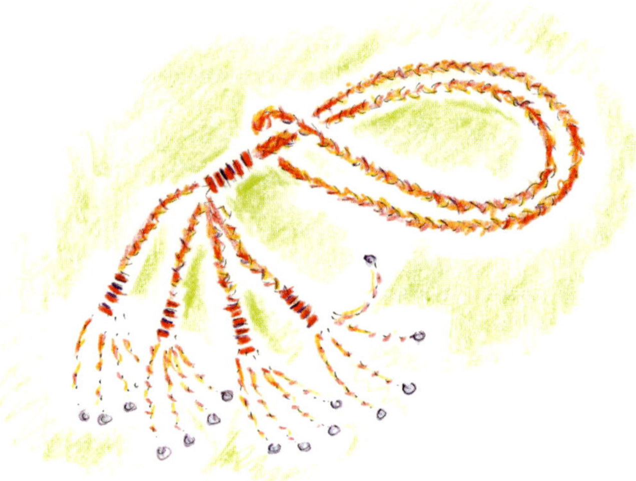

YOU WILL NEED

- Brightly coloured wool in 3 tones that blend well – 24 pieces, 3.5m/11' long
- Scissors
- Large-eyed needle
- Clothes pegs
- 16 small bells (optional)

1. Line up all the lengths of wool. Leave 55cm/21" at one end unplaited then start plaiting until there is 55cm/21" left at the other end. Knot some wool around both ends of the plaiting to stop it unravelling. Hook your work over a door handle or a coat hook to stabilise it and bring the ends together.

2. Divide the lengths of wool into four bunches of 12 threads each – use clothes pegs to keep these bunches separate. Plait each bunch halfway and knot some wool around the end of each one. Divide each of the four bunches again into four and plait each one to the end – tie a knot around each of the 16 ends.

3. Wind some wool neatly around the knots covering all the loose ends – this winding can be about 2cm/¾" wide. Thread in the ends with a needle.

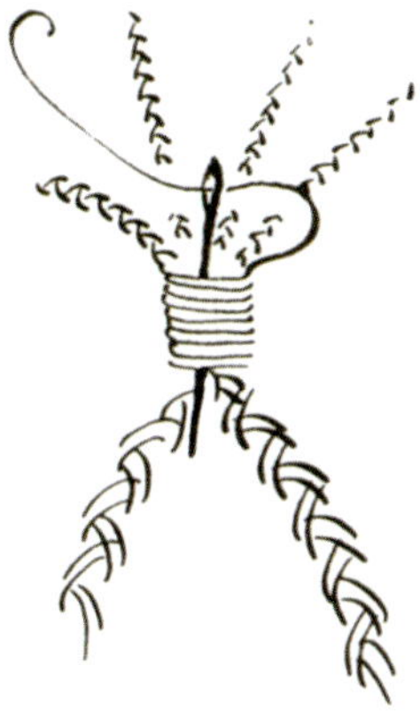

The tiny bells at the ends add a musical note!

Knitted Piglet

This cheeky little piglet will bring a smile to your face. The body is knitted on four needles and the snout is quite fiddly, so it is not a project for beginners.

YOU WILL NEED

- Pig pink DK wool
- 4 knitting needles, 3mm/US size 2
- Fleece for stuffing

1. FOR THE BODY

Cast on 14 sts on 3 knitting needles (5 sts on two needles, 4 sts on one needle)

For the head, knit in rounds [k1, p1] until you have 3.5cm/1¼"

Next round: double the number of sts by [k1 inc 1] until the end of the round (28 sts)

Continue on in plain knitting until work measures 7cm/2¾" from where you increased.

Start decreasing in the next round as follows: K1, k2 sts tog, k5, k2 tog, k5, k2 tog, k5, k2 tog, k5 (24 sts).

Next round: *[K2 tog, k4] *rep to end of round (20 sts)

Next round: *[K2 tog, k3], *rep to end of round (16 sts)

Next round: *[K2 tog, k2], rep to end of round (12 sts)

Next round: *[K2 tog, k1], *rep to end of round (8 sts)

2. Break the thread and gather these 8 sts on a needle and draw together tightly. Sew the thread in on the wrong side of the pig's body.

3. FOR THE LEGS

Use 2 needles only:
Cast on 10 sts
Knit 10 rows, st st
Break wool with a little extra length and gather the sts – pull together and sew up back seam.
Make 3 more so he can stand up!

4. FOR THE EARS

Use 2 needles only:
Cast on 8 sts
Row 1: K to end
Row 2: P to end
Row 3: K1, k2tog, k2, k2tog, k1
Row 4: P to end of row
Row 5: K1, k2tog, k2tog
Cast off

5. Make another ear and stuff the body with fleece. Make the snout by threading a piece of wool on a darning needle and draw it through the very front of the face with a tiny running stitch, as shown below.

6. Fold the ear in half and sew it together at the bottom. Sew ears in place and open up.

7. Stuff the legs and sew them onto the body. Make a short tail with pink wool by twisting a cord (see page 120) and sew it in place.

Any piglet brothers and sisters next?

Knitted Cat

This sweet little cat can be knitted in various colours – grey, white or brown. It looks especially good in soft fluffy wool like mohair. An easy knitting project.

YOU WILL NEED

- Cat colour DK wool, about 25gm/1oz
- 2 knitting needles, 3mm/US size 2
- Fleece for stuffing
- 2 threads of wool for the face, 1 pink and 1 blue or green
- A tiny bell on a ribbon to put around the neck (optional)

1. FOR THE BODY

Cast on 24 sts and knit 52 rows
Cast off

2. FOR THE HEAD

Cast on 14 sts
K 14 rows
K2tog, k to end
K 3 rows, as above
Inc 1, k to end
K 3 rows, as above
K 14 rows
Cast off

3. FOR THE TAIL

Cast on 16 sts
1st row: K to end
2nd row: K 10 sts and turn (leaving 6 sts unworked)
3rd row: K to end (this row is shorter now)
Repeat these 3 rows 3 times
Cast off

4. TO SEW THE BODY TOGETHER

Corners 1, 2, 3, 4 are the feet.

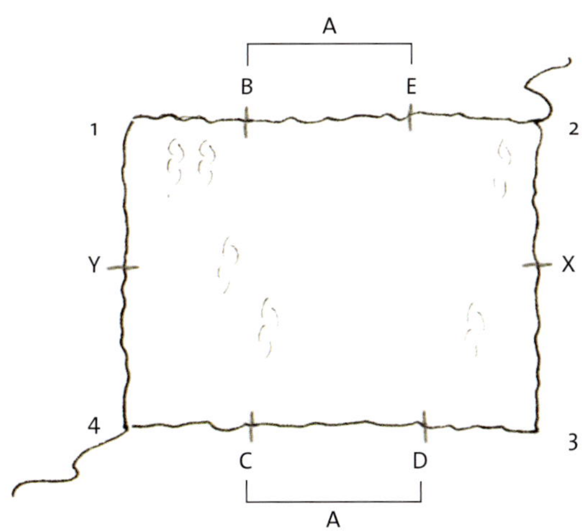

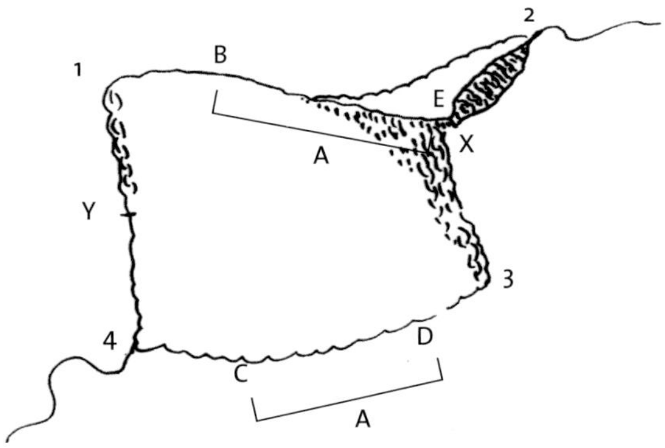

5. Fold E to X and B to Y. Sew the leg seams.
Sew the leg seams on the other side in same way (C to Y and D to X). Then stuff the body and close by sewing up the seam at A.

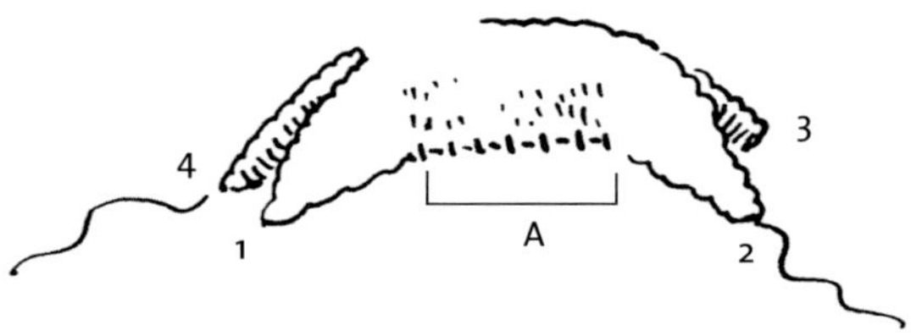

6. Now fold the headpiece in half and sew up both side seams.

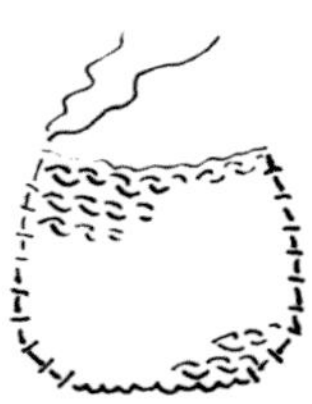

Fold

7. Stuff the head and close the top seam. Sew diagonally across the corners with a small running stitch to make the ears. Embroider the face.

8. Sew the head onto the front of the body.

9. Sew up the tail and sew in place – see above.

If you like, tie a tiny bell on a ribbon around the neck. He is ready for a cuddle!

Bootees, Socks and Slippers

These are all cosy, pretty and easy to knit. With the same basic pattern, there are several possibilities! Make either tiny baby bootees, or socks and slippers for a toddler. The pattern is so simple that an older child could make any of these quite easily. Here is your chance to make striped socks if you like these and have just the right left-over colours.

Bootees for a Newborn Baby

YOU WILL NEED

- 4 ply baby-soft wool, 20gm/1oz
- 2 knitting needles, 3mm/US size 2

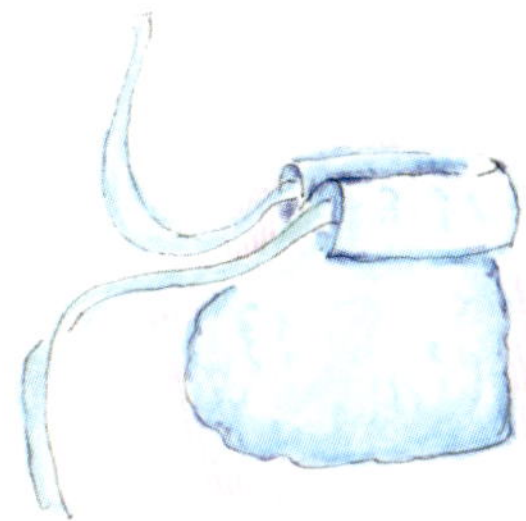

1. Cast on 56 sts
K 26 rows in st st
Cast off 12 st and k to end
Repeat row above (32 sts)
Knit 22 rows
Decrease as follows:
Next row: [K2tog] to end of row (16 sts)
Next row: P to end
Next row: K2tog and rep to the end of the row (8 sts)
Next row: P to the end

2. Break the wool, leaving about 15cm/6". Run the wool through the 8 sts, pull together and sew in securely on the wrong side of the sock. You have two choices. You can sew up the middle front section (X–Y) and back seam (A–B) as in the diagram below.

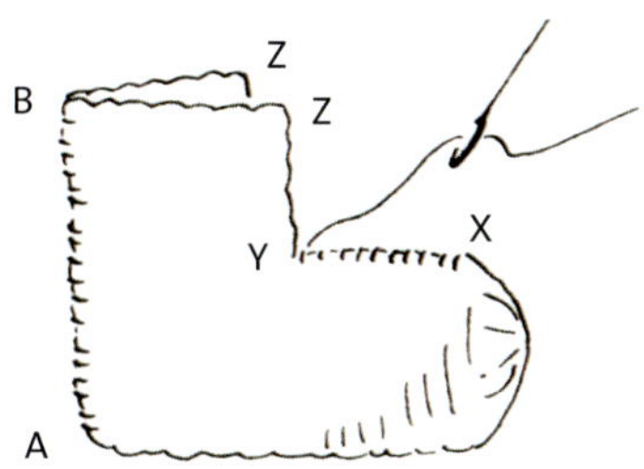

Or, if you would like it to be a sock, you can sew up the back seam (A–B) and then the front seam Y–Z, as shown here:

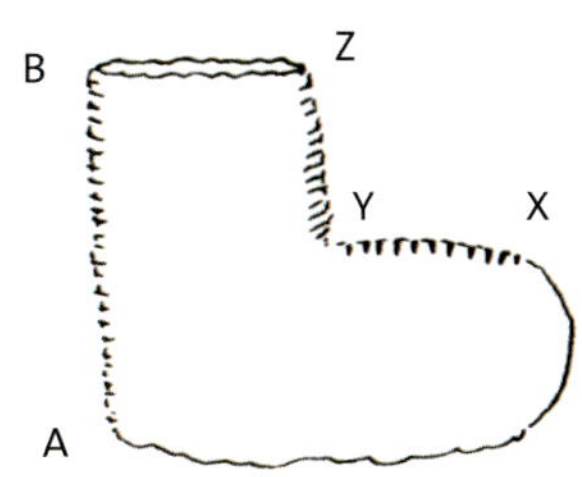

If you would like it to be a bootee with a ribbon, fold the top edge (Z–B) down, sew it into the sock and thread a piece of ribbon through it, as shown:

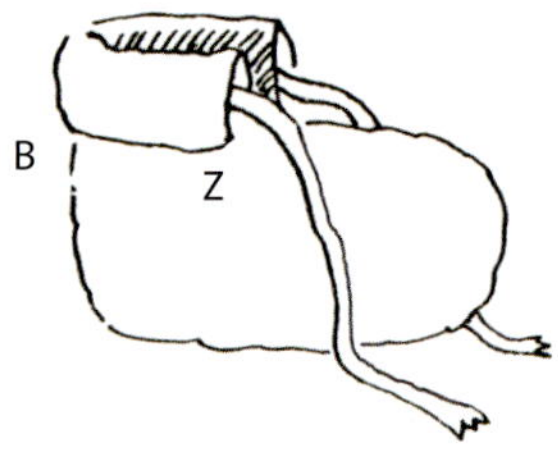

Socks or Slippers for a Toddler

YOU WILL NEED

- DK wool, 50gm/2oz
- 2 knitting needles, 4mm/US size 6
- 1 piece of thin leather, about 15 x 15cm/6 x 6" (eg window cleaning leather)
- Sharp scissors
- Strong thread and needle

1. Follow the instructions given for the baby bootee. As you are using bigger knitting needles and thicker wool, your sock will be much bigger with the same number of stitches given for the bootee. Follow the sewing-up instructions above for slippers or socks.

2. For the slipper soles, put one sock on your child's foot and stand the child on a piece of paper. Then draw around the foot with a pencil to make the pattern. Cut out the paper pattern and draw round it on the leather. Turn the paper over and draw round it again.

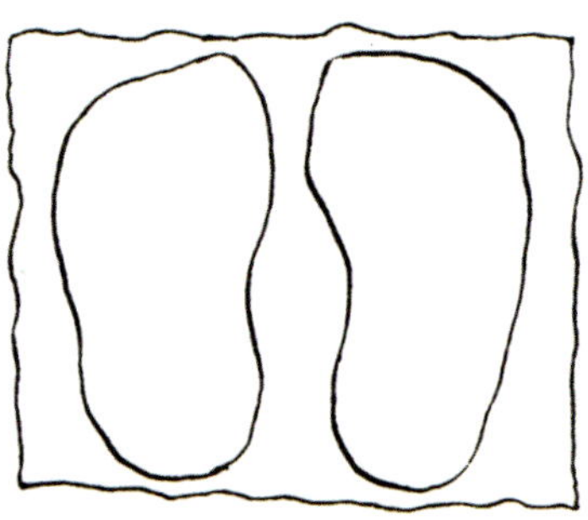

3. Cut out the two leather soles. With some strong thread, sew the soles onto the bottom of the socks using an overstitch.

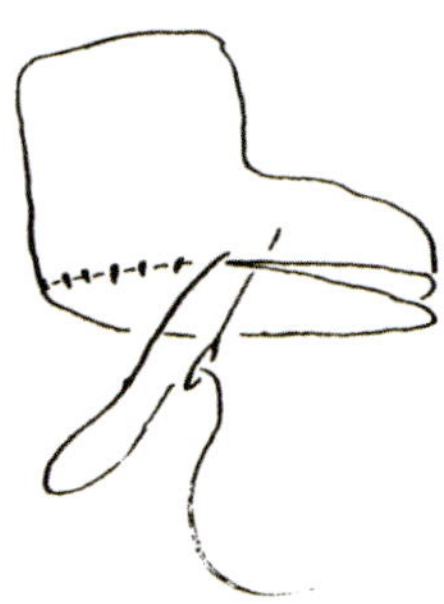

You may want to make a pom-pom (see p 231) from the same wool that you used to knit the slipper, and sew it into the front of the slipper as a decoration.

Crocheted Slippers

Here is your chance to make warm and colourful slippers in just the colour you want!

With the same basic pattern, you can make any size you wish. As you can see from the illustrations, the slippers can be finished off in quite a few different ways. Choose the one that suits you best.

The slippers have sheepskin soles and can be crocheted either plain or in several colours. If you cannot get hold of any sheepskin, you can crochet the soles.

For teenagers and adults to make.

YOU WILL NEED

- For UK junior shoe size 8, Euro 25 or US 9
- Sheepskin, 20 x 18cm/8 x 7"
- DK wool, 50gm/2oz
- Crochet hook, 3.5mm/US size E
- Leather punch
- Paper, pencil and scissors

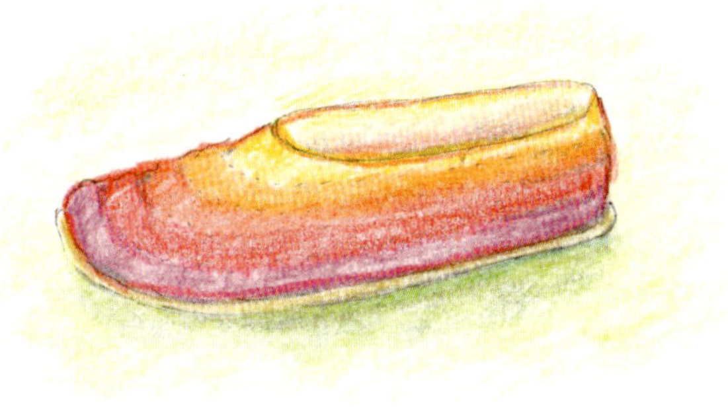

1. Put the paper on the floor and draw round the wearer's foot with a pencil to make a paper pattern for the soles; allow a little extra space. Cut out the pattern and lay it on the smooth side of the sheepskin. Then draw round the pattern with a pencil or marker. Turn the pattern over and draw round it again.

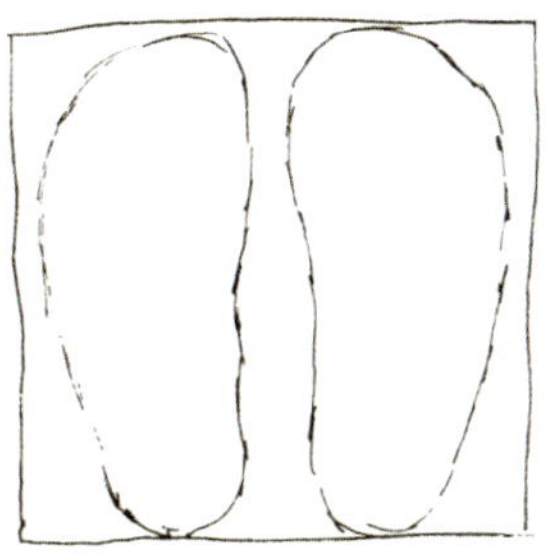

2. Cut out the two soles from the sheepskin. Make holes round the edge of the soles with the punch, 3mm/1/8" diameter, about 5mm/1/4" apart.

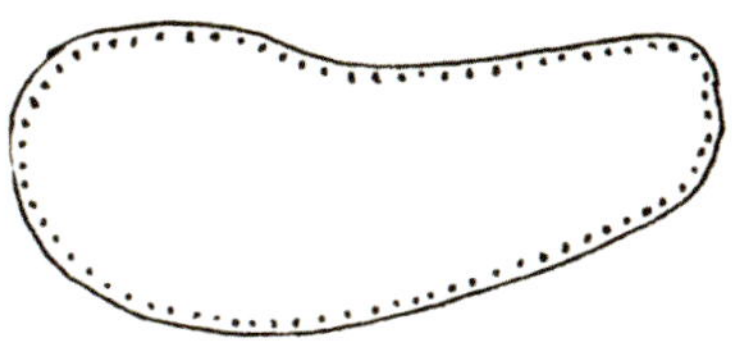

3. Start crocheting at the centre of the heel, using triple crochet stitch.
Go round the sole, one stitch in each hole
Work a 2nd row on top of the 1st row
Work the 3rd row to the front of the slipper
Start to shape the toe by working 3 sts into 5 sts, missing out every other stitch.

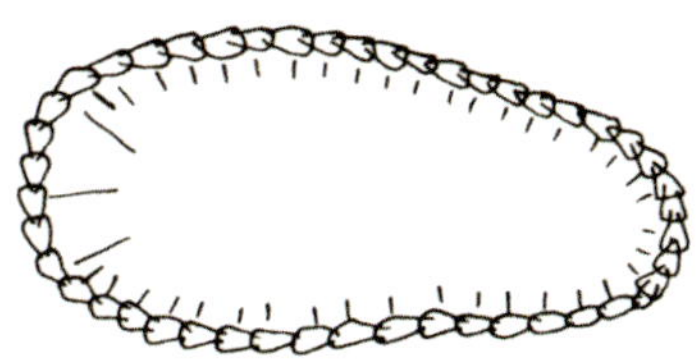

4. For 3 rows, dec 5 sts at the toe end, as above (miss out every other st 5 times).

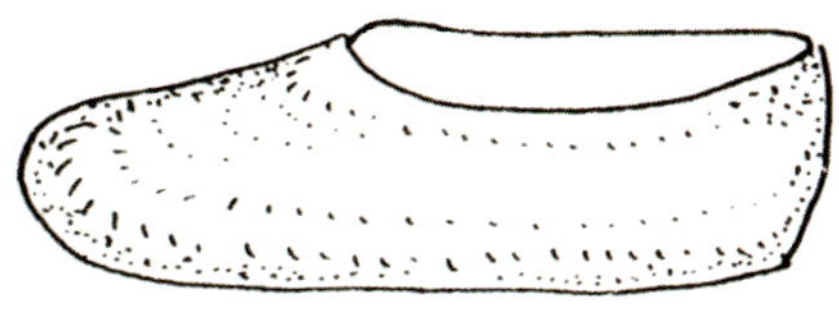

For slip-on slippers, you have finished here.

To make a strap-on slipper, crochet a strap and sew it in the appropriate place.

Crocheted slipper variations

1. To make bootees for a baby or toddler, follow the above instructions but measure to the baby's foot. Add more rows round the ankle.

2. For very small bootees you can thread elastic or ribbon through the ankle opening to stop them being kicked off.

3. For larger slippers, the opening around the ankle should be big enough for the child to put them on easily. Crochet backwards and forwards around the ankle and leave the centre front open. Sew up the gap created in the centre front with a few stitches and continue adding rows going round the leg opening until it is high enough.

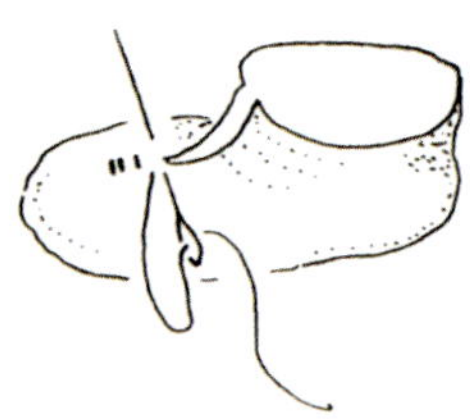

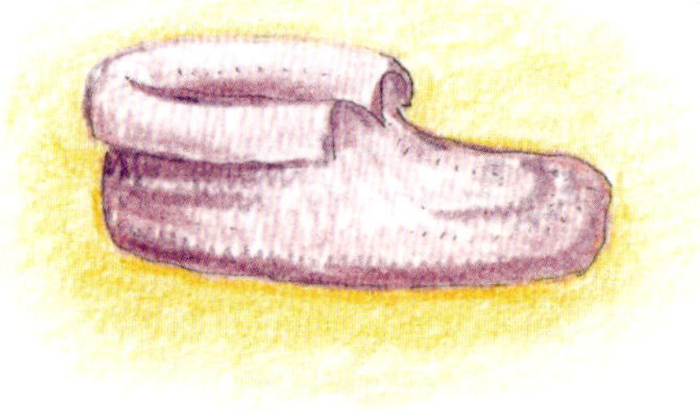

Crocheted sole

1. Make a length of chain stitch with double-thick wool, which is as long as the required sole, minus the width.

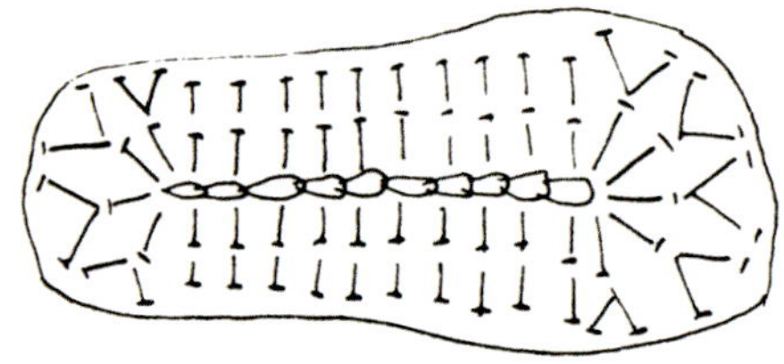

2. Work along this base chain as if you were working in rows. Into the last chain work enough extra stitches to make a fan shape, creating a semicircle. Continue working stitches into the chain and make a fan shape at the other end. Join the last stitch to the starting stitch. Work more rows (increasing only at each end) until the sole is the size required.

Finger Puppets

Finger puppets are lovely presents for children and good fun to make, as they do not take very long. The characters for a whole story or fairy tale could be made. We have even seen an ill child in hospital who had a set of nurses, doctor and a patient! At night time they can be the child's alter ego who re-lives the day's adventures.

For knitters who can use 4 needles.

YOU WILL NEED

- Scraps of DK wool in various colours – for faces use beige, brown or pale pink
- 4 knitting needles, 3mm/US size 2
- Crochet hook, 3mm/US C
- Fleece or cotton wool for stuffing
- 2 small bells for the jester
- Gold ribbon for the princess's crown

1. BASIC PATTERN FOR ALL PUPPETS

Cast on 18 sts over two knitting needles (to make sure that the bottom edge is not too tight)

Distribute the 18 sts over three knitting needles (6 sts on each)

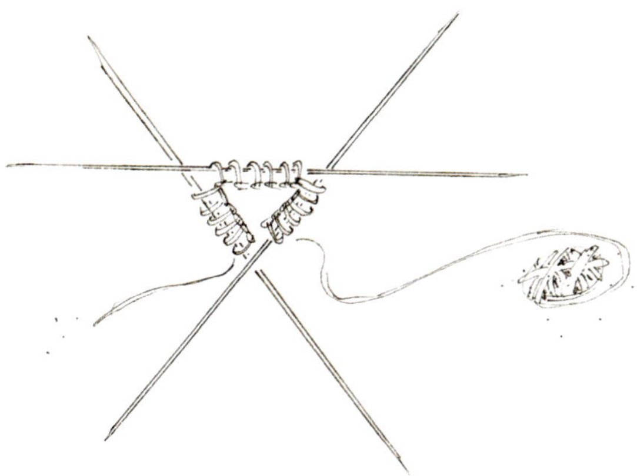

K 26 rounds in one of your body colours (it will come out as st st in the round)
Change to face colour and k 10 rounds
For puppets with hats, change to the hat colour and finish as for the animals etc below.
For the animals or puppets without hats:
Next row: Ktog 1st and 2nd st of each needle
Repeat for the next 2 rounds (9 sts)

2. Break the yarn and thread it through the 9 sts with a needle. Pull the stitches together, closing the top of the head. Stuff the head. Thread a piece of wool through the top of the body where it meets with the face and draw together tightly to form the head. Secure the thread with a knot and sew the ends in securely.

3. Many kinds of hairstyle are possible. They are all sewn on in the same way. Choose the colour of the hair and thread a length of that wool onto a big darning needle. Make a loop (a big one for long hair, a small one for shorter hair) and right next to it make a small backstitch to stop the loop from sliding.

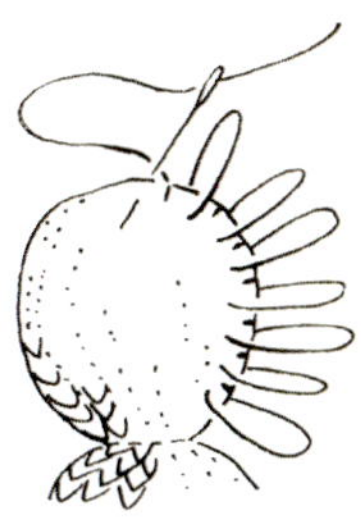

4. Continue with these loops until the head is covered. For some dolls you will need very little hair around the hats; for others you may want to cut the loops open.

Here are a few characters for your cast of finger puppets.

Boy (a lovely rascal)

1. Following the basic pattern (see page 167), start the body with 16 rounds in dark green and then 10 rounds in yellow. Knit the head in a face colour.

2. For the hat use red and knit 3 rounds. On the 4th and 5th rounds, decrease by knitting together the 1st and 2nd stitch of each needle, also as above. Cut your wool, leaving 15cm/6" and thread this through the remaining stitches. Draw up tightly and sew securely on the inside of the puppet. Stuff the puppet and finish as shown in basic pattern.

3. The boy has short brown hair (leaving the hair loops uncut makes his hair looks curly).

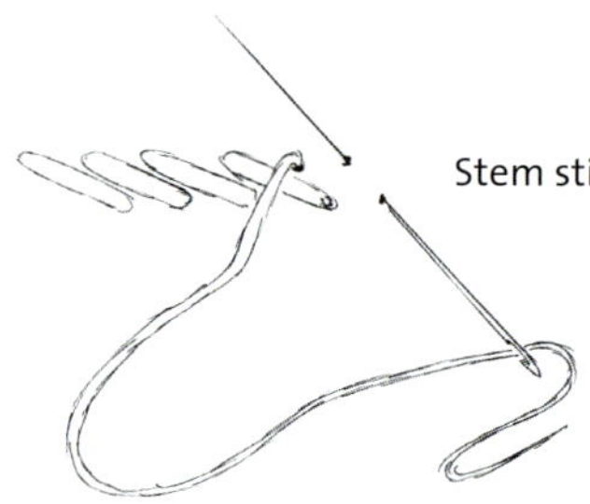
Stem stitch

4. Embroider braces over the yellow jumper using green thread in stem stitch (see right). The eyes and mouth can be embroidered, if required.

Princess

1. The body of this beautiful puppet is knitted in a soft pink or blue and the head in face colour, as described in the basic pattern. Follow the pattern for stuffing and finishing the puppet. She has long hair and around her head she wears a crown made from a piece of gold ribbon, which is sewn together at the back of the head.

2. Her eyes and a mouth can be embroidered. Use pins to see where to put the features, with the eyes halfway down and forming a triangle with the small mouth.

Lion

1. Knit the body and the head in golden yellow as described in the pattern. Stuff and divide the head from the body.

2. TO MAKE THE EARS
With the crochet hook, pick up the first stitch at the side of the head
Pull the yarn through and crochet 2 chain sts
Make 3 treble sts into the 1st chain st
Cut the yarn and pull through last st
Sew the ear onto the head

3. Make one more ear for the other side, then embroider the face and make the mane with thick, dark brown wool.

Elephant

1. Knit the basic body and head with grey wool. Stuff and divide the head from the body as described in the pattern.

2. TO MAKE THE TRUNK:
Cast on 6 sts over three needles (2 on each) – you can use cocktail sticks as needles
K until it reaches 1½cm/⅝"
To decrease:
K2tog, k to end of round
K 5 rounds
K2tog, k to end of round
K 4 rounds

3. Cut the yarn, leaving 10cm/4" and thread this through the remaining 4 stitches and pull together, sewing the thread in securely.

4. Carefully sew the trunk onto the middle of the elephant's face.

5. TO MAKE THE EARS (USING TWO NEEDLES)
Cast on 3 sts
1st row: K to end
2nd row: Inc 1, k to last st, inc 1
3rd row: Repeat previous row (7 sts)
K 18 rows
To decrease:
22nd row: Dec 1, k to last st, dec 1
23rd row: Repeat previous row (3 sts)
K 1 row
Cast off

6. Make another ear. Then sew the ears onto the sides of the head and embroider the eyes with black yarn.

Witch

Here is a not-really-scary witch!

1. Knit the body in purple and the face in yellowish-white, using the basic pattern above. Stuff and divide the head from the body as described.

2. TO MAKE A HEADSCARF (USING 2 NEEDLES)
With some very bright green wool, cast on 1 st
Working in st st, inc 1 st at each end of every alternate row until you have 28 sts
Cast off

3. Sew the headscarf onto the head. Make some hair with orange wool, cutting the loops open, as described in the basic pattern.

4. TO MAKE THE WITCH'S NOSE:
Pick up a st in the middle of the face with the crochet hook (use the same method as the lion's ears)
Crochet 4 chain sts

5. Break the yarn, pull the end through the last chain st and sew onto the face, as shown.

The witch could have green eyes and a rather large mouth.

Jester

1. Following the basic pattern, knit 16 rounds for the body with plain red wool. On the next round knit with yellow wool and then alternate red and yellow rounds until there are 26 rounds (5 yellow ones), ending on a red round. Knit 10 rounds in face colour then change to yellow.

2. TO MAKE THE HAT
Pick up 9 stitches on a safety pin
Divide the 9 over 3 needles (you can use cocktail sticks as needles)

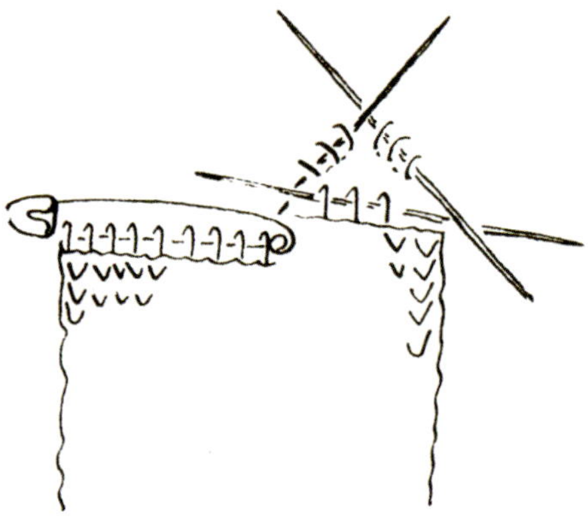

K 8 rounds, alternating red and yellow
9th row: (decrease) k to last 2 sts, k2tog (7 sts)
K 3 rounds
13th row: (decrease) k to last 2 sts, k2tog (5 sts)
K 3 rounds
17th row:, (decrease) k to last 2 sts, k2tog (3 sts)

3. Break the thread and pull it through the remaining 3 sts and tightly draw together. Sew a little bell onto the end of the hat. Then pick up the 9 sts from the safety pin and knit the other side of the hat as described above, starting with yellow wool.

4. Stuff and finish the puppet as shown in the basic pattern above. He has a ring of short brown hair around his hat. The eyes and a mouth can be embroidered onto his face.

Give all your finger puppets a home and see how creative your storytelling can become.

Long Woolly Hat

Most young children love to wear a real gnome's hat! Parents are happy with that too, as it really covers the ears and does not keep falling off. You can knit it in just one colour or you can do it in stripes or even in a simple Fair Isle pattern. The size given fits a 1–6-year-old. For teenagers and adults to make.

YOU WILL NEED

- DK wool, 80gm/3oz
- 2 knitting needles for ribbing, 3mm/US size 3
- 2 knitting needles, 4mm/US 6
- 1 button
- 1 crochet hook, 3.50mm/US size E

1. Cast on 98 sts on 3mm needles
K 20 rows [k1, p1]
Change to larger knitting needles (if you plan to knit in more than one colour, start the pattern or stripes here)
K 54 rows st st
Next row: Cast off 6 sts at the beg of next row (92 sts)
Repeat (86 sts)
K 2 rows
Next row: Cast off 6 sts at the beg of next row (80 sts)
Repeat (74 sts)
K 2 rows
Next row: Cast off 6 sts at the beg of next row (68 sts)
Repeat (62 sts)
On next right side row: k2tog, k to last 2 sts, k2tog (60 sts)
Knit 7 rows
Repeat previous 8 rows 16 more times (28 sts)
K 3 rows
Next row: [k2tog, k4] to end
K 3 rows
Next row: [k2tog, k3] to end
K 3 rows
Next row: [k2tog, k1] to end
K 3 rows
Next row: [k2tog] to end

2. Break the thread and run it through the remaining 5 stitches. Pull together and sew in securely. Fold the hat in half and sew the two edges together as shown.

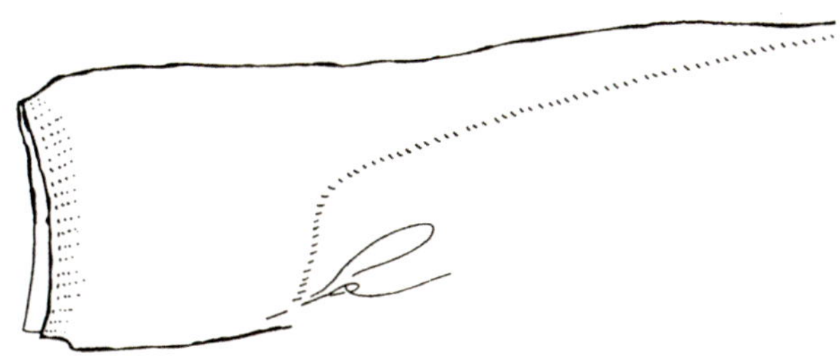

3. To neaten the neck edge, crochet around it using a crochet hook. Crochet a loop big enough to take the button, at the front corner of the neck edge on one side. Sew the button on the front corner of the neck edge on the other side. Make a pompom (see p 231) and fix it onto the end of the hat.

Ready to enjoy the cold winter fun!

Baby and Toddler's Sleeping Bag

In this bag your little one will always feel cosy and will never lie there cold and uncovered. It also stops lively toddlers from climbing out of their cots. The larger one has an open-ended zip, which runs from top to bottom and cannot be easily undone by your child. The smaller bag – for babies – can be made from thick woollen material which makes it ideal for going out in the pram on a cold day.

As the child will spend many hours in the bag, it is very important to use natural fabrics so that the child's skin can breathe. Suitable fabrics are: fine wool, brushed cotton, flannelette, Viyella or quilted cotton (the last of which does not need lining).

The small size is for a baby, about 4–9 months.
The large size is for a toddler, about 1–3 years.

YOU WILL NEED

FOR THE SMALL SIZE

- Outer fabric, 80 x 90cm/32 x 36", and lining fabric the same size
- Matching thread
- 1 zip, 50cm/20" long
- Bias binding in contrasting colour, 12mm/½" wide, 220cm/86" long

FOR THE LARGE SIZE

- Outer fabric, 220 x 90cm/86 x36", and lining fabric the same size
- Matching thread
- 1 open-ended zip, 60cm/24" long
- Bias binding in contrasting colour, 12mm/½" wide, 300cm/108" long

1. Make up the pattern (see page 173) and cut out all the pieces from the outer fabric and the lining (if you are using one). Putting the right sides together, pin and sew up both side seams from the under-arm edge to the bottom edge of the bag. Pin and sew shoulder seams. Pin and sew the centre front seam from the bottom edge to X. Sew along the bottom edge. Press seams open.

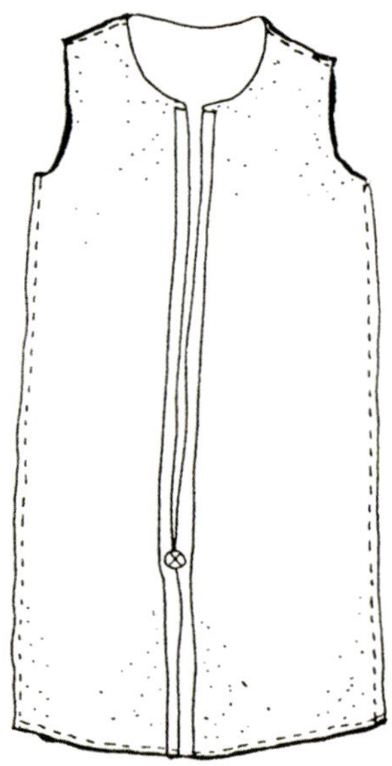

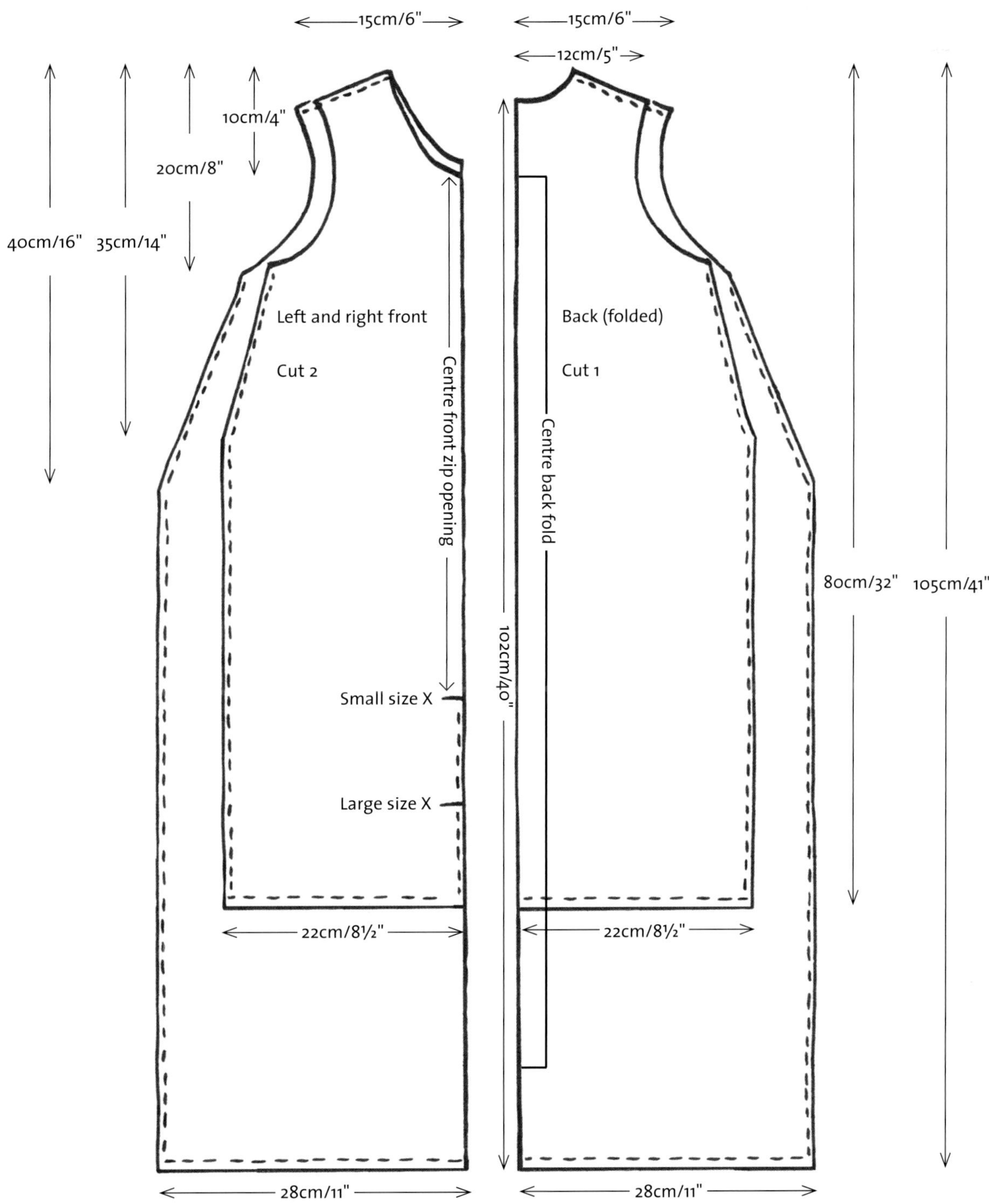

15cm/6"
15cm/6"
12cm/5"
10cm/4"
20cm/8"
40cm/16"
35cm/14"
Left and right front
Cut 2
Centre front zip opening
Small size X
Large size X
22cm/8½"
28cm/11"
Back (folded)
Cut 1
Centre back fold
102cm/40"
80cm/32"
105cm/41"
22cm/8½"
28cm/11"

2. Repeat this with the lining pieces. Turn only the outer fabric bag right side out. Push the lining into the outer bag then pin the lining into the outer bag with wrong sides together, matching all edges and seams. Tack around the neck edge and armholes. Turn in the edges along the zip opening and tack them together. Bind the armholes, neck edge and both edges of the zip opening with bias binding.

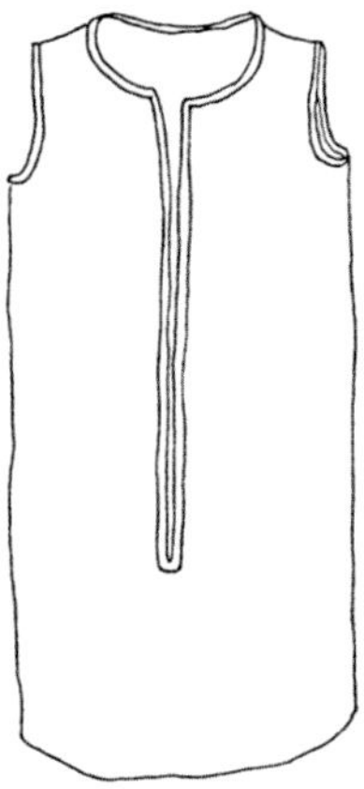

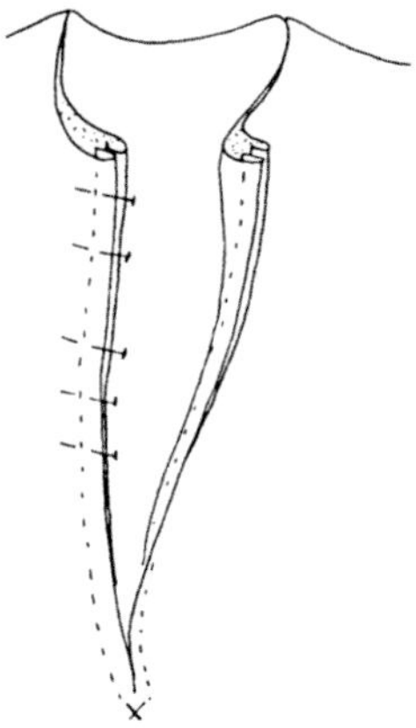

3. Pin, tack and sew the zip into the centre front opening.

Please note: For the large sleeping bag only, sew the open-ended zip to the bag so that it closes at the foot end. You pull the zip downwards to close it.

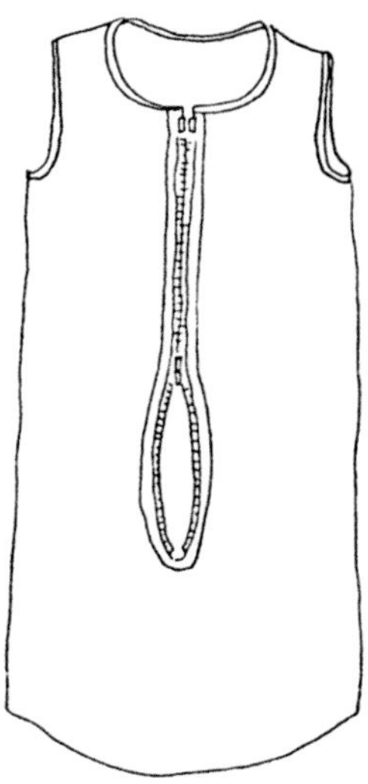

Ready for a bedtime story.

Basic Jumper

Knitting these not-so-large panels is fun. Use 100% pure wool in a child's pastel colour for utter cosy happiness. Don't forget to look at the washing instructions on the wool label.

The jumper has ribbing at the bottom, around the cuffs and across the shoulders. You can decide how wide you want the neck opening to be and sew together the front and back along the shoulder accordingly. For a young child, sew one or two buttons onto each shoulder front and make corresponding loops on the shoulder back to attach and close.

Easy knitting, so suitable for beginners.

How to knit a jumper to size

Once you know how to work out your own pattern, knitting becomes really enjoyable! Here is the basic pattern for a jumper, which can be made with or without sleeves.

It looks great on a baby or an adult. You can use thick or thin wool or cotton.

To be sure the new jumper will fit properly measure an existing one that fits well. Draw a sketch of the jumper and enter all the basic measurements.

1. To judge how much wool you will need, weigh the jumper – as long as it is knitted with the same kind of wool you are going to use for the new jumper. (If you don't have a similar jumper, enquire at your local wool shop or knitting club.) As stitch tensions differ from person to person, you must find out how many stitches you knit to the centimetre/inch.

2. To do this, knit a sample piece: cast on about 30 stitches (not so many for thick wool and large needles, and more with the fine yarn and small needles). The sample piece should be at least 12cm/5" wide and about 5cm/2" long. Lay the knitting on a flat surface – do not to stretch it. Insert two pins 10cm/4" apart.

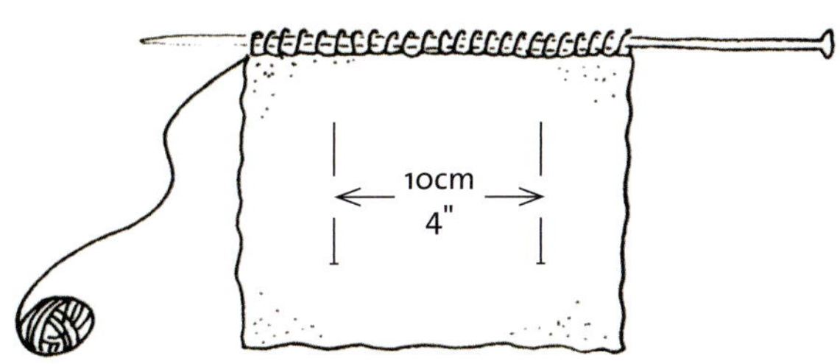

3. Count the number of stitches between the pins, divide this number by 10 for cm or 4 for inches and you will know how many stitches you need per centimetre/inch. You can now work out how many stitches you need to make your home-designed jumper in the right size.

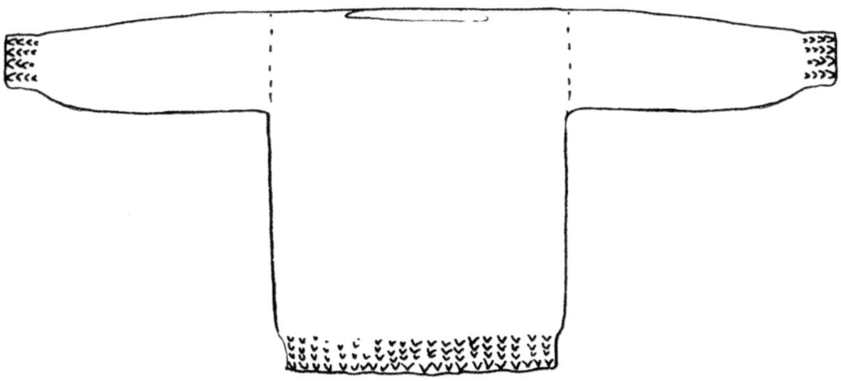

1. FRONT AND BACK

Cast on the number of sts needed to get the right width (see page 175)
[K1, p1] until it reaches 5cm/2" (for a baby's jumper to 3cm/1¼" in [k1, p1])
Continue in st st until 7cm/2¾" below the shoulder line (for a baby's jumper, knit to 4cm/1½" below the shoulder line)
Next row: [K1, p1] to end
Cast off loosely and repeat

2. TO MAKE THE SLEEVES:

Cast on the number of sts needed for the width of the sleeve around the armhole (see page 175)
Knit the length of the sleeve minus the ribbing around the cuff in st st, ending on a wrong side row
Next row: [k2, k2tog] to end of row
Continue knitting in [k1, p1] for another 4cm/1½" for the cuff (for baby's jumper only 2½cm/1" long)

3. TO MAKE UP

Sew the shoulder seams together on each side as far as you wish towards the neck opening. Sew in the sleeve then join the sleeve and side seams. If you use buttons, sew them onto the jumper front and make corresponding loops on the back.

Mittens

These mittens make a lovely present and they are simple and straightforward to make.

The pattern is for a child 6–8 years old. Sizes for 1 -year-olds and 2–3-year-olds are given in brackets. This is an easy knitting project.

YOU WILL NEED

- Warm colour DK wool, 50gm/2oz
- 2 knitting needles for ribbing, 3mm/US size 2
- 2 knitting needles, 3.5mm/US size 4

1. Using 3mm needles, cast on 48 (34, 40) sts
Work 38 (30, 34) rows in [k2, p2]
Change to 3.5mm and work in garter stitch
Inc 1 st, k to end
Repeat previous row
K14 (8, 10) rows

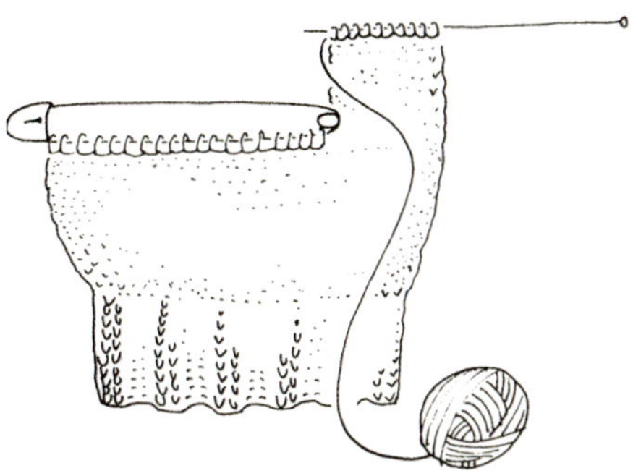

2. TO SHAPE THE THUMB
Next row: Work with the first 14 (10, 12) sts only, leaving the other 36 (26, 30) on a stitch holder*
K 18 (12, 14) rows
Next row: [K2tog] to end
Next row: P to end
Break thread and draw through remaining sts and sew in securely
Pick up sts from stitch holder and knit 36 (24, 28) rows
Next row: [K2tog] to end
Next row: P to end
Next row: [K2tog] to end
Next row: P to end
Break thread and draw through remaining sts and sew in securely.

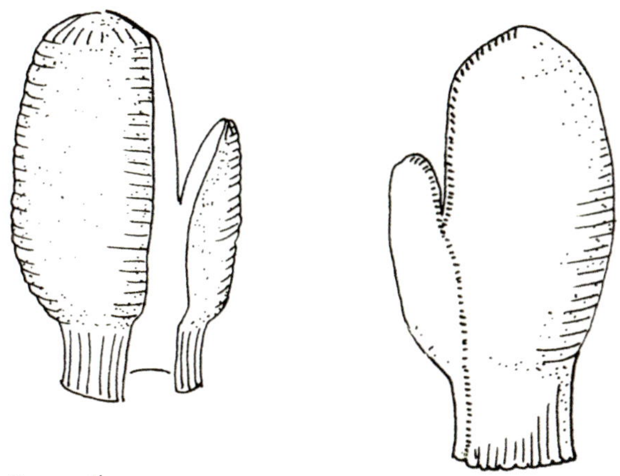

3. Sew up the seams

For the other mitten use the same pattern but with the thumb on the other side.
at * start by leaving the first 36 (26, 30) sts on a stitch holder and knit with the last 14 (10, 12) sts.

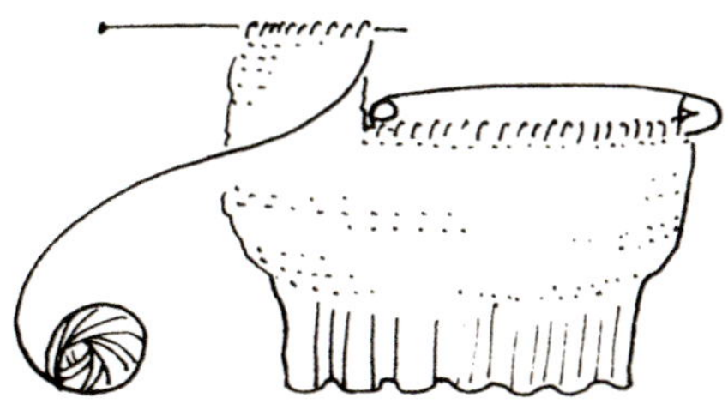

Ready for Jack Frost!

Halloween Lantern

Autumn's dying down gesture is celebrated, as it promises new life in spring within each seed. However, a balanced approach is required here, especially for very small children.

Here is a friendly Jack o' Lantern.

YOU WILL NEED

- A pumpkin
- A knife and a spoon
- A night-light candle

1. Cut a large circle in one piece, out of the top of the pumpkin – hold your knife at an angle so when you put the cut piece back it does not fall through the hole. This is his hat.

2. Gouge out all the seeds and flesh as far as you can, without making a hole in the outside. The flesh can be used to make a delicious warming soup and you can roast the seeds to make tasty nibbles.

3. Mark a friendly face on the side of the pumpkin and cut it out. Place the night-light in the bottom and light it when it is dark.

Your Jack o' Lantern is ready to be put on a windowsill to show his golden light – and the Halloweeners will knock on your door!

Hanging Pockets

These can be made to match your children's bedroom colours. They are great for tidying up bits and bobs, small dolls, hats and gloves – you name it! There are two sizes. These can made by older teenagers or adults.

Smaller pockets

YOU WILL NEED

- Plain calico (your choice of colour), 40 x 63cm/16 x 25" for the backing
- Matching gingham, 36 x 51cm/14 x 20" for the pockets
- Optional trimmings, such as rick rack or broderie anglaise
- Wooden dowel, 6mm/¼" diameter, 40cm/16" long
- Thin cord, 50cm/20" long
- Sewing machine and sewing cotton

1. Fold over 1cm/½" on all four sides of the calico backing. Press then fold over another 1cm/½" on the two long sides and one short side at the bottom. Press and tack. Turn over the top short side by 5cm/2" then press and tack. This will be the channel for your dowling.

2. Cut the gingham across the width into three strips. Each strip is 36cm/14" long and there are three widths: 14cm, 17cm and 20cm (5½, 6½ and 8"). Fold over 1cm/½" on all four sides of each strip then press and tack. Tack the optional trim to one long side of each strip then machine it.

3. Tack the widest strip to the bottom of the calico on three sides, leaving the top open. Pin the middle strip to the calico 3cm/1¼" above the first strip and tack as before. Pin the narrowest strip to the calico 3cm/1¼" above the middle strip and tack it. Machine all the seams.

4. Decide how wide the pockets should be and machine from the top to the bottom of the strips accordingly.

5. For further decoration, cut out felt names, hearts, flowers, etc and fix them on the space at the top. Slide the dowel through the seam at the top. Tie the cord to each end so you can hang up the pockets.

Larger pockets

YOU WILL NEED

- Cotton drill or denim, 90 x 70cm/36 x 28" for the backing
- Cotton drill in a different colour, 114 x 66cm/45 x 26" for the pockets
- Wooden dowel, 2cm/¾" diameter, 1m/40" long

1. Hem the backing denim as the calico for the smaller pockets with a wide seam on one long edge to form the top tube.

2. Cut the fabric for the pockets down the length into three strips, 20cm/8" wide. Assuming you are making four generous pockets on each strip, allow 3cm/1¼" on each side of a pocket to make a pleat.

3. Hem all four sides of each strip as with the smaller pockets. Mark the width of each pocket and its pleats and pin it together. Tack the first strip to the bottom of the backing. Measure 2cm/¾" up and pin the middle strip to the backing then tack it on. Repeat for the top strip and tack it on. Machine all seams.

4. Slide the dowel through the seam at the top of the pockets then hang the projecting ends on two hooks fixed to the wall.

Sandman

Friendly dreams will come very quickly when this soft cuddly sandman shares a child's pillow. For a teenager or adult to make.

YOU WILL NEED

- Pale blue brushed cotton or flannelette (for softness), 50 x 40cm/20 x 16"
- Scraps of soft yellow and peach felt
- Teased and washed fleece
- Needle and thread
- Embroidery thread

1. Fold the flannelette fabric in half and cut the two main pattern pieces.

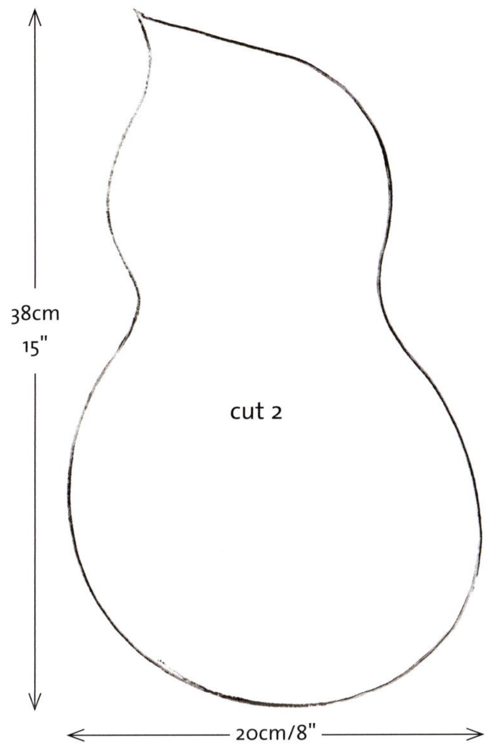

2. Cut four small and two large stars and the moon from the yellow felt. Cut the face and hands from the peach felt. Pin in position as shown on the pattern. Stitch in place using a small running stitch.

3. Sew the face in stem stitch using pale blue embroidery thread. With right sides together, sew the body pieces together, leaving an opening at the bottom.

4. Fill lightly with fleece. Close the opening, turning in raw edges.

Goodnight and sweet dreams!

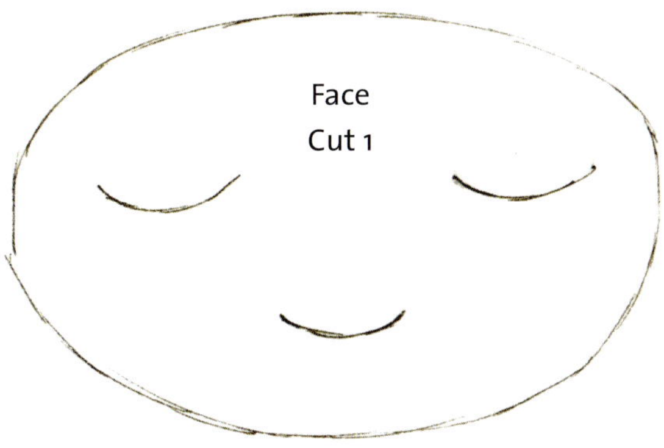

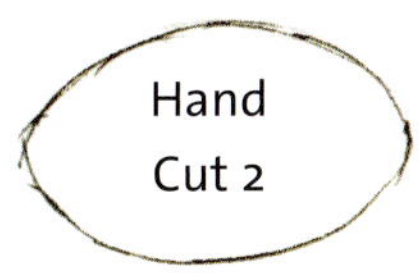

NB: Pattern pieces are actual size.

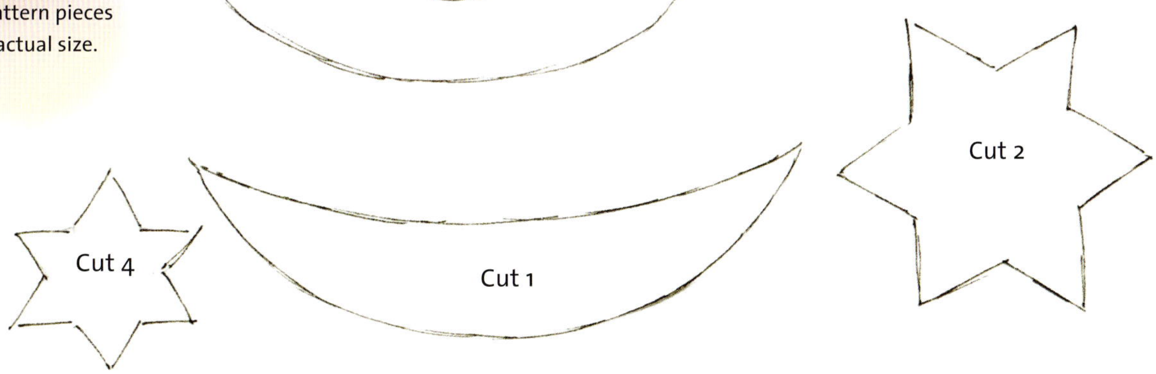

Magic Ball of Wool

This is a most original present, especially loved by children who enjoy knitting. The idea is that as the child knits, little presents appear and fall out of the ball of wool. It is best made from double knitting wool – as always, choose a nice colour!

The little presents should be chosen to suit the age, taste and interests of the child. The presents can be either wrapped up in pretty paper or used just as they are. For a young knitter to make.

YOU WILL NEED

- Ball of DK wool
- Little bits and pieces, such as: little stones, hairclips, necklaces, tiny toys, bells, shells, coins, shiny buttons, sweets (chocolates may melt), flowerseeds, little candles, ribbons, bits of lace, charms, crayons, notepad, spinning top, yo-yo, beads, tiny animals made from clay or wood, little soaps, etc Use your imagination!

1. Start by putting the most special or precious present in the middle of the ball.

2. Wrap the wool around it and keep adding more presents as you wind the wool into a magic ball.

Candle Lake

Imagine a darkened room with lots of greenery, heavy with the scent of resin and wax. Small candles light up a glistening, sparkling little lake on a table. Crystals and pebbles shine as if alight themselves. Quiet small faces are transfixed by the magic.

YOU WILL NEED

- A large bowl, a baby bath or large deep plastic tray (could be a photographic tray)
- A low table
- Aluminium cooking foil
- Crystals, pebbles, shells, small stones, 1 or 2 large stones
- Sprigs of evergreen in small vases
- Dark blue fabric to drape around the outside
- Night-light candles – 1 or 2 for each child – don't remove them from their aluminium case
- Pins, tape, Blu-Tack

1. Keep all your children out of the room till you are quite ready – that way it will be a real surprise. Put the bowl onto the low table. Drape the cloth around the outside of the bowl and secure with tape, pins, Blu-Tack.

2. Cover the inside of the bowl with aluminium foil and wrap it over the rim to cover the top edge of the blue cloth. Place pebbles and shells across the bottom of the bowl and make some little hills with the stones.

3. Fill the bowl with water, leaving the tops of the islands dry, until it looks right.

4. Put the greenery and crystals on the islands and around the edge if your bowl has one. When it is completely dark outside, place one candle in the water and light it.

5. Switch off all the lights. Quietly welcome everyone in to see the candle lake. Give each child their own candle, light it and then they can float it in the warm quiet.

Pure magic!

Please note: Never leave a lit candle unattended.

Winter

Soon after the equinox – when night and day are equals – the darkness quickly gains the upper hand. Every afternoon gets shorter and darker. Storms batter the land and when the pale sun briefly appears it slants down from between deep purple clouds. Soon the cold overtakes the wet. Now the trees' bare branches are sharply silhouetted against a pale mauve sky – the wind is nippy.

During the long night the stars sparkle brightly in a gigantic crisp sky. Down below, the first iced-over puddles crack underfoot. The Earth crystallises in shivery cold. A deep hush falls over the land. High time to hurry home and make it as warm and cosy as possible.

But not before we have gathered some winter greenery. In this seemingly dead world the fresh evergreens seem to have eternal life. There is the fragrantly festive upright pine with its strong symmetry and glossy, spiky needles; the prickly holly with its blood red berries; the mistletoe, bringer of love and friendship; and the ivy which, like most of us, needs a strong base to grow.

There are many festivals during this time, so I have included many different tables.

Advent Table

Every year I am impressed by the rapid succession of festivals during this time. They have evolved over centuries and they all keep us busy in an indoors and inward way. The festivals are partly from pre-Christian times and partly from Christian times, as well as from the West and the East.

The biggest festival is of course Christmas and the preparation time for that is Advent. Advent starts on the fourth Sunday before Christmas. Christmas is a fixed date. When it falls on a Sunday then Advent will be longest: 28 days (four weeks). When Christmas is on a Monday then Advent will be shortest: 22 days long (three weeks and one day).

The Advent table can be made meaningful by starting very sparsely and slowly and building it up in four stages around a star path over the whole Advent period.

YOU WILL NEED

- Deep royal blue (ultramarine) fabric sufficient to cover the table and the backdrop
- Backdrop construction materials (see nature table scenery, page 11)
- A few small logs between 20cm/8" and 30cm/12" long
- Stick-on gold stars
- Mary and Joseph (see crib figures, page 192)

1. Drape the backdrop with the blue fabric. Make a simple stable, using a few small logs. It can be quite primitive; it is not a major construction! Mark out a meandering star path across the table from one edge to the stable. Remember to leave space for new features to be added later. Stick gold stars onto the blue material to mark the route. Each star represents one day of Advent.

2. Every day Mary and Joseph take one step on this star path towards the stable where, on Christmas Day, the holy child will join them. As they make their journey, the table can be built up slowly over the four consecutive weeks.

3. The four realms of Nature appear one after the other on each Sunday. The first week shows the mineral world; so now you can find a special place for your crystals and a gnome. A tea light can bring a little light to the darkest week of the Advent table.

On the second Sunday the plant world joins the table; add some flowers from your garden or a little house plant. Large pine cones, set point upwards, look like pine trees in the background.

The third Sunday sees the animal world join in; here you can display small wooden, clay or knitted animals.

Christmas in the fourth week completes the journey with the world of humankind: see the Christmas festival table on page 187.

Christmas Festival Table

On Christmas Eve you can place a festive red cloth under and in front of the stable. Mary and Joseph move into the stable. Rearrange your plants, crystals and animals to accommodate them.

On Christmas Day in the early morning the Christ child arrives, brought by an angel, which is suspended above the stable. The shepherds and their sheep join them too. Traditionally, the Three Kings arrive on 6 January.

During the twelve holy nights the table can remain to be admired and children will love to rearrange the animals.

When things start to look a little tired it can be discreetly refreshed.

The Christmas table can be followed by the Three Kings table, a snow table, if the weather is right, or you can set up a small simple winter table.

Three Kings Table

On Christmas Day the shepherds gather around the holy family in the stable. Traditionally, the Three Kings start their journey to follow the Star from far-away lands and arrive on 6 January, which is Epiphany – the Festival of the Three Kings.

The Christmas festival table is changed into quite a different setting. You can make it smaller and use a magenta or peach blossom cloth as a background. To complete the setting, fix a large star to the backdrop and add a beautiful seasonal flowering plant, a white candle and a crystal.

The Three Kings bring their offerings.

Simple Winter Table

If we want just a little reminder for ourselves, for teenagers or for older people, we can simply follow nature's colour mood with a few extras. You can use a deep royal blue (ultramarine) table mat or a felt square (30 x 30cm/12 x 12") with the corners rounded off. Place on it a simple vase that holds some beautiful twigs, like crack willow, bright red maple or dogwood, with some evergreens.

You can display an art card depicting a wintery scene. A white or purple quartz crystal and a white candle can complete your creation.

Snow Table

If the weather changes dramatically to snow, your winter table can change too. Snow brings fun.

Smooth white silk spread around an 'icy' mirror makes a frozen pond where gnomes and small folk frolic. Use pale grey material for the backdrop. Snow crystals in the form of straw stars can hang from bare branches.

Towards Valentine's Day, red hearts (see page 225) can be added. Snowdrops are out by now and can be added too – the whole can be lit by tea lights or electric tree lights.

Advent Wreath

Christmas seems to move forward every year. In shops one can buy Christmas trees already at the beginning of Advent. It is very difficult to find the patience to wait until Christmas to put up the Christmas tree but traditionally it only belongs to the twelve holy nights. Advent is a lot easier to celebrate if you have an Advent wreath and a calendar.

On the wreath are four candles. If you have time, it is very nice to set a few minutes aside, just before the children's bedtime, to have the rooms darkened and the candles lit.

Just one is lit in the first week, two in the second week, three in the third and in the last week before Christmas there are four candles shining out into the dark to herald the coming of the light in the darkness.

A simple Advent song is all that is needed to make a much appreciated ceremony.

YOU WILL NEED

- A wreath base, which can be bought in a florist (or use a cheap plastic wreath and remove the artificial greenery)
- Clean, fresh branches of spruce (the Christmas tree type). You will need more than you think!
- Green twine
- Secateurs
- 4 red ribbons, each approx 70cm/28" long
- 4 red candles
- 4 Advent wreath candle holders or firm copper wire, about 40cm/16" long
- Pair of pliers

1. It is easier to work on the kitchen worktop, as a lot of greenery will fall off.

2. Cut small sprigs of greenery. Using the base as a foundation, and always laying them in the same direction, place several sprigs together around it and tie them on with twine.

3. Repeat this process, filling it out nicely and evenly into a firm, well-proportioned wreath. Always cover up the twine with new sprigs. The last ones are a bit more difficult to fit in – just push them into place. Turn the wreath over and repeat the process so that it becomes evenly rounded all over. Tie the red ribbons to the wreath with bows, equally spaced around it. Then place the candles in their holders in the space between the ribbons.

4. Alternatively, you can make your own fixing using the copper wire. Cut the wire into four pieces as long as the depth of the wreath plus 2cm/1". Using the pliers, heat one end of the copper over a fire until the wire is very hot.

5. Hold the candle and steadily push the very hot wire into the base of the candle to a depth of 3cm/1½". Allow it to cool and push the wire straight into the wreath. If you have no space on a sideboard or shelf, you can suspend the wreath from the ceiling using much longer red ribbons.

On Christmas Eve the wreath makes way for the tree, which in its turn lasts through the twelve holy nights.

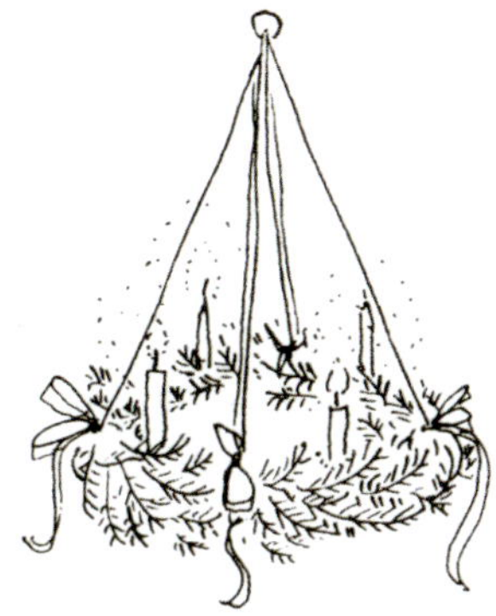

Please note: Never leave a lit candle unattended.

Christmas Door Wreath

Welcome your visitors with a festive sight by hanging a slightly different wreath on your front door.

YOU WILL NEED

- A wreath base, available at florists, or use a cheap plastic wreath with the artificial greenery removed
- Clean, fresh branches of spruce (the Christmas tree type). You will need more than you think!
- Green twine and florist wire
- Secateurs
- 4 red ribbons, each approx 70cm/28" long
- Assorted natural decorations, such as red berries, dried orange slices, cinnamon sticks, pine cones, dried Japanese lantern flowers.

Make the base as in the previous wreath (above). Tie the red ribbons to the wreath with bows, equally spaced around it. Fix the decorations all around the wreath, using the string or wire. This wreath will last longer if it is not directly exposed to the wind and rain.

Crib Figures

These figures are the focal point of the Advent and Christmas tables. They require medium ability in cutting and sewing. Baby Jesus is very small and delicate and the most difficult to make.

Mary

YOU WILL NEED

- Firm bundle of fleece, 11cm/4½" long and about 2.5cm/1" diameter
- Piece of red felt for dress, 9 x 13cm/3½ x 5"
- Piece of blue felt for cloak, 13 x 16cm/5 x 6¼"
- Piece of pink stockinette, 8 x 12cm/3 x 4"
- Thread
- Scraps of light yellow fleece or wool for hair

1. Wind some thread around the fleece to keep it in shape. Form a head shape at the top end by tightly tying around the neck, about 2.5cm/1" from the end. Cut an 8cm/3" square of stockinette and tie this over the head.

2. Fold the piece of red felt in half by bringing the short sides together and sew up the seam. Run a gathering thread around the edge at one end then put the dress over the roll of wool, with the seam at the back, and draw the gathering thread tight around the neck and secure. The figure should stand up.

3. Place some light yellow wool on the head for hair and sew in place with a few stitches. Lay the piece of blue felt horizontally, wrap it around the head and shoulders and secure it in place with a few small stitches.

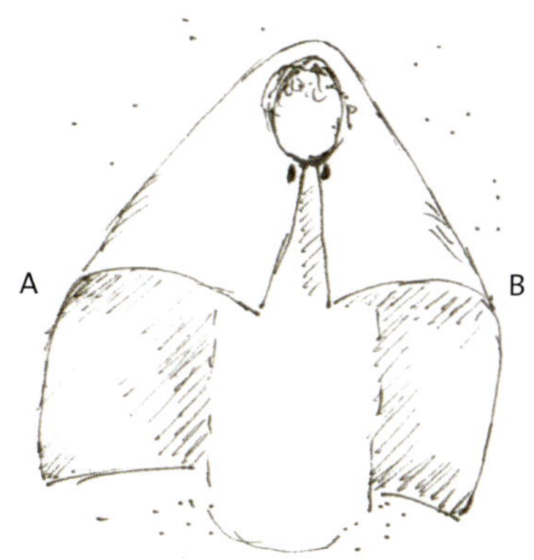

4. Bring A and B towards the middle forming a 'wrist' in each fold.

5. Make the hands by tying two tiny bits of fleece into scraps of stockinette. Sew the hands into the 'wrist' folds of the cloak then round off the corners of the cloak at the bottom in the front, as shown right.

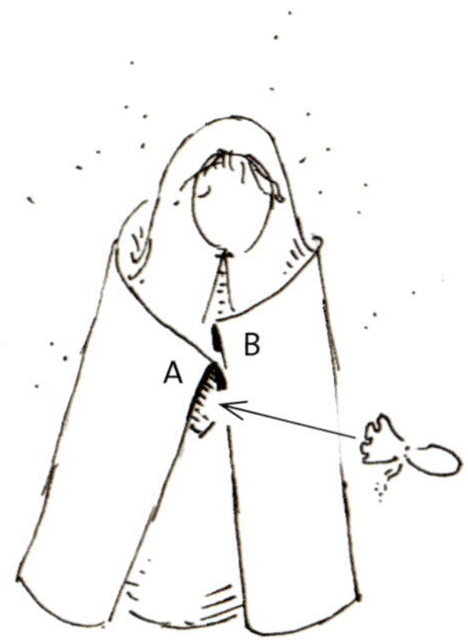

Baby Jesus

YOU WILL NEED

- Piece of fleece, 6cm/2½" long and about 1.5cm/¾" diameter
- Piece of pink stockinette, 6 x 6cm/2½ x 2½"
- Piece of white silk or fine cotton material, 24 x 12cm/9 x 5"
- Light-coloured embroidery cotton
- Needle and white cotton thread
- Pin

1. Form a head shape at the top end of the fleece by tightly tying around the neck. Cover the head with the square of stockinette and tie it around the neck (see Mary on page 193). Fold the silk (or cotton) in half to make a square, wrap it around the head and stitch in place under the chin.

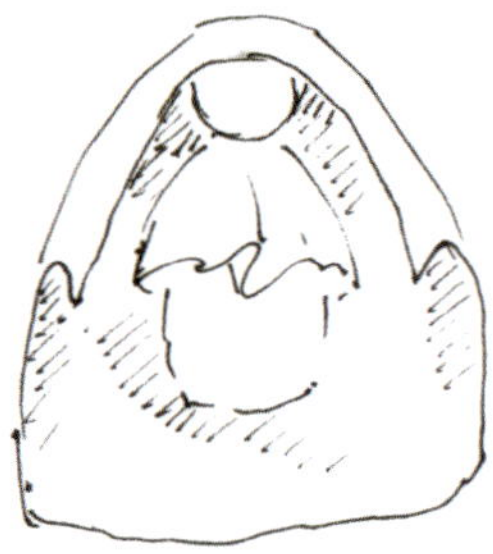

2. Fold the bottom of the silk over the body. Tuck under raw edges, tightly bundle up the little one with the seam at the back and pin it in place. Sew it up and swaddle with embroidery silk

Joseph

YOU WILL NEED

- Firm bundle of fleece, 11cm/4½" long and about 2.5cm/1" diameter
- Piece of medium brown felt, 20 x 11cm/8 x 4½" for the robe
- Piece of dark brown felt, 9 x 12cm/3½ x 8¼" for the cloak
- Piece of stockinette, 8 x 10cm/3 x 4"
- Brown thread
- Scraps of grey fleece (or white) for beard and hair
- Pipe cleaner
- Small twig or stick for Joseph to hold

1. Make the head and body in the same way as described on page 193 for Mary. Push the pipe-cleaner through the wool roll just below the head, to make the arms.

2. Fold the brown piece of felt in half and cut out the robe (see below). Sew up the side seams and turn it inside out.

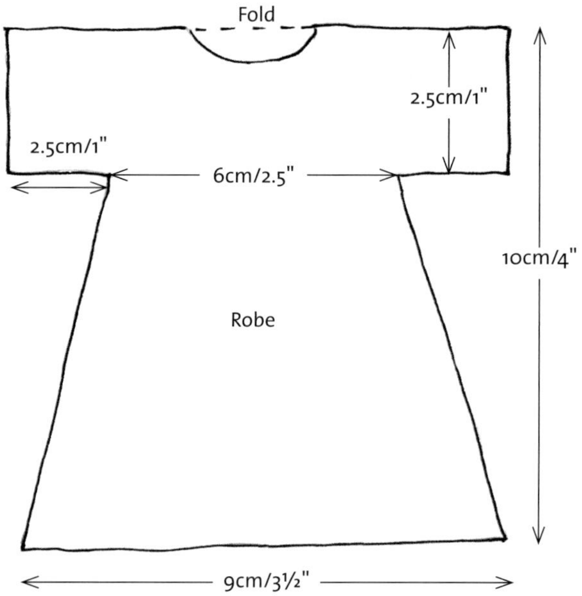

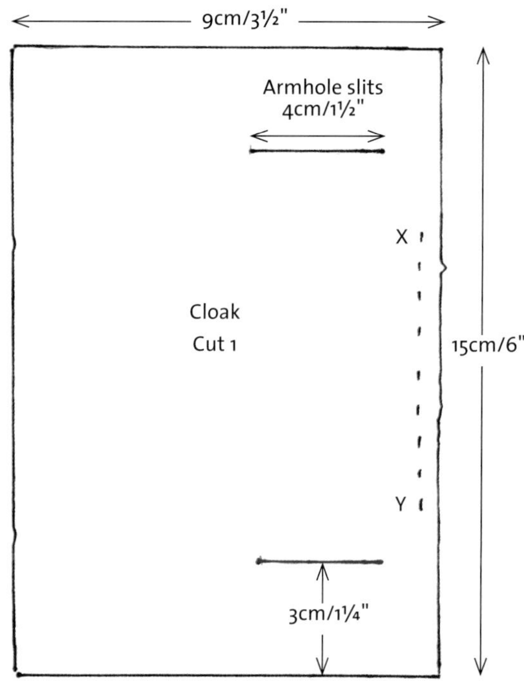

3. Run a gathering thread around the edge of the neck opening and put the robe on Joseph. Draw the gathering thread together tightly around the neck and secure it. Bend back the pipe cleaner if necessary so that the arms are the right length. Put a bit of fleece around the end of each pipe cleaner and tie some stockinette over it to make hands. Sew the sleeves around the hands with tiny stitches. Sew some hair and a beard to Joseph's head then make a cloak from the dark brown felt cut as shown (right).

4. Run a gathering thread from X to Y. Put the cloak around Joseph with his arms through the armhole slits. Draw in the gathering thread to fit round the neck at the back. Fold the front of the cloak as shown.

5. Hold the cloak together with a small stitch and round off the corners at the bottom.

6. To make the hat, cut a circle with a diameter of 6cm/2½" from the dark brown felt and run a gathering thread around this circle 1cm/½" from the edge. Draw the thread together slightly and sew the hat on Joseph's head.

7. Sew the stick to one of Joseph's hands with a few stitches.

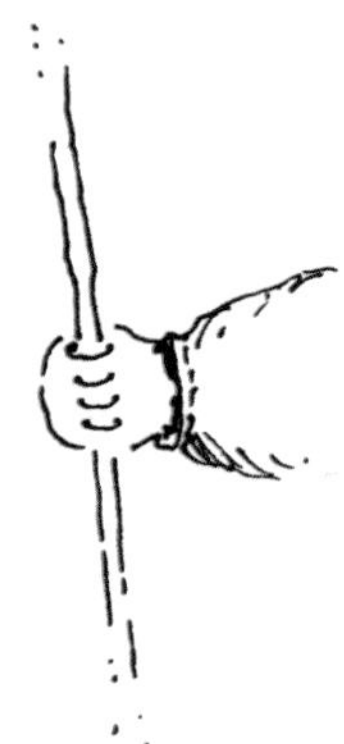

Shepherds can be made in the same way as Joseph, but use sheepskin instead of felt as a cloak.

The Three Kings

These are to be placed on the Three Kings table. They are made using the same base as the other crib figures.

The body and robes are made just like Joseph's (pages 194–5), only in different colours. Traditionally, Balthazar, the oldest, has white hair and a beard, and a blue robe and cloak. Melchior has brown hair, and a red robe and cloak. Caspar, the youngest, has dark skin and hair, and a green robe and cloak.

YOU WILL NEED

- Fleece (as for Joseph)
- Mid-red felt, 20 x 11cm/8 x 4½"
- Blue felt, 20 x 11cm/8 x 4½"
- Green felt, 20 x 11cm/8 x 4½"
- Silk matching the red, 20 x 14cm/8 x 5½"
- Silk matching the blue, 20 x 14cm/8 x 5½"
- Silk matching the green, 20 x 14cm/8 x 5½"
- Stockinette (as for Joseph)
- Red, blue and green thread
- Fleece scraps for beard and hair – white, brown and black
- Pipe cleaner
- Embroidery silk, 30cm/12" – red, blue and green
- Gold paper for crowns and gifts
- Watercolour paint to use as a dye if some of the colours are not available

1. Make the bodies and robes the same as for Joseph. Follow the suggestions for the colour of hair given above. If you do not have the right colour fleece you can dye it. Lay the piece on a non-staining surface and paint it with the watercolour and leave to dry. If necessary dye the silk in the same way and leave to dry.

2. To make the cloaks, hem the short ends, hem the bottom and make a seam for the top and insert the embroidery silk to create a cloak.

3. Make simple gold crowns and gifts and fix them in place.

Ox, Ass and Sheep

These animals are the humble witnesses in the Nativity stable. They are easy to make once the unusual method has been mastered. They are for teenagers or adults to make.

YOU WILL NEED

- A couple of lengths of pipe cleaner, about 20cm/8" long
- Half a handful of fleece

It's a good idea to practise the technique first. Pull off a little thin tuft of fleece and lay it on the top 2cm/¾" of the pipe cleaner and wrap it firmly around it once. Gently let go so that the fleece holds onto the cleaner and itself. Repeat this wrapping process adding the fleece gradually and evenly. The finished result should be smooth – neither too thin like knitting wool nor too fat with a loose bulge.

Once the technique is mastered it is easy to create the animals. These steps apply to all the animals.

1. Start by covering the individual bits of pipe cleaner with one layer of fleece.

2. Following the diagram, shape the outline of the head – find the right proportions and dimensions. Tightly wrap a thin layer of fleece around the head to give it volume.

3. Fold the legs in half and just lay them in place over the back. Fix them by wrapping with a bit of fleece.

4. Fix the ears and horns in the same way. Wrap more thin layers of fleece tightly but gently around the tummy and neck until the right volume has been reached.

Ox

YOU WILL NEED

- Red-brown teased wool fleece
- Pipe cleaner – 1 piece 20cm/8" long – for head, neck, body , tail all in one piece
- Pipe cleaner – 2 pieces 13cm/5"long – for the legs
- Pipe cleaner – 1 piece 8cm/3" long – for the ears
- Pipe cleaner – 1 piece 8cm/3" long – for the horns

Look at the diagrams for the animal's body stance and proportions – all legs are skinny at the hoof and fatter towards the body. The ox has a straight back with a head at right-angles facing down – its body mass is mainly around the neck and shoulders. The ass has a slightly curved back, longish neck and legs. The sheep has a straight back, very short neck and plenty of fleece!

Pipe cleaner

Fleece

Ass

YOU WILL NEED

- Grey teased wool fleece
- Pipe cleaner – 1 piece 18cm/7" long – for head, neck, body, tail all in one piece
- Pipe cleaner – 2 pieces 14cm/5½" long – for the legs
- Pipe cleaner – 1 piece 6cm/2½" long – for the ears

Sheep

YOU WILL NEED

- White teased wool fleece
- Pipe cleaner – 1 piece 11cm/4½" long – for head, neck, body , tail all in one piece
- Pipe cleaner – 2 pieces 8cm/3" long – for the legs
- Pipe cleaner – 1 piece 4cm/1½" long – for the ears

Fleece Wool Angel

This is a truly angelic creation. It can go at the top of your Christmas tree or, better still, above the Nativity crib. For nimble fingers.

YOU WILL NEED

- 50cm/20" of special wool fleece called 'roving' or tops (available from craft shops) torn or teased from a long length. You want the ends to be uneven not cut.
- White cotton thread
- Gold or silver thread
- Scissors
- A tiny gold or silver star small enough to go on the head (optional)

1. For the head and body, tease 30cm/12" from the wool roving and fold it in half. Tie a knot in the middle and carefully pull it tight.

2. Bring the two lengths together to form the body below the head – make sure one is at the front and one is at the back. Also make sure the 'head' and the 'hair' are facing you.

3. Wind the cotton two or three times round the neck and tie at the back, then knot the two loose ends together to form a loop for hanging up the finished angel.

4. Tease off two 10cm/4" pieces of fleece. Separate the front from the back and place the new short piece in between. Push it up to just beneath the head. This piece will be the arms and the wings.

5. Hold it all temporarily together with a clothes peg underneath the waist. Lay a 50cm/20" length of gold/silver thread round the back of the neck and pull it forward like a scarf.

6. Gently pull each end diagonally down across the chest to under the arms and then up diagonally across the back, continue over the shoulder to the front again and diagonally across the chest again, round the waist twice and tie a knot at the back and cut off the excess thread. Remove the peg.

7. To make the arms and wings, separate out one piece on either side to form the arms. Slightly twist the ends to keep them temporarily in shape.

8. Fold about 2cm/1" of fleece back on itself to form a small loop for the hands and then firmly tie it with the gold/silver thread to form the wrists.

Spread out the wings behind and above the head then spread the skirt into shape. If you have a tiny star, fix it on the hair above the forehead. Now your little angel is ready to enchant everyone.

Tissue Paper Angel

This delicate angel looks beautiful suspended over the stable or over a child's bed. Though it is simple, it is very delicate and requires precision cutting and tying.

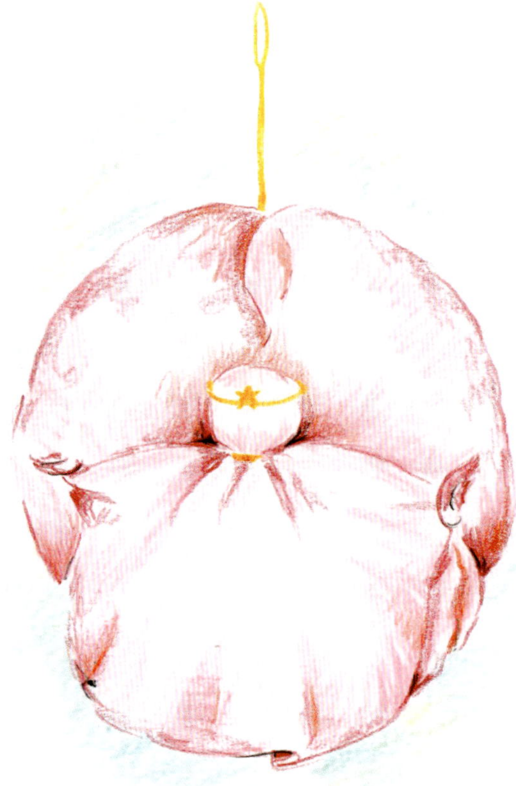

YOU WILL NEED

- Piece of tissue paper, 30 x 18cm/12 x 7" – pastel colour
- Small piece of fleece or cotton wool for the angel's head
- Gold or silver thread
- Tiny star/sequin (optional)
- Glue
- Scissors, compass and a ruler

1. Draw a circle on the tissue paper (diameter 16cm/6¼"). Cut it out within the pencil line, so the line does not show. Shape the fleece or cotton wool into the size of a marble and put this little ball of wool into the centre of the tissue paper circle. Wrap the tissue paper around the wool and tie under the head with some thread.

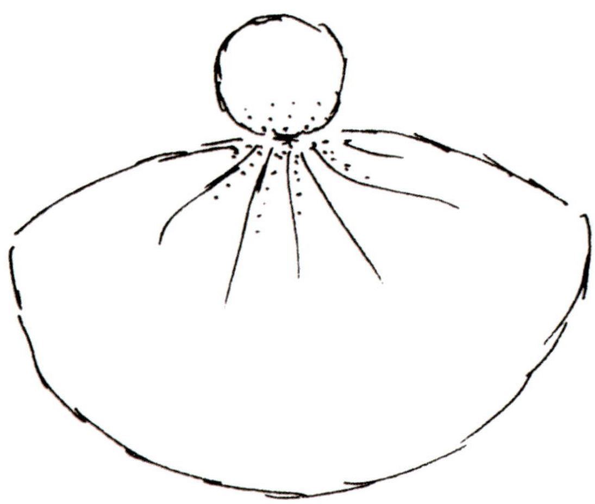

2. Make a little twist in the tissue paper at each side to form the arms and hands.

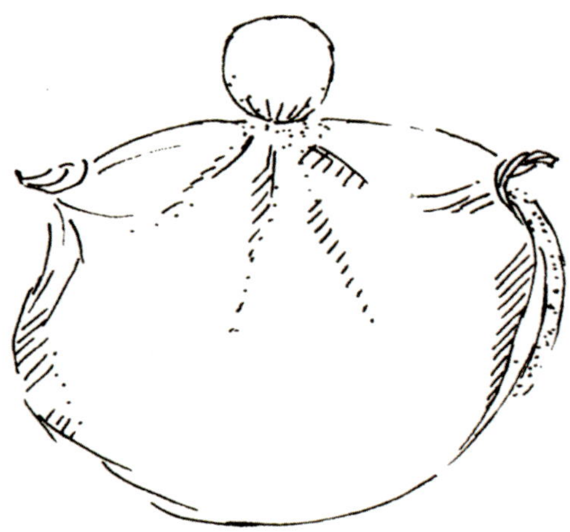

3. Arrange the dress at the back with two folds so that the wings can later be fixed more easily.

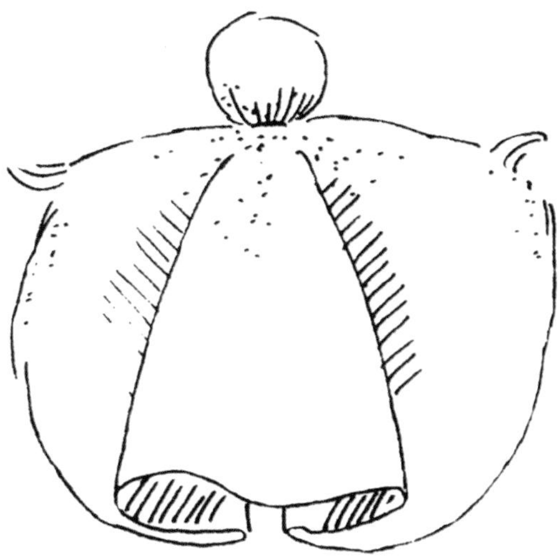

4. Cut out another circle from the tissue paper (diameter 14cm/5½") then fold the circle in half and shape it by cutting it as shown below.

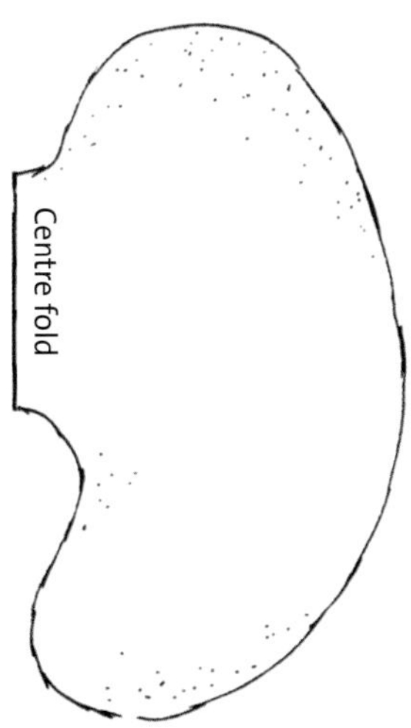

5. Bunch together the middle fold and tie some thread around it.

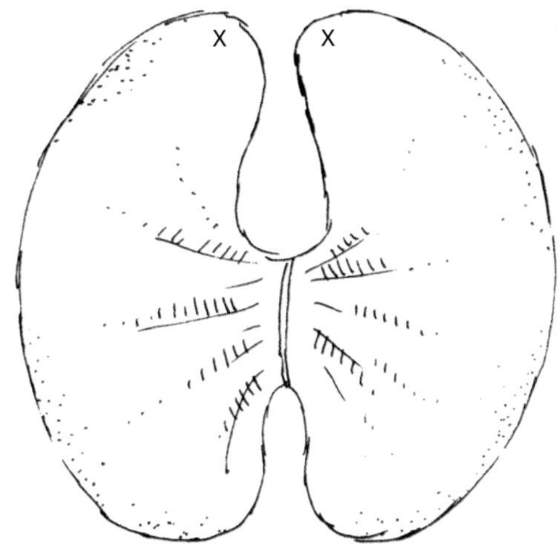

6. Tie the wings around the neck with a length of gold thread. Leave one end of the thread long so that the angel can hang from it. The thread must go behind the head and in front of the wings to keep the angel flying nicely. Use a little gold thread to tie around the angel's head for a crown. The knot must be at the back of the head.

7. Stick the tiny star onto the angel's forehead. Put a spot of glue at point X on the wings and glue them together. If you want to make a mobile, hang three or more angels on a piece of cane or covered ring.

Tissue Paper Stars

These stars look most effective in the window and really brighten up a grey, misty winter's day! An older child can make them but great care must be taken over folding them, as each fold must be very exact. After making one or two basic-shaped stars, it is great fun to experiment and make many variations by just folding the paper slightly differently. By altering the length of the sides of the paper or by adding twice as many points to the star, you will get surprising results. Here are some ideas.

Basic eight-pointed star

YOU WILL NEED

- Kite paper (or tissue paper) any size but 30 x 25cm/12 x 10" or 23 x 19cm/9 x 7½" are good starting sizes
- Glue stick
- A4 sheet of white paper
- Sharp scissors

NB: Always work on the white paper when making the folds. This allows you to see clearly where to overlap the tissue paper.

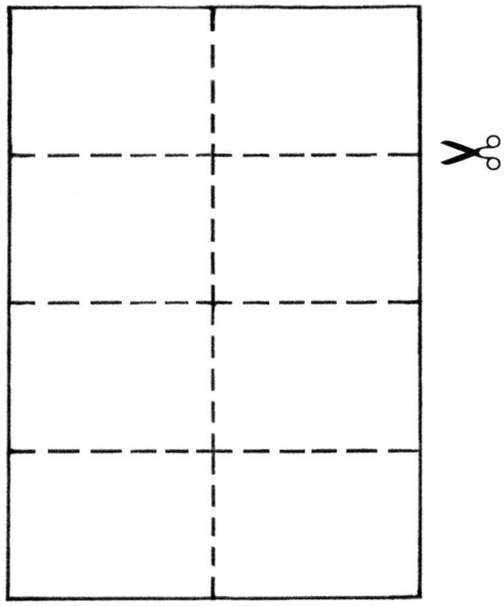

1. Fold and cut eight pieces of tissue paper as shown.

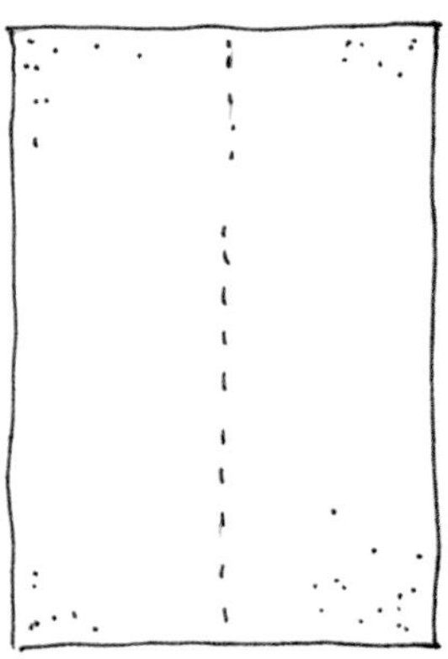

2. Fold each piece in half lengthwise (bringing the long sides together) and unfold again.

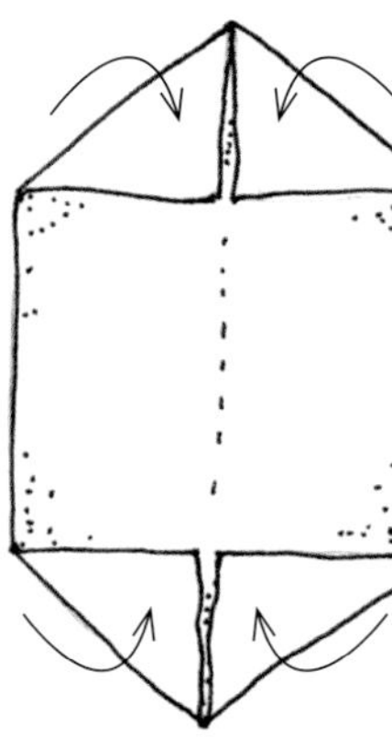

3. On each piece fold all four corners onto the middle crease.

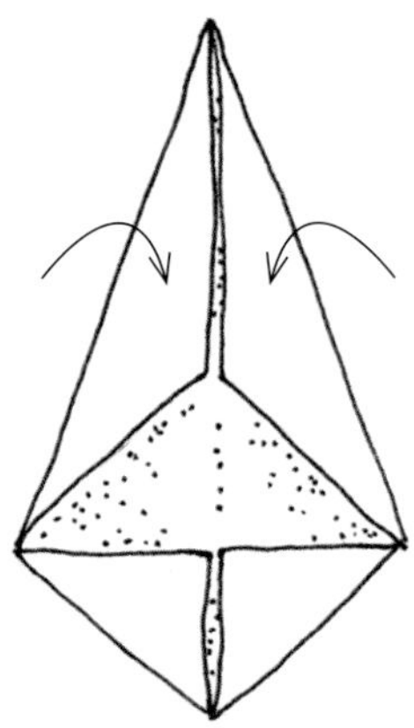

4. On each piece fold two of the corners once again so that they meet at the crease.

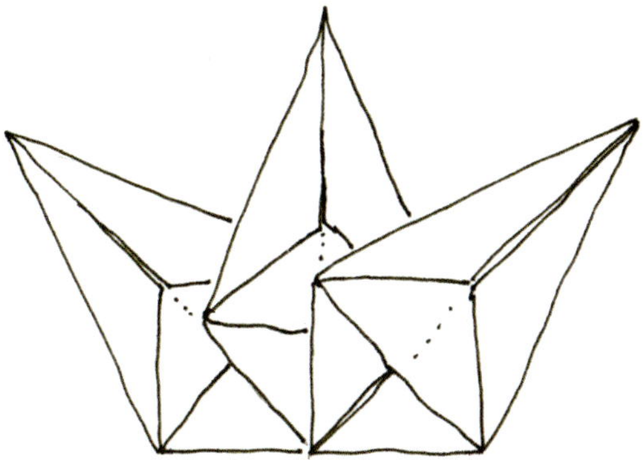

5. Place three folded paper pieces as above and glue neatly where they overlap.

6. Continue adding pieces and gluing them until you have done seven. Now, one edge on the first and on the seventh piece should touch. Lift the first piece and slide one half of the eighth piece underneath it so that it completes the star. Glue neatly where they overlap. You may have to apply an extra bit of glue if some of the corners do not lie flat.

Rainbow star

Repeat the basic eight-pointed star but use a different colour for each point. Glue the points together in this order: red, orange, yellow, light green, dark green, blue, purple, pink.

Sixteen-pointed star

YOU WILL NEED

- Kite paper (or tissue paper) any size but 50 x 30cm/20 x 12" is a good starting point
- Glue stick
- Sheet of white paper
- Sharp scissors

1. Cut each sheet as in the basic eight-pointed star to make 16 identical rectangular pieces. Follow the instructions for the basic star up to step 4.

2. Fold the bottom half over to the middle, the same as the top – ie with one more fold. Glue the star together like the basic star as in steps 5 and 6.

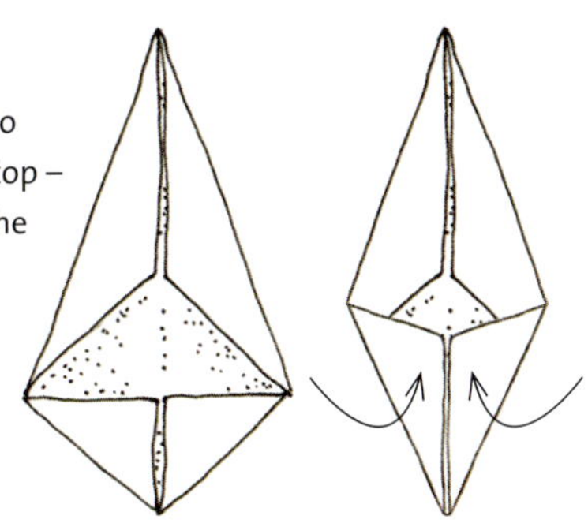

Transparencies

What a gorgeous sight it is when the sun shines through stained glass windows! Here are some tissue paper versions which are just as beguiling.

Whilst you work on these projects you must check to see if your colours and shapes go together, as everything depends on how the colours blend. So test your colours on top of each other by holding them to the light before you start your project. Together they should create a uniquely vibrant glowing image.

Here are four different ways to achieve this:

1. The most child-friendly way is to work on your table near a window and hold your project up to it.
2. If you have a glass-topped table put a light under it.
3. Temporarily fix the work directly onto a window.
4. Use a readymade light box.

Remember that prolonged exposure to bright sunlight will make the colours in tissue paper fade. If your window is likely to attract condensation you should make the completed transparency water resistant by applying self-adhesive plastic film to the back.

Easy transparency

YOU WILL NEED

- Firm thin card, about A4 size – 30 x 20cm/12 x 8"
- Tissue paper in different pale colours – they should blend well when overlapped
- Glue stick
- Sharp scissors or cutting knife and board (for the adult)
- Blu-Tack

NB: The best 'firm thin card' to use for transparencies is 220gsm (US 80lbs)

1. Cut a pleasingly shaped frame from the card.

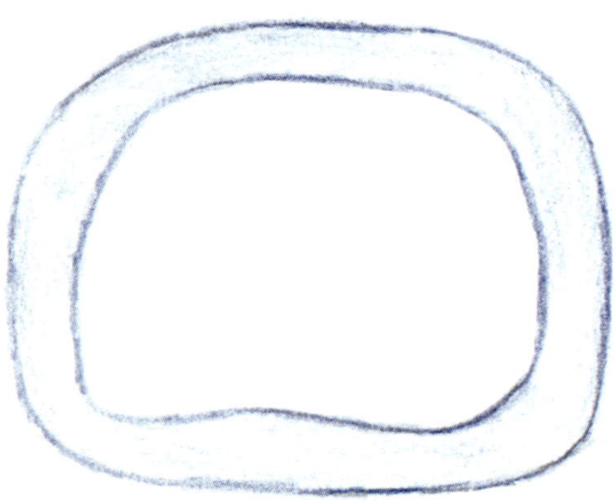

2. Spread glue sparingly on the back of the frame and cover the whole of it with one piece of very pale-coloured tissue paper. Trim off any overhanging edges. This forms the base for the rest of the work. Now your child can do the rest – still working on the back.

3. Tear the tissue paper into some random shapes and stick them with a small amount of glue onto the base. Matching colours work best. Keep holding the frame up to the light to check your progress. The tissue paper can overlap, thus creating a wonderful range of new shapes and colours.

5. When you have finished sticking, trim any overhanging edges on the frame. Stick it, frame side to you, onto the window with Blu-Tack.

This is a wonderful introduction to transparency making for you and your children. Young children will love to repeat the process many times – let them go for it!

Grand festival transparency

The previous approach of tearing, overlapping and designing with tissue paper can be used to great effect by parents and teachers working on a much larger scale. I have used this with young adults as a work of social art – several people working together on one piece.

Replace the A4 size frame with a whole window or a glazed door. Big is beautiful too!

YOU WILL NEED

- Translucent paper big enough to fill the window. Tissue paper is not strong enough for this. It could be kite paper (up to A1 size), tracing paper (up to A0 size), even greaseproof paper in as many colours as possible.
- Glue stick
- Blu-Tack

1. Fix the translucent sheet directly to the glass with Blu-Tack. Tear and glue large pieces of kite/tissue paper onto the 'base'. When you work for a festival, use the colours associated with it – see the The Colour Year (page 9). The beauty of your design relies on how well you match and overlap your colours. Your theme could be a simple colour mood – light colours at the top, through medium strong ones to darkest at the bottom. Or you can build up images with lots of pieces rather like a mosaic, but slightly overlapping them.

2. Relate your images to the festival figures. Start with the background and use the palest colours first. Slowly make the colours slightly darker and stronger starting around the outside and then do the same for the images. As with all transparencies, the glowing colour effect depends on combining matching colours.

Scissor transparency

This is a slightly more difficult version of the easy transparency especially for those children who have just started using scissors.

YOU WILL NEED

- The same as easy transparency (page 206) except replace tissue paper with kite paper. This is slightly stiffer and therefore easier to cut
- A pair of proper children's scissors

Cut the 'base' as in easy transparency (page 206). Your child can cut all the coloured shapes instead of tearing. Stick them onto the base as before. This version will develop scissor skills without requiring much accuracy.

Rosette window

These circular (doily-like) windows are radiant with their transparent, patterned designs. They are just a bit more difficult than the scissor transparency so are suitable for 5-year-olds upwards.

YOU WILL NEED

- 3 squares of kite or tissue paper, about 20 x 20cm/8 x 8" in light matching colours
- Glue stick
- Nail scissors
- Blu-Tack

1. Take one sheet of paper and start by folding it in half as shown below. Bring A to D and B to C.

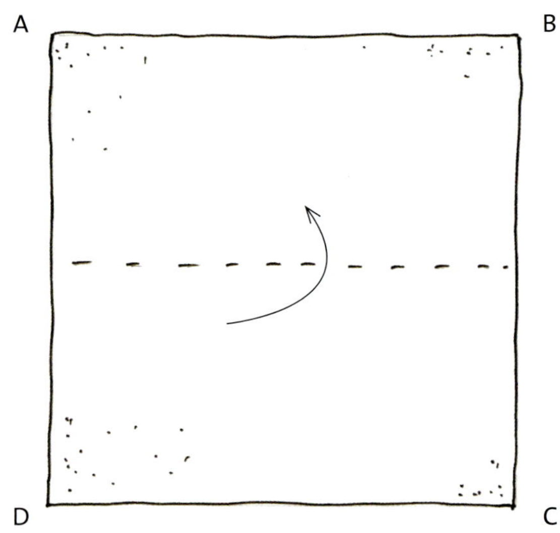

2. Carry on folding as shown in the four diagrams below. X marks the centre of the sheet.

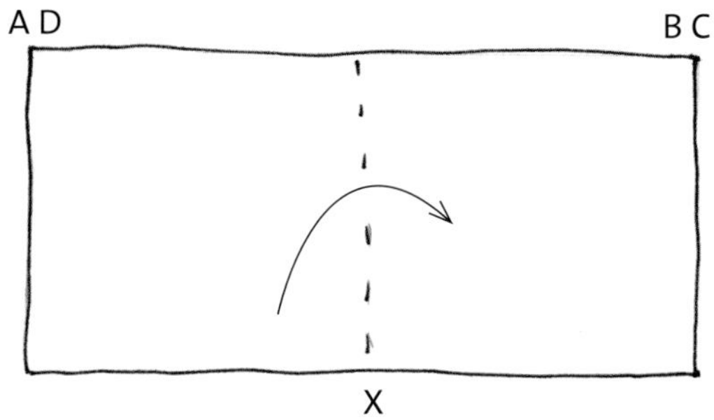

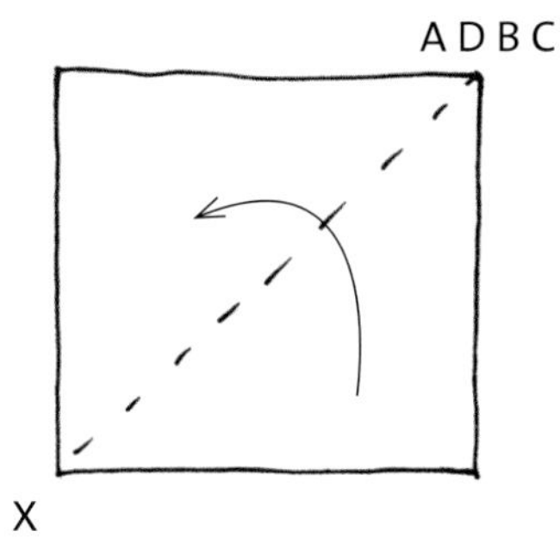

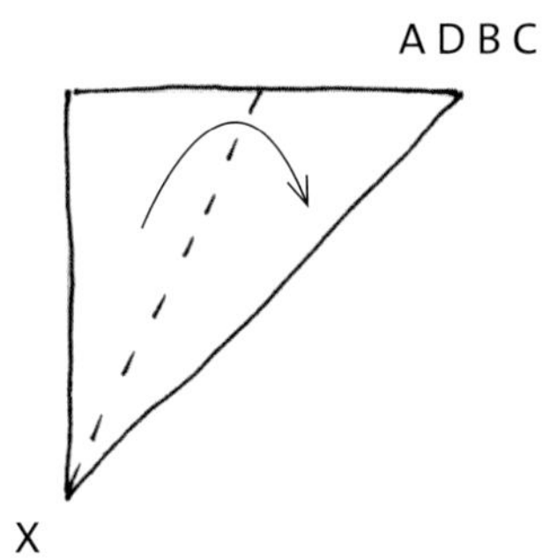

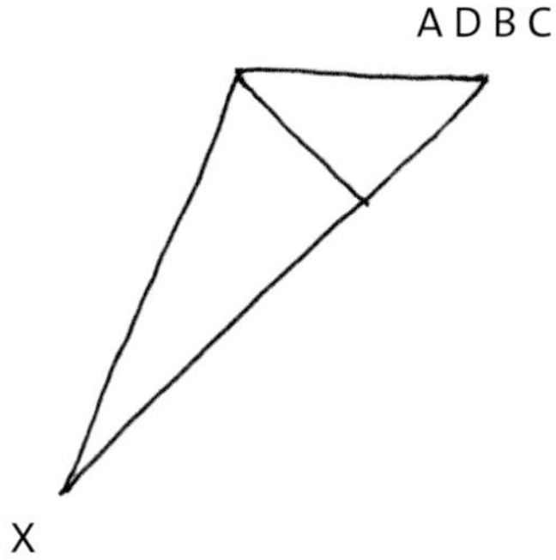

3. Round off the top. and cut out small shapes something like the shaded areas in the diagram below.

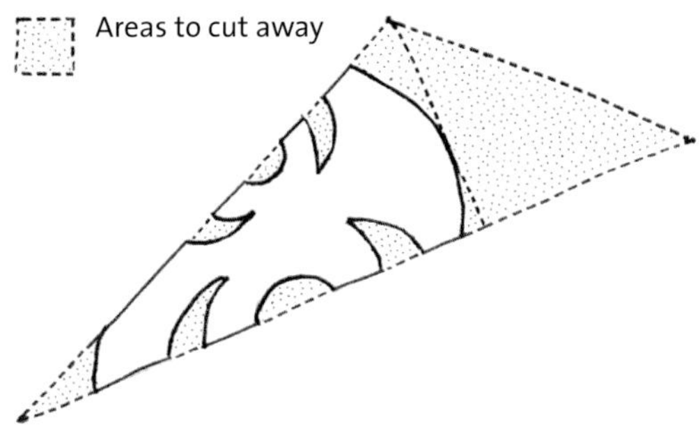

4. Take care not to cut right across from side to side as your rosette will fall apart. Open it up and lay it flat – gently smooth it with a warm iron set on 'cool' or 'silk' – don't worry if some folds still show. Repeat the process with the other two sheets using different cut-outs. Cut away most paper from the darkest sheet something like the diagram below.

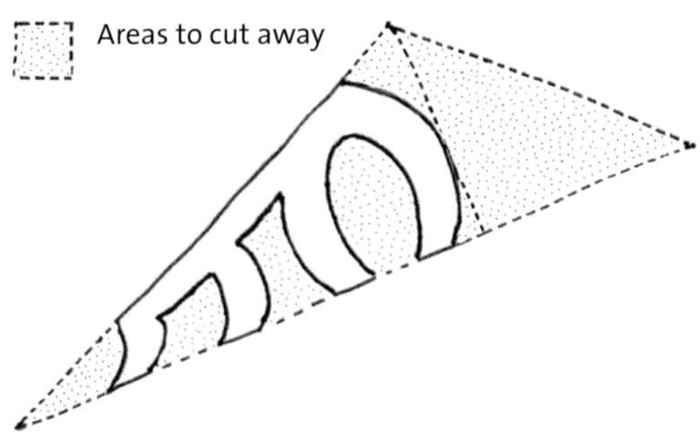

5. Overlay the three sheets and sparingly glue them together with the folds lining up where possible. Fix it to the window with Blu-Tack.

6. Stand back and admire! For a presentation window cut a round frame out of dark blue card, outside diameter 24cm/9½" with a hole 19cm/7½". Glue the already assembled rosette neatly onto the back of the frame.

Nimble fingers transparency

This version requires neat cutting and design skill so is not suitable for very young children to make. It is more difficult, as it requires recognizable shapes, for example people, animals and trees.

YOU WILL NEED

- Firm thin card, about A6 size (15 x 10cm/6 x 4")
- Kite paper in many different colours
- Glue stick
- Sharp scissors and a cutting knife and board
- Pencil
- Blu-Tack

1. Cut a pleasingly shaped frame from the card – either landscape or portrait. Spread glue sparingly on the back of the frame and cover the whole of it with one piece of very pale-coloured kite paper. Trim off any overhanging edges. This forms the base for the rest of the work. Turn it over and work on the front.

2. On a matching colour draw or trace your chosen shape. Cut it out, making sure that you cut away the pencil lines, otherwise these will show up very clearly. Stick with a little dab of glue. Add details in different matching colours, including overlapping to make a richer picture. Then add torn pieces as background – mountains, clouds, etc where needed. When you have finished sticking, trim any overhanging edges on the frame and fix down any loose bits of paper. Stick it on to your window with Blu-Tack.

Cut-out transparency

These are made by cutting one whole shape out of the card, or several parts that make up the whole design. The open parts are then covered with tissue or kite paper. These small transparencies can also be used as greeting cards. Some refined cutting skills are required.

YOU WILL NEED

- Firm thin dark blue card, about 15 x 10cm/6 x 4"
- Tissue or kite paper
- Tracing paper
- Hard pencil
- Paper clips
- Glue stick
- Scissors
- Cutting knife and board
- Blu-Tack

1. Sketch your design on a piece of paper making sure each colour is a separate shape. Copy your design onto the tracing paper. Fix the tracing paper onto the card with paper clips and with the hard pencil draw over the line, pressing firmly to give an imprint.

2. Cut out the shape, turn it over and stick different-coloured bits of tissue or kite paper onto the various openings.

3. Now fix it onto a window, stand back and admire your handiwork or send it to your friend.

Silhouette transparency

These beautiful images contrast a card cut-out with a freely torn tissue or kite paper background. They are the most difficult transparencies to make, as they require precision cutting and some design skill. For teenagers and upwards.

The following is for a free-standing transparency to stand on a window sill or in front of a table lamp.

YOU WILL NEED

- Dark blue firm thin card, about 30 x 15cm/12 x 6"
- Tracing paper, also about 30 x 15cm/12 x 6"
- Tissue paper in suitable matching colours
- Glue stick
- Cutting knife and board
- Scissors
- Hard pencil
- A few paper clips

1. Draw the enlarged design, including the frame, or your own design, onto the tracing paper. Attach the tracing paper to the blue card with the paper clips.

2. Pressing firmly with the hard pencil, draw along the shape on the tracing paper to transfer the design onto the blue card to leave an indentation but no pencil line. Remove the tracing paper and cut out the shapes on the blue card. Make sure that the figures (or your design) remain attached to the ground edge of the card.

3. Turn the card over, glue sparingly all over the back and cover with the palest shade of tissue.

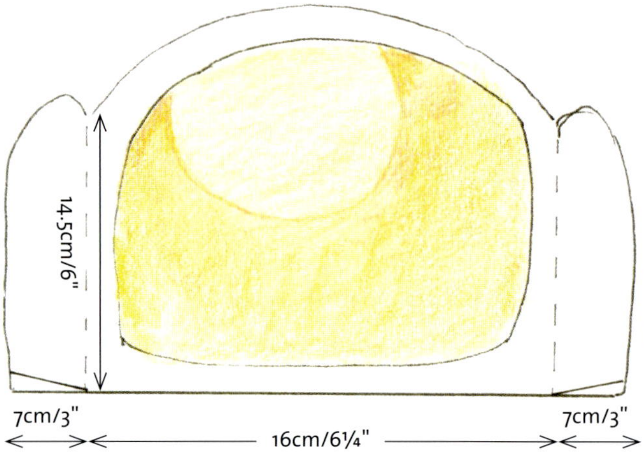

4. For the next colour layer, lay the same shade or a slightly darker but matching shade over the whole image. Before gluing, tear out the top left part so that the first colour layer is still visible. Glue sparingly the second layer on to the edge of the card, and also use a tiny bit of glue on the tissue paper.

5. Take the third layer and repeat the last process, making sure that you tear away a larger part so that the second layer is visible.

6. Continue adding colour layers in this way but do not lose the silhouette. Check your progress by holding it up to the light – stop when you are happy with the result. Score the side panel lines at the front.

7. Bend the two side panels, along the scored lines, towards the back of the transparency so that it can stand. Trim 1cm/½" at an angle from the side panels. Trim off or glue down any loose bits and place it front of a light or window.

8. If you want to make a transparency to fix directly to a window, follow the above instructions, but omit the two side panels.

Advent Calendar

This Advent calendar is magical. Its transparent windows glow in the winter light, warming even the coldest day.It has 28 windows; the bottom half are card silhouettes with tissue paper backgrounds. The other half (the top and the Nativity) are made entirely of tissue or kite paper. Advent starts on the Sunday four weeks before Christmas and therefore varies in length. The 28 windows allow for the longest Advent.

This design uses all techniques found in earlier projects – it is therefore suitable for experienced nimble fingers with lots of patience (not beginners). It also requires a lot of work, so you are well advised to start well in advance of Advent.

It can be used free-standing with the side flaps and an electric light behind it. Or without the side flaps it can be stuck to a condensation-free window away from direct sunshine (which can bleach out colours).

Put it away somewhere safe when you have finished with it – our one has lasted already into the next generation and has heralded countless Christmases.

YOU WILL NEED

- 2 large (A1) sheets of thin, dark blue firm card, 220gsm (US 80lbs)
- Kite paper or tissue paper in as many different colours as possible
- Glue stick
- Sharp pointed scissors
- Craft knife and a cutting board
- Greaseproof paper, 55 x 60cm/22 x 24"
- Small, self-adhesive gold stars
- White pencil
- Hard pencil
- Paper clips
- Blu-Tack
- Light box or a glass table with a light under it (optional)

1. Take one sheet of card and lightly mark out the whole perimeter of the calendar with the white pencil, following the measurements as shown.

2. Cut around it, score the side wings, fold them back once and then open them out flat again.

T = Transparency
S = Silhouette

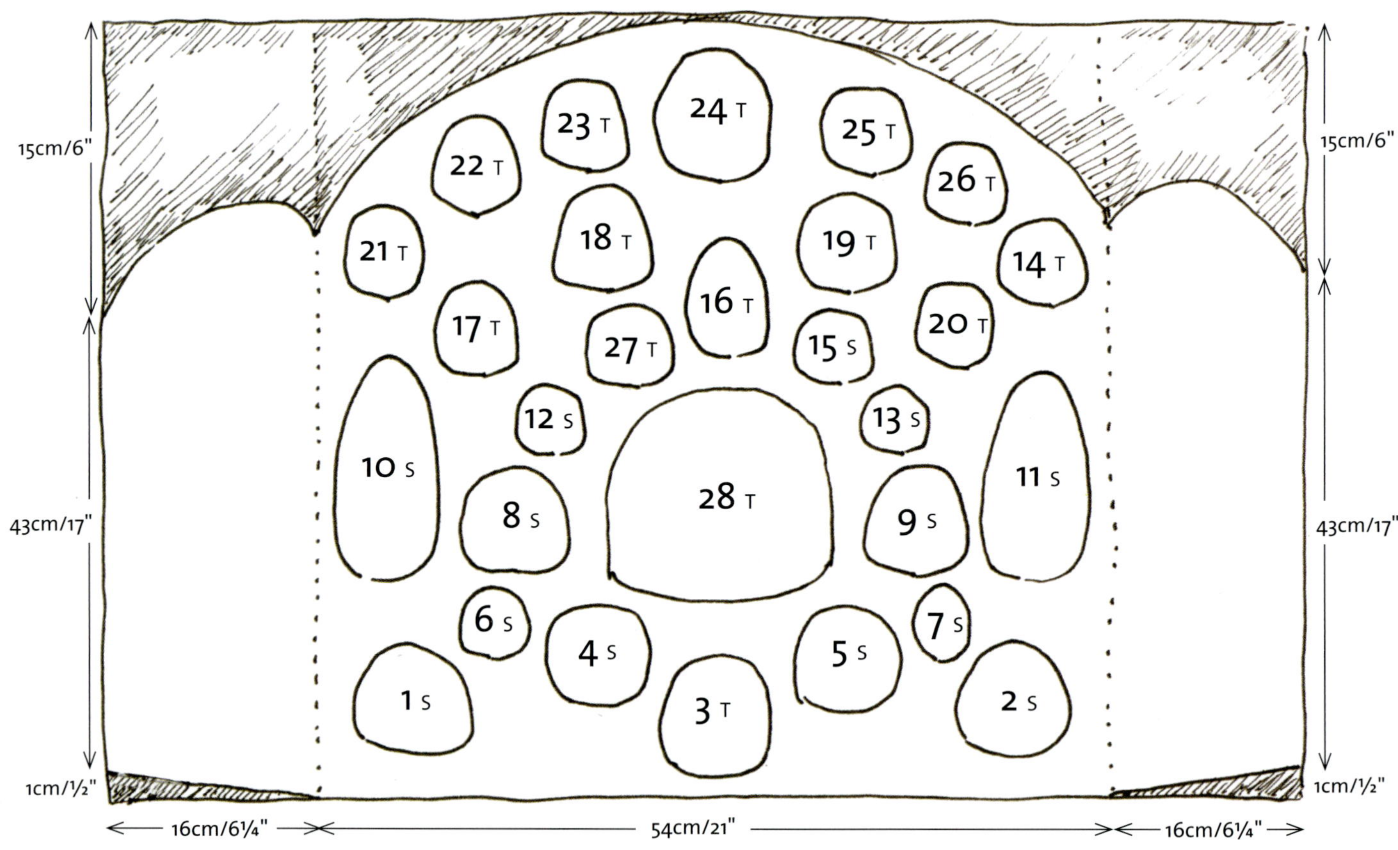

3. Use the white pencil to lightly draw freehand the outline of all 28 windows. Refer to the illustration to give you the rough size. The larger the window, the greater the light, but the weaker the construction.

4. Write the number (not the letter) under the window and on the window 'cover'. Write clearly and neatly, as this will be an important part of the finished project.

5. Cut out the windows with the knife and keep them safe, as they will be put back when all is finished. So now you have 28 holes in your card and 28 'covers'.

Now you are going to make 28 individual transparencies!

6. Fix greaseproof paper with paper clips on to the card and trace all the window openings. The windows marked S are silhouettes cut out of card with a light-coloured kite or tissue paper background.

7. Trace all the S-marked window images (see below and page 216) onto the same piece of greaseproof paper in the correct place. Paper-clip the greaseproof paper onto the other sheet of blue card. With the hard pencil, draw firmly over the traced images to make an imprint on the card beneath.

8. Cut out the silhouettes carefully – leave them attached to the blue card frame. There should be 13 altogether. Don't worry if it goes wrong – you can always make a new one and glue it in place.

1 S

4 S

2 S

5 S

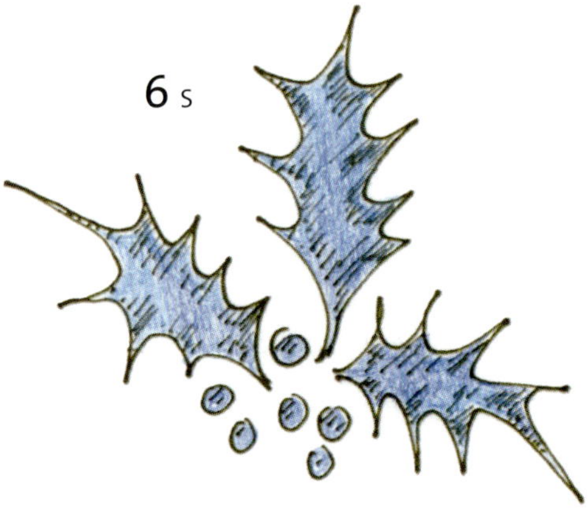

6 s

9 s

11 s

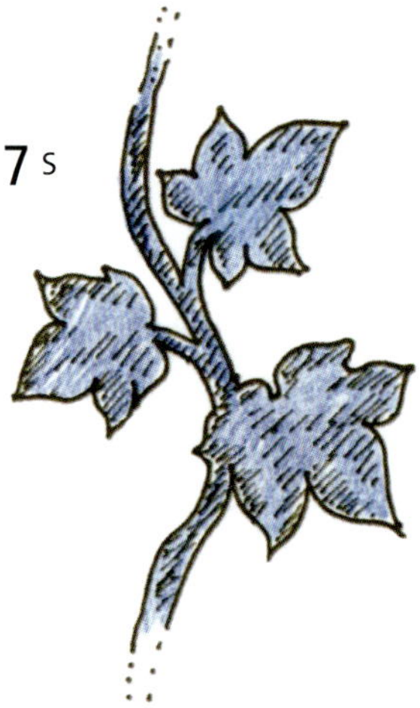

7 s

10 s

8 s

15 s

12 s

13 s

9. Turn over the card so you are working on the back. Glue a piece of light-coloured tissue paper over each individual silhouette. Where possible use different colours for this first layer to bring variation and contrast. Add more layers of torn coloured paper for the ground and the sky, thus making a silhouette transparency for each window.

10. Cut out all T window openings and glue a different piece of light-coloured tissue paper over each of the remaining windows (the T ones are all small 'nimble finger transparencies'; see page 210).

11. Trace all the T examples (see below and page 218) onto suitably coloured tissue or kite paper. Cut out carefully, taking care not to leave the pencil lines. Turn over the card and stick the images onto the front of the coloured background. For the moon and stars (numbers 14, 21 and 27) you can use a white background and then cut away the image from a darker colour paper that you glue to the back – the image will shine white.

You can make the colours even more beautiful by adding matching colours in or around the images on the back. But only do this to enhance the image.

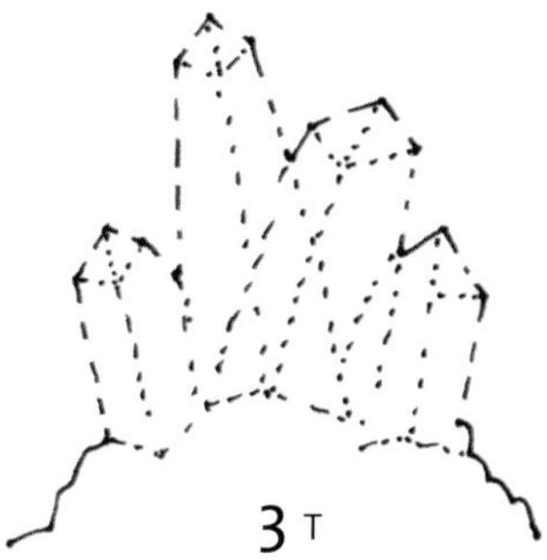

3 T

14 T

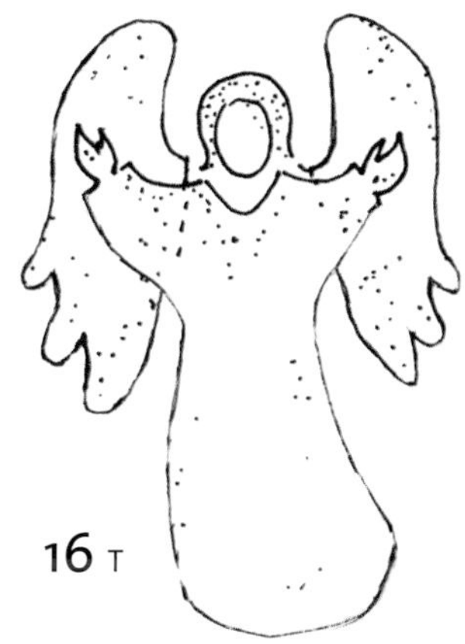

16 T

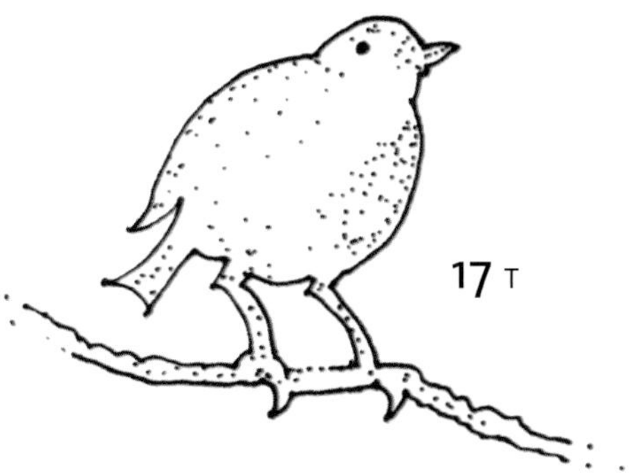

17 T

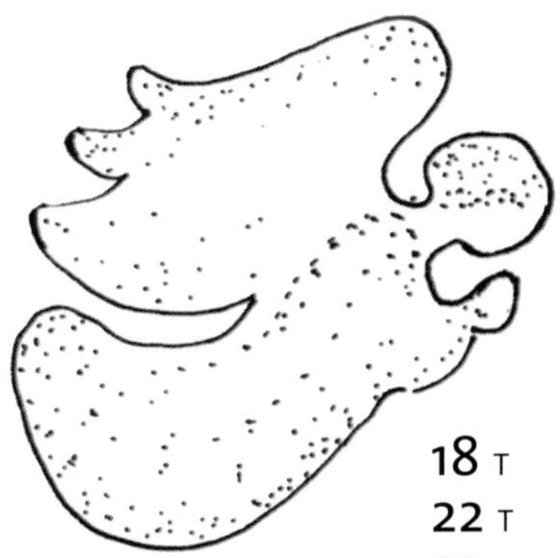

18 T
22 T
23 T

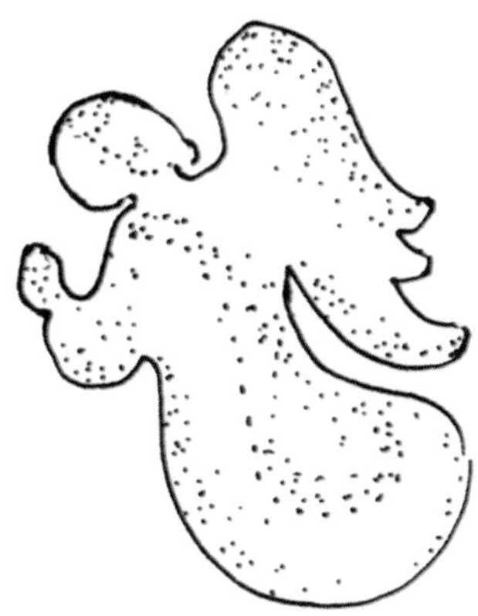

19 T
25 T
26 T

20 T

21 T

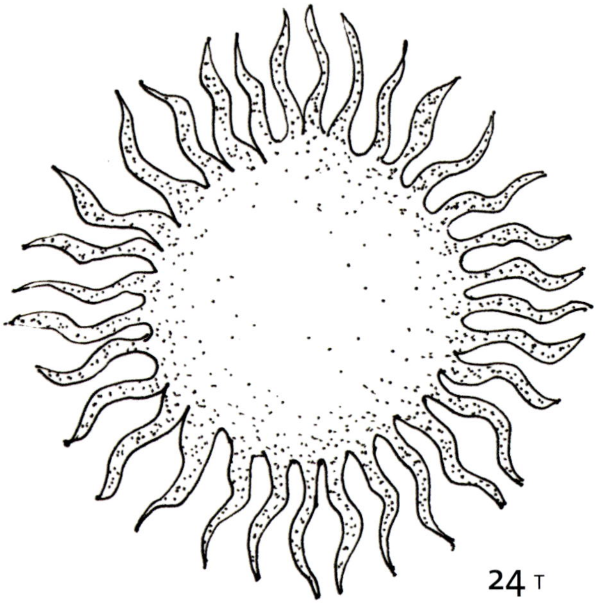

24 T

27 T

12. Start the large Nativity scene (28 T) with white on the back and build up the rest on the front, layer after layer.

You can also cut out stars here from the darker paper as empty negative spaces. The figures can be built up out of different-coloured kite or tissue paper on the front. Neaten up any loose bits on the back then glue the two blue cards together (A and B) with the cut-outs on the front facing the right way up, making sure that everything lines up.

13. Attach the 'covers' onto the front of the windows with two or three gold stars. You are now ready for Advent. On the first Sunday open the first window. Next day open the second window, etc For a short Advent you can open extra windows at the start so that your last one is open on Christmas Day. On that day all the windows will be open with the biggest and most beautiful one showing the Nativity scene.

(NB: Keep the calendar and all the offcuts of card and paper together in a folder so that next year you can repair it easily if necessary.)

28 T

Walnuts

Most people break open a walnut so they can eat the kernel inside – normally with nutcrackers or even a hammer. As a crafter you can eat the insides and then make things with the two empty half shells.

To open a walnut neatly, hold it in your gloved hand (until you have practised a bit) and then push a square-ended screwdriver firmly into the joint and twist it. It should open easily as two separate pieces.

As soft as silk
As white as milk
As bitter as gall
A thick wall
And a green coat over all.

Old riddle

Gift box

A wrapped walnut must surely hide something precious.

This is a very special wrapping for a tiny present but is not suitable for young children to make.

YOU WILL NEED

- A walnut cut in half
- Glue
- Pretty ribbon

1. Put the tiny present into the nut. Now put a tiny drop of glue or a bit of Blu-Tack on each side of the shell to make sure it will not open by itself.

2. Paint the nut gold, if you like, and tie the ribbon round it.

Tooth fairy purse

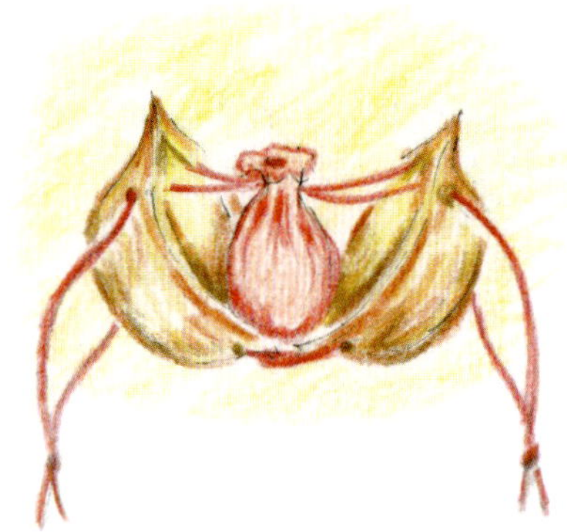

A tiny little purse hidden in a walnut is an ideal place to put a child's tooth for the tooth fairy to find. Will she come and exchange the tooth for a shiny penny or some other treasure?

YOU WILL NEED

- A walnut shell cut in 2 halves
- A scrap of cotton fabric
- Needle and matching thread
- Very narrow ribbon, 35cm/14"
- A drill and a small drillbit

1. Drill four small holes in each walnut half.

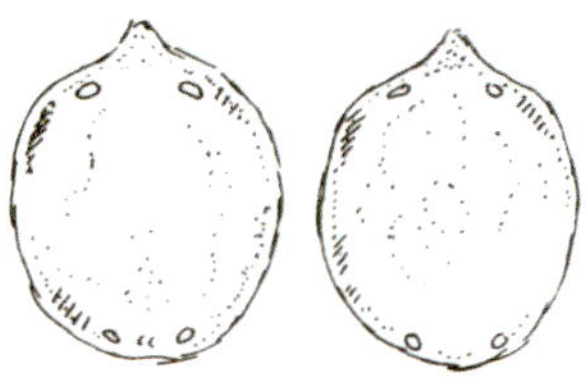

2. Cut out and sew a small purse from the fabric to fit into the walnut and hem each edge as shown.

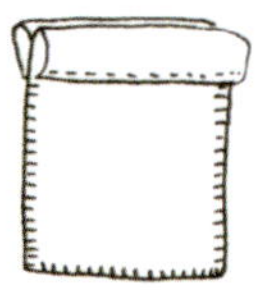

3. Thread the ribbon through the two holes in the bottom of both shells to act as a hinge then cut off and tie the two ends together.

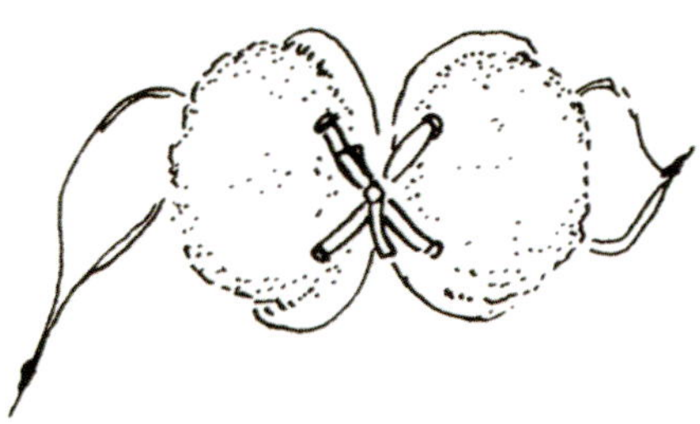

4. Cut the remaining ribbon in half and thread each length through the hem of the purse as shown.

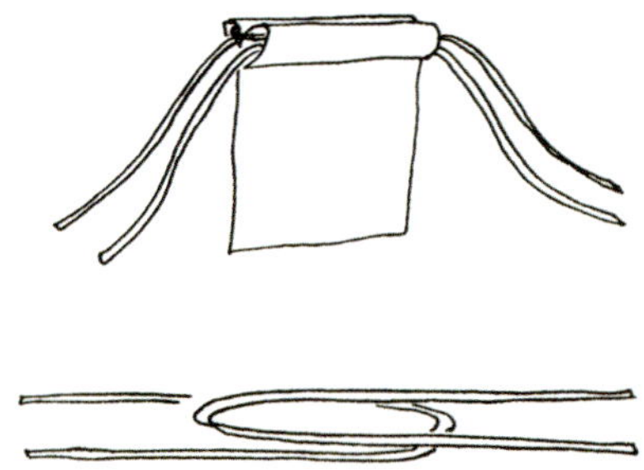

5. Put the purse in the nut and thread one ribbon through each hole in the top of the two shells. Tie the ends of the ribbons together to prevent them slipping out again.

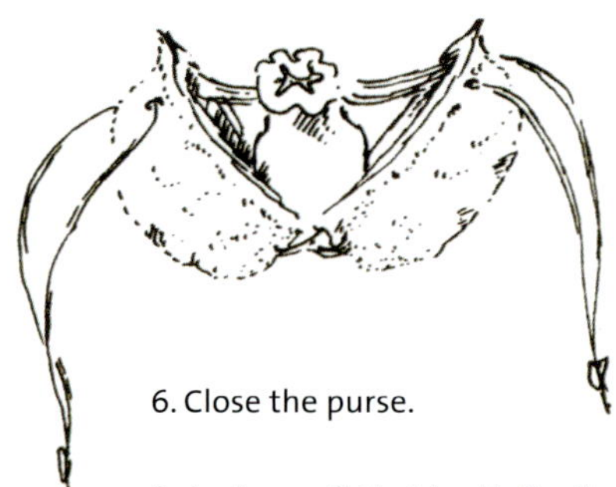

6. Close the purse.

But when will that tooth finally come out?

Tiny table decoration

YOU WILL NEED

- Half a walnut shell
- Some small dried flowers or a holly leaf for Christmas
- Tiny bit of plasticine or wax
- Small candle
- Tiny piece of card
- Glue

Press a small amount of plasticine or wax into the walnut shell. Put the candle firmly into the middle. Arrange the dried flowers and holly leaf around the candle. Cut out a small star from the card and glue the walnut half onto the star to stop it falling over.

Cradle

This must be the smallest-ever cradle for a doll's house!

YOU WILL NEED

- Half a walnut
- Scrap of cotton fabric in a plain pastel colour
- Scrap of fleece or cotton wool
- Needle and thread

Put a layer of fleece or cotton wool into the shell to make a mattress. Make a tiny pillow and cover. You have a rocking cradle for a doll's house. You might find another slightly bigger shell that is just the right size to fit together with your cradle.

Candle Holders

Children love to feel that the darkness is held back by the soft and mysterious light of a few candles. Better still if they can help with the making of the holders of the little lights.

The object of this project is to make an interesting wooden base with a candle-sized hole in it. It is a good project for a young woodworker.

Your design depends on the piece of wood you choose.

YOU WILL NEED

- A small log, or a short branch minimum about 5cm/2" diameter, or a short workshop offcut of timber, or any interesting piece from the wood pile
- Plane or rasp
- Pencil
- Handsaw
- Sandpaper
- Household candles
- Drill brace and a bit the same diameter as the candle
- Linseed oil and a rag

Simple branch with various candles

Take a short branch, minimum diameter 5cm/2", and find which way it lies flat. Leaving it flat, drill a hole in the upper side of it and gently push in the candle. You can make as many holes as will fit comfortably.

Short round upright log

Choose the top and turn it over and use the rasp/plane to smooth the bottom surface so that it will stand up. Drill a hole in the upper side of it and gently push in the candle.

Log slice

1. Select a log at least 7cm/3" diameter. Choose which piece will be your slice and mark the cut with a pencil. Cut off the slice you fancy, stand it on the table and choose the top. Sand down the top and bottom. Leave the bark on the sides or, if you prefer, plane/rasp it off and sand the sides too.

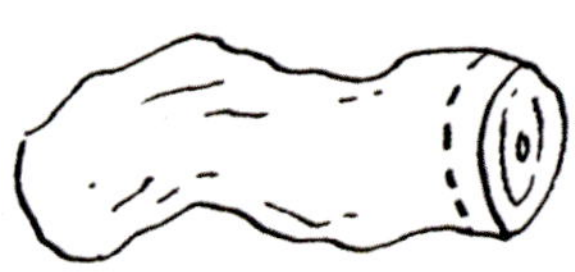

2. Find the centre of the top and drill a hole in it and gently push in the candle.

Fancy shape

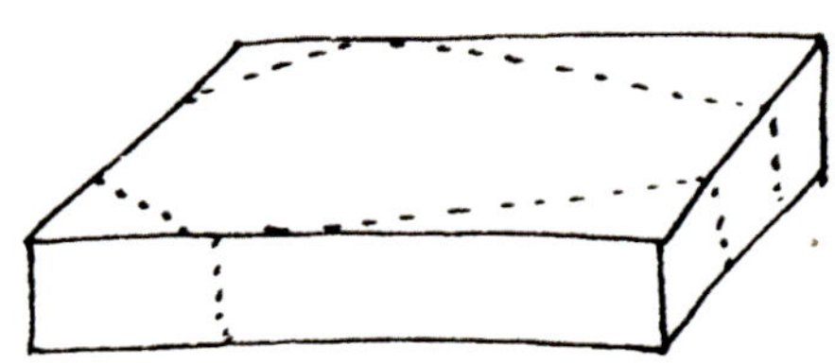

1. Take your workshop offcut and choose the top. Mark the final shape you want with a pencil then carefully cut it – you may need to hold it steady in a vice or clamp it to something solid. Drill the candle hole in the top. Sand it smooth.

2. You may want to paint it with transparent watercolour – yellows and reds go well with candlelight. When it is completely dry, you can oil it with linseed oil (several thin coats) or you can wax it and polish it (several thin coats). Gently push in the candle.

Candle Decoration

This simple candle decoration adds a festive touch to your Christmas table. Red beads and green felt make a lovely 'holly' effect. This is an easy present that children can make in a few minutes.

YOU WILL NEED

(To fit a medium-sized candle)

- 7 red round wooden beads, 1cm/½" diameter
- Scraps of green felt
- Some elastic thread and a needle to suit

1. Cut out seven leaves from the felt.

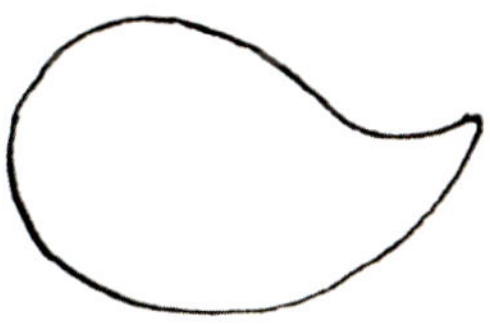

NB: The pattern piece for the leaf is actual size.

2. Using the needle, thread the beads and felt leaves onto a double thickness of elastic thread.

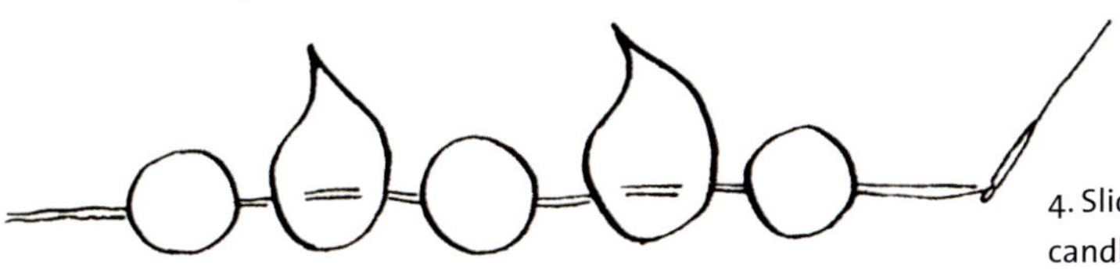

3. When all seven leaves and beads are threaded up, tie the elastic thread in a circle, stretching the thread slightly.

4. Slide the decoration over the bottom of a candle and put the candle into a holder

Twelve Days of Christmas Calendar

After the climax of Christmas, children sometimes feel a kind of emptiness that can be filled by continuing the present-giving with this calendar, which lasts from Boxing Day to Three Kings' Day – 6 January.

Each boot contains a small present, one to be opened on each new day. It looks especially good if the colours of the boots are those of the rainbow (light yellow, dark yellow, orange, red, purple, dark blue, light blue, green).

YOU WILL NEED

- 12 pieces of felt, 12 x 6cm/5 x 2½", rainbow colours if possible
- Embroidery cotton in matching colours
- Wooden ring, diameter 20cm/8"
- Red ribbon, 220cm/90", about 1cm/½" wide – the exact length will depend on where you hang it
- 12 little gifts to put in each boot

1. Cut out 24 boot shapes using the pattern.

NB: The pattern piece for the boot is actual size.

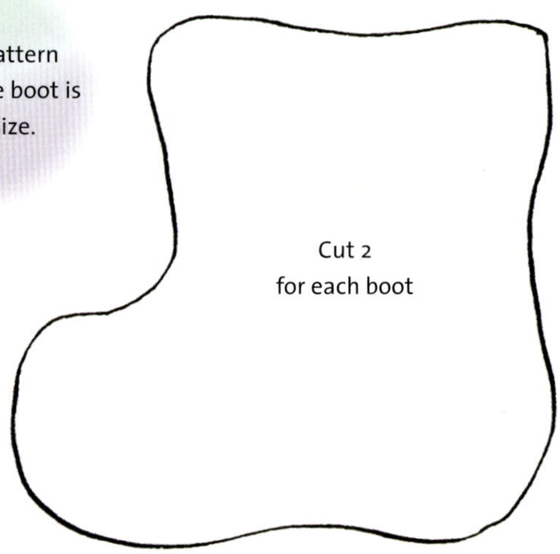

2. Sew around each pair of boot shapes with a blanket stitch. Start at the top of the front and finish at the top at the back. Leave a long thread that can be used to hang the boot on the ring.

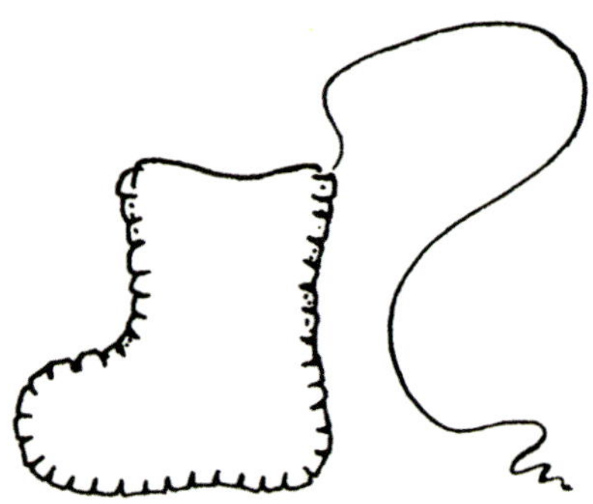

3. Hang the boots on the ring, spacing them evenly (see the suggestion above for the succession of colours). You may want to put a drop of glue on the ring for each boot to stop it sliding about. Put a little gift into each boot, cut the ribbon into four equal lengths, tie them to the ring in four places and hang it up.

Felt Hearts and Woolly Balls Mobile

This ring looks attractive and is especially festive for Christmas using strong red and green colours.

YOU WILL NEED

- Metal or bamboo ring, diameter about 23cm/9" obtainable from any craft shop
- Card for the woolly balls; a cereal packet is the right thickness
- Compass and ruler
- Green wool
- Small quantity of red wool
- 2 squares of red felt, 23 x 23cm/9 x 9"
- Larch cones (optional)
- UHU glue
- Small scissors
- Darning needle

1. If you use a metal ring, bind it with red wool until the metal does not show through. Attach four pieces of red wool about 45cm/18" long around the ring equal distance apart. Tie the ends together and hang it up.

2. Make at least four green woolly balls by following the pompom-making instructions on page 231. Attach them to the ring equal distance apart in between the red wool.

3. To make the heart chains, cut out three sizes of hearts, two pieces for each heart, so that you have small, medium and large.

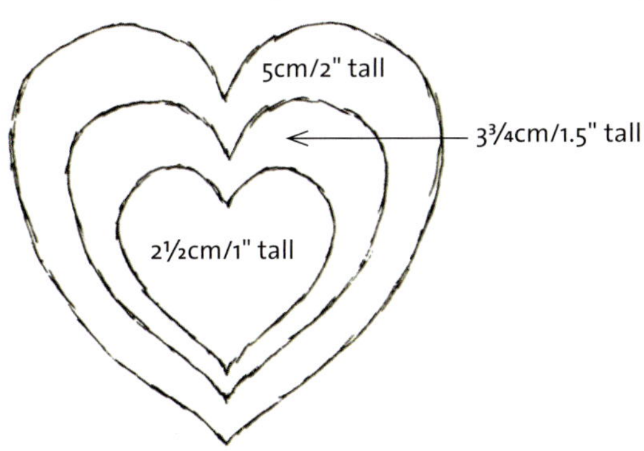

4. Take a piece of red wool about 35cm/14" long and glue the two sides of the smallest heart together with the wool in between. Leave a 5cm/2" gap and glue the next two sides of the medium-sized heart together further along the same piece of wool. Leave another 5cm/2" gap and do the same with the large heart.

5. Make three more chains and tie each one to the ring at the points where the red wool is attached. Glue the larch cones around the ring on top.

Card Stand

Sometimes one receives a very beautiful card: for instance a homemade one or a good reproduction of a great painting. To do it justice and to display it well you can use this card stand. Very young woodworkers can make this as a first project. They can do it so easily that we found the whole family was provided for very quickly!

1. Cut the wood the right size then remove the rough edges with the plane or rasp. This can be done very simply by just rounding off the two top edges; or in a slightly more difficult way by making sloping surfaces.

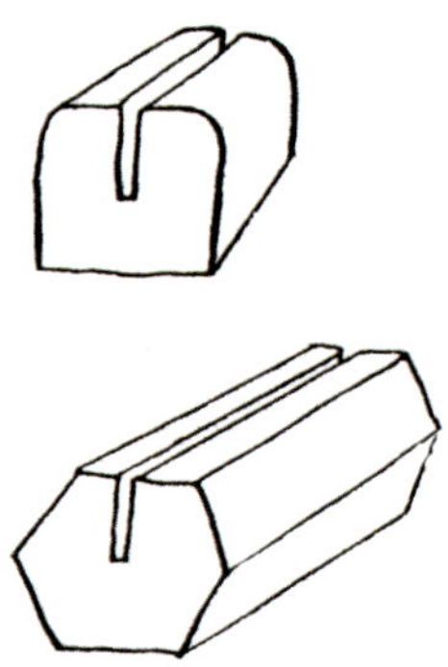

2. Make a cut down the length as shown. This may need extra supervision. This cut takes the card. Sand down again any sharp splinters, oil the piece sparingly several times to bring out the grain, and allow to dry overnight.

YOU WILL NEED

- Small off-cut of softwood, about 15 x 2 x 2cm/6 x 1 x 1"
- Handsaw
- Plane or rasp
- Sandpaper, medium and fine
- Linseed oil and a rag for applying it

Bird Table

This bird table can be made in a short time and it is exciting for the child to watch the birds feeding from it.

But once you start feeding birds please do keep it up, as they rely on it.

If plywood is used, make sure it is external ply. Our six-year-old son enjoyed drilling the holes with a big hand-drill best of all!

YOU WILL NEED

- A piece of wood, about 30 x 30cm/12 x 12"or a slice of tree truck of similar size
- Rope 6mm/¼" diameter, 2.8m/9' long
- Drill and 12mm/½" drill bit

1. Sand the piece of wood until it is nice and smooth. Depending on the shape of the wood, drill three or four holes about 2 cm (¾") from the edges.

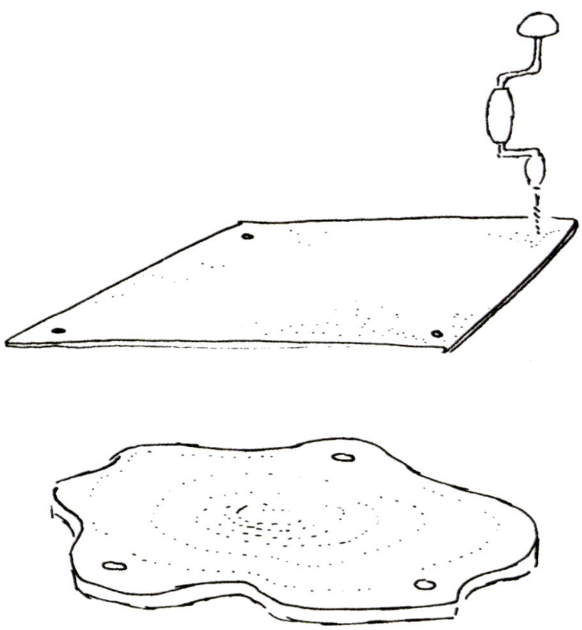

2. Thread the rope through each one of the holes and make a knot underneath the board. Gather the cords together at the top and make a knot. Hang your bird table outside the window.

Nest Box for Garden Birds

Nature needs all the help we can give it, so why not welcome birds to your garden with this lovely nest box

Make it of wood – the easiest to use is plywood or MDF. But a softwood board will be fine too – 15mm /5/8" thick. You will have to increase the width of the front and the back to allow for thicker wood. To make a home for small blue tits, make the entrance hole 25mm/1" diameter. For larger sparrows, make it 32mm/1¼" diameter.

This project requires carpentry skills. Children can learn by watching the process unfold. They can help out where appropriate.

YOU WILL NEED

- A piece of MDF 12mm/½" thick – it must be moisture resistant or a piece of plywood 12mm/½" thick (again it must be exterior quality), 50 x 50cm/20 x 20"
- PVA wood glue
- About 30 nails (panel pins) 30mm/1¼" long
- About 10 screws, 3 x 30mm/6 x 1¼"
- 2 mirror plates
- Water-based paint or preservative
- Small paint brush
- Hand saw
- Hammer
- Drill, bit and screwdriver for the screws
- Brace and bit for the entrance hole
- Ruler and pencil
- Carpenter's square

1. Carefully mark out each piece shown below, taking care to allow for the thickness of the saw cut when you measure.

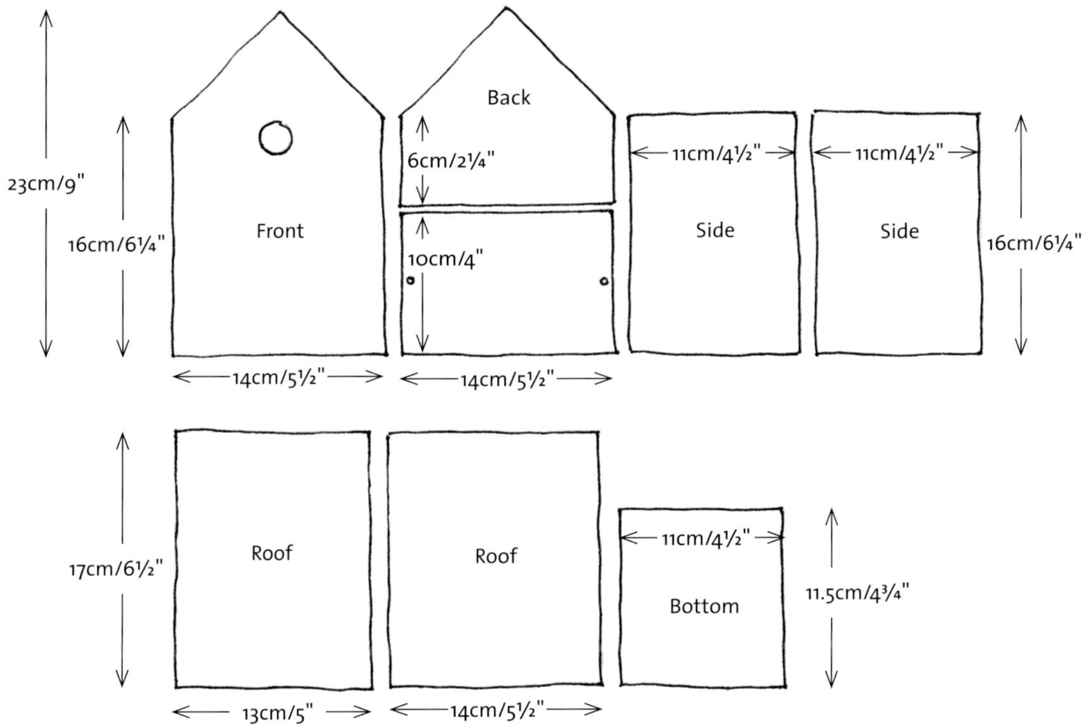

2. Cut out the pieces, making square edges as far as possible. Leave the back as one piece until later. Drill the entrance hole in the front panel – it should be at least 12.5cm/5" above the bottom floor. Glue and nail the two sides to the front.

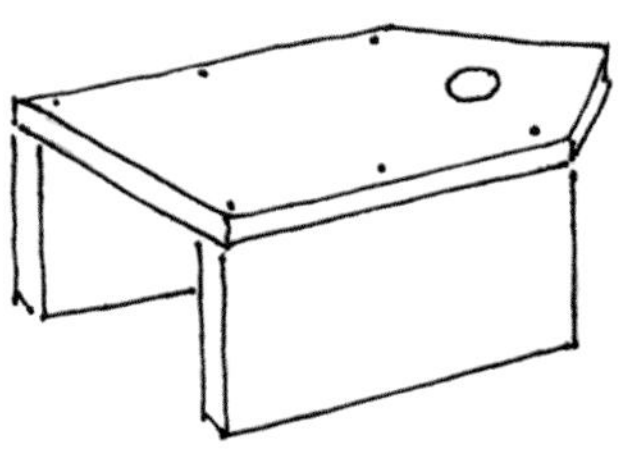

3. Check to see if the bottom fits and adjust as necessary. Glue and nail it into place.

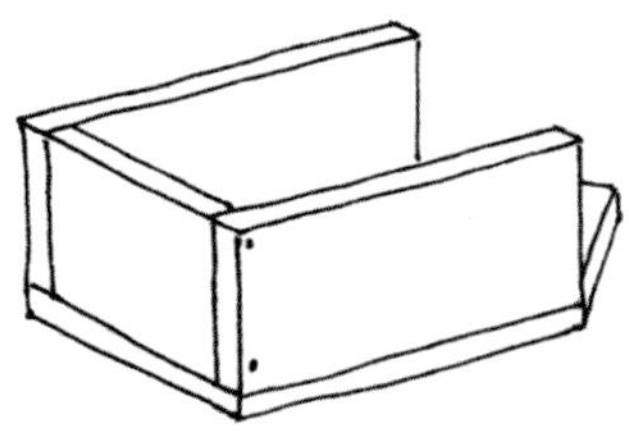

4. Check to see if the back fits and adjust as necessary. Cut it into the two pieces shown on previous page. Glue and nail the upper piece to the top of the box.

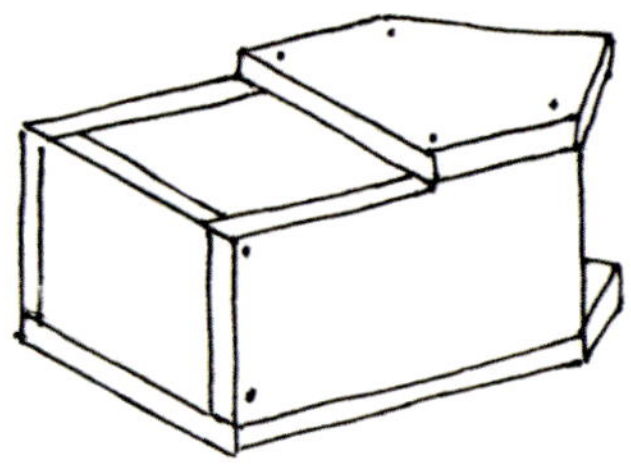

5. Drill and screw the lower piece to the bottom of the box – make sure that the recent cut edges are together. This forms the removable panel needed for annual cleaning. Check to see if the two roof panels fit onto the walls – the longer one overlaps the shorter one. Adjust as necessary.

6. Glue and nail the roof panels into place – make sure you glue the joint at the ridge. Drill two small drainage holes in the bottom. Fix the two mirror plates to the top and bottom or to both sides. Apply two coats of paint but don't paint the inside of the box.

7. Fix the box in the chosen location. You can thread wire through the mirror plates and tie it to your tree if you prefer not to screw into a tree trunk. Then locate your box in a quiet part of the garden at least 2m/6' above the ground, sheltered from the prevailing wind and out of direct midday sunshine where possible.

The birds want to fly straight to the box from their local perches so there should be perching branches and shrubs in the garden, but not too close. Please persuade children not to peep into the box because they will scare the birds away. Best to watch from indoors or at least 10m/30' away.

The box can be used year after year, but remember to remove the box in November to clean it out with very hot water – but no detergent. Keep it in the house until the inside is quite dry. You may want to put it back outside because birds sometimes roost (sleep) in it during the winter.

If you don't want to do this, make sure it is back outside well before St Valentines Day (14 February), when the birds start hunting for nesting places again. Honestly!

Caterpillar Bookmark

This is a little present that a child can make in a short time.

YOU WILL NEED

- A scrap of DK wool
- Crochet hook, 3.5mm/US size E
- 2 very small glass eyes or black beads
- Glue or thread for fixing eyes

1. Crochet a length of chain (using chain stitch) as long as you want your bookmark to be. A good average length is 23cm/9". Turn at the end of the chain and, starting into the second stitch from the hook, work four trebles into one chain stitch (look online for more information).

2. Repeat this about ten times. You will find that the crochet stitches will twist around the chain and your caterpillar will emerge. Sew in the thread and glue on the glass eyes or sew on the beads in the appropriate places.

3. If you want to make a 'hairy' animal, thread short lengths of wool through the face of the caterpillar, knot them and cut them off.

Another suggestion is to make one caterpillar at each end of a chain and use them for tying around a girl's pony tail.

Pompom or Woolly Ball

Making a pompom brings a smile to any face as, before your unexpecting eyes, a flat shape turns into a ball! They can be made in various sizes and colours. They look great at the top of a gnome's hat, very small ones can be attached to ribbon or twisted cord on babies' bootees or they can be hung from a mobile.

They can also just be the first balls for throwing, as they are easy to pick up for little fingers.

They are easy for young children to make – with adult help for finishing and perseverance. But what a great achievement when they are finished.

YOU WILL NEED

- Wool in a bright colour
- Card – a cereal box is the right thickness
- Compass and ruler
- Small scissors
- Darning needle

1. Draw and cut out two cardboard circles 5cm/2" in diameter. Cut a small hole in the centre of both circles 1cm/½" diameter. Take the two circles, pass lengths of green wool through the hole and wrap it round the card until there is no space left in the centre.

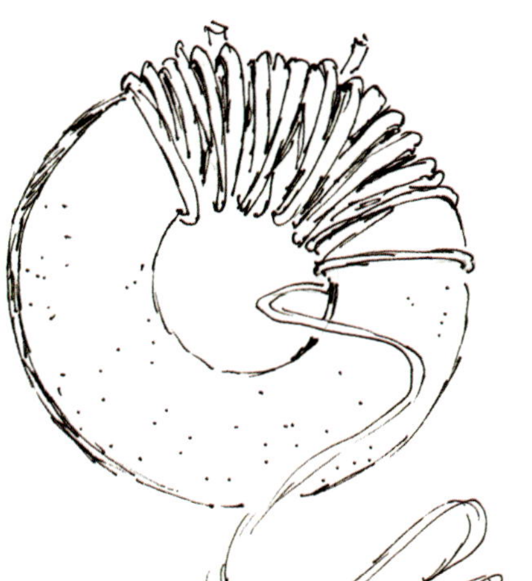

2. Towards the end you will find it necessary to thread the wool onto a needle in order to get it through the small hole.

3. Cut the wool all round the outer edge of the circle.

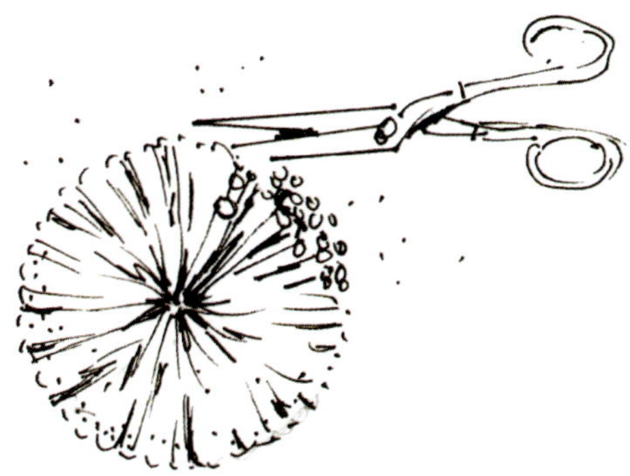

4. Tie a length of wool as tightly as possible round the centre in between the two pieces of card. If you plan to use it for a mobile, leave the ends long so that the ball can be easily attached. Remove the cardboard and fluff out the woolly ball, trimming it where necessary.

Enjoy!

Felt Ball

This is a lovely present for a toddler, soft to hold, made with pretty colours and with a jingling bell hidden in the middle. It is made out of 12 pentagons, which together make a dodecahedron. It requires some precision cutting and sewing to look good. The tricky part is the sewing together of the panels.

This is a good project for teenagers to make.

YOU WILL NEED

- Felt in 4 different rainbow colours – each colour 20 x 7cm/8 x 3"
- Cotton thread that goes with all the colours
- Wool fleece
- 1 tiny bell
- Cardboard, 7 x 7cm/3 x 3"
- Scissors

1. Draw a pentagram (see page 148) to the size indicated below:

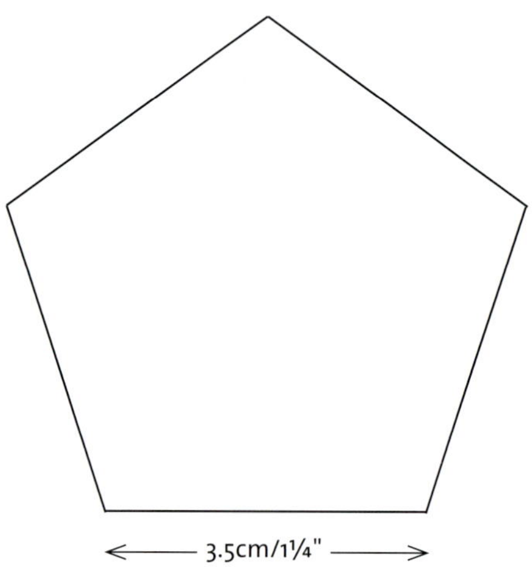

NB: The pattern piece for the ball is actual size.

2. Transfer to the cardboard and cut the card to make the pentagon template. Mark 12 pentagons on the felt – three on each of the four colours. Carefully cut them out. It is easiest to make two separate halves so start by laying out a colour design. You can do it so that no two colours will be neighbours. (NB: The centre pentagons are not the same colour.)

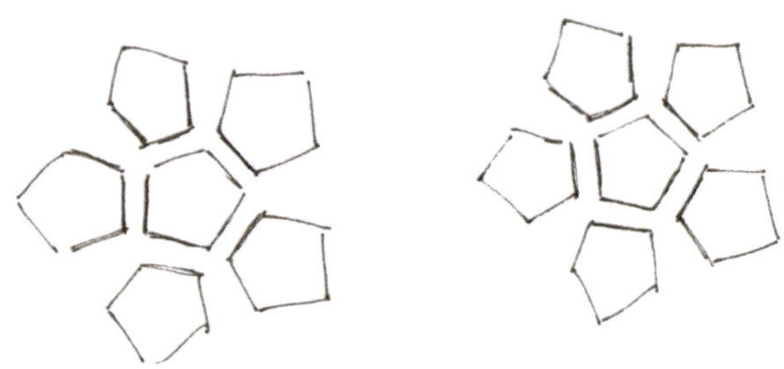

3. Sew the 'petals' onto the centre pentagon for each half then sew their edges together to form a half ball. Sew the two halves together, making sure to follow the drawing so that the two halves interlock.

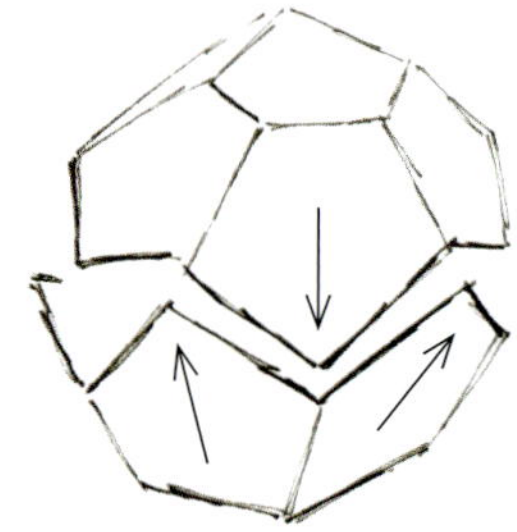

4. Leave an opening for stuffing and the bell and firmly stuff the ball, making sure that the bell is towards the outside. Finish sewing.

The ball is ready for play!

Felt Crown

These beautiful crowns can stimulate creative play. Together with veils (page 14) they are ideal for dressing up as kings, queens, princesses and the birthday child. They are great just as they are, but if you want to decorate them, who is to stop you?

They require precision cutting and very hot ironing but they are easy to make for an experienced crafter. Little children like to watch and can help with decorating.

YOU WILL NEED

- 2 pieces of natural felt. Each piece could be a different colour but they should go together, for example pink and lavender or orange and yellow; all 63 x 9cm/25 x 3½"
- Double-sided paper interfacing (iron on), same size as above
- Cartridge paper, also same size as above
- Pencil
- Sharp scissors
- A few paper clips
- Damp cloth
- Tailor's chalk or a fabric marking pencil
- PVA craft glue
- Decorations – ribbon (plain or sequinned), little beads, 'sparkles', cut felt shapes, etc

1. Place the interfacing rough side down onto the felt, fix with paper clips and iron at setting two (medium hot). Pull off the paper and discard. Now place the other felt on the just-ironed-on interfacing and cover with a damp cloth and iron at setting 3 (hot). Leave to cool for 15 minutes.

2. Trace the template (see page 234) onto the cartridge paper.

3. Cut out the shape and place the cut-out paper crown onto the felt and secure it with paper clips. Draw around it with the chalk then remove the paper and cut out the crown, keeping the cut-out triangles for decorations.

4. If you want to decorate the crown, you should do that now. Use the felt triangles, ribbon and sparkles – and any other decorations you choose. Most can be successfully stuck onto felt with PVA glue. Make sure the glue is dry before going to the next stage.

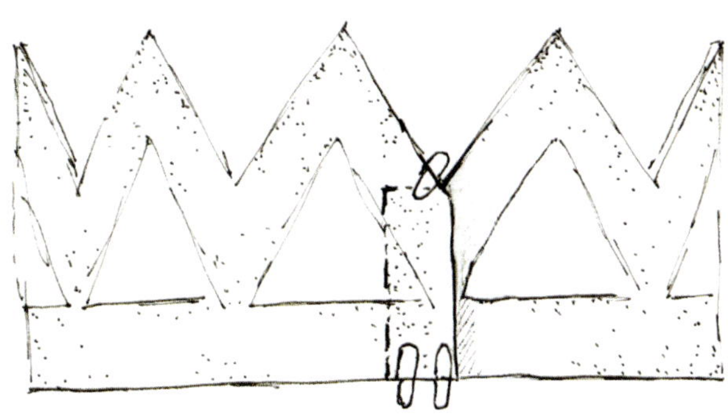

5. Fit the crown around your child's head and fix it together with paper clips. Lift it off and glue the overlapping pieces. Slide on some paper clips and leave to dry.

Let the coronation begin!

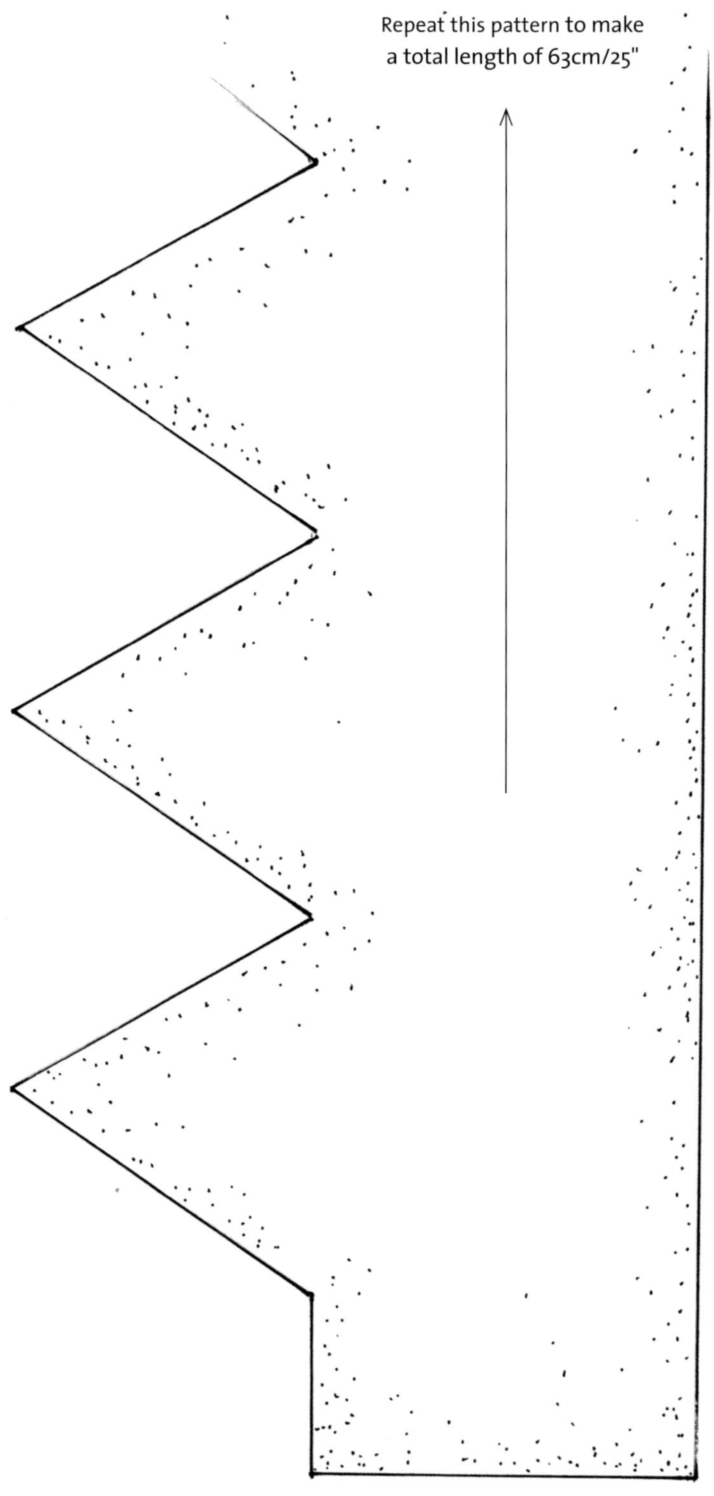
Repeat this pattern to make
a total length of 63cm/25"
9cm/3½"

Small Presents

Whereas it can be good fun to receive or give an expensive bought gift, it is much more personal and thoughtful to replace it with a homemade one.

Buy some seeds or collect your own in the autumn. If bought, take them out of the packet and wrap a few in tissue paper. Staple them onto written instructions. Let the result be a surprise.

Our four-year-old received a marvellous birthday present from his girlfriend. It was a large opened-up pine cone, which had a Smartie on every scale. What a pretty, delicious thing!

Little wooden figures are an ideal present, as they can be used in the seasonal tables. Many crystal shops sell tiny bits of semi-precious stone. These too can be used in the seasonal displays. They can be given in a small homemade bag.

But, best of all, see the many items throughout this book which will be the best presents ever received by any grandparents or friends.

Happy crafting!

Resources

For all types of silk:

www.rainbowsilks.co.uk

For eco-friendly craft materials, including wool, fleece, kite paper, doll-making materials, paints:
www.myriadonline.co.uk

Locally, I would like thank:

Sew & So, 1 Lansdown, Stroud, Gloucestershire GL5 1BB

Mother Goose, 10A Market Street, Nailsworth, Gloucestershire GL6 0BX
www.mothergooseonline.co.uk

Many of the materials can be found in craft chains and discount stores as well.

Acknowledgements

I would like to give my special thanks to: Christine Fynes Clinton for taking time out from her busy teaching schedule to write up her beautiful new doll projects – the star, the clutch and the soft doll; Stephanie Cooper for revisiting the hip horse project with her granddaughter; and both Christine and Stephanie for co-creating the original *The Children's Year* so long ago!

I would love to thank our lovely grandchildren with their shining faces as they eagerly engaged in craft projects from the book and all our friends who generously gave us their wonderful advice.

Thank you to Martin Large of Hawthorn Press for asking me to give the original a thorough overhaul, Lucy Guenot for her artistic interpretations of my text and drawings, and Christine Kidney for keeping a watchful eye on my logic and English.

Most of all I thank Tom for his patient processing and countless re-processing of my endless, messy scribbles – even trying to follow where K2 and P3 would lead to ...

Select Bibliography

Bob Clay, *Shaping the Flame,* Art Books International, Hove, 2000

A Druitt, C Fynes-Clinton, M Rowling, *All Year Round*, Hawthorn Press, Stroud, 1995

Maria Schindler, *Goethe's Theory of Colour*, New Knowledge Books, East Grinstead, 1964

R Steiner, *The Festivals and their Meaning*, Rudolf Steiner Press, London, 1981

R Steiner, *The Four Seasons and the Archangels*, Rudolf Steiner Press, London, 1984

M van Leeuwen, J Moeskops, *The Nature Corner*, Floris Books, Edinburgh, 2008

V von Holstein, *Nature Spirits and What They Say*, Floris Books, Edinburgh, 2004

Index

Ordering Books

If you have difficulties ordering Hawthorn Press books from a bookshop, you can order direct from our website **www.hawthornpress.com** or the following distributors:

UNITED KINGDOM
BookSource
50 Cambuslang Road,
Glasgow, G32 8NB
Tel: (0845) 370 0063
Email: orders@booksource.net

USA/NORTH AMERICA
Steiner Books
PO Box 960, Herndon,
VA 20172-0960, USA
Tel: (800) 856 8664
Email: service@steinerbooks.org
www.steinerbooks.org

Waldorf Books
Phil & Angela's Company, Inc.
1271 NE Hwy 99W #196, McMinnville,
Oregon 97128, USA
Tel: (503) 472-4610
Email: info@waldorfbooks.com
www.waldorfbooks.com

AUSTRALIA & NEW ZEALAND
Footprint Books Pty Ltd
4 /8 Jubilee Avenue,
Warriewood,
NSW 2102, Australia
Tel: (02) 9997 3973
Email: info@footprint.com.au
www.footprint.com.au

Hawthorn Press
www.hawthornpress.com